STAR WARS

KNIGHT ERRANT

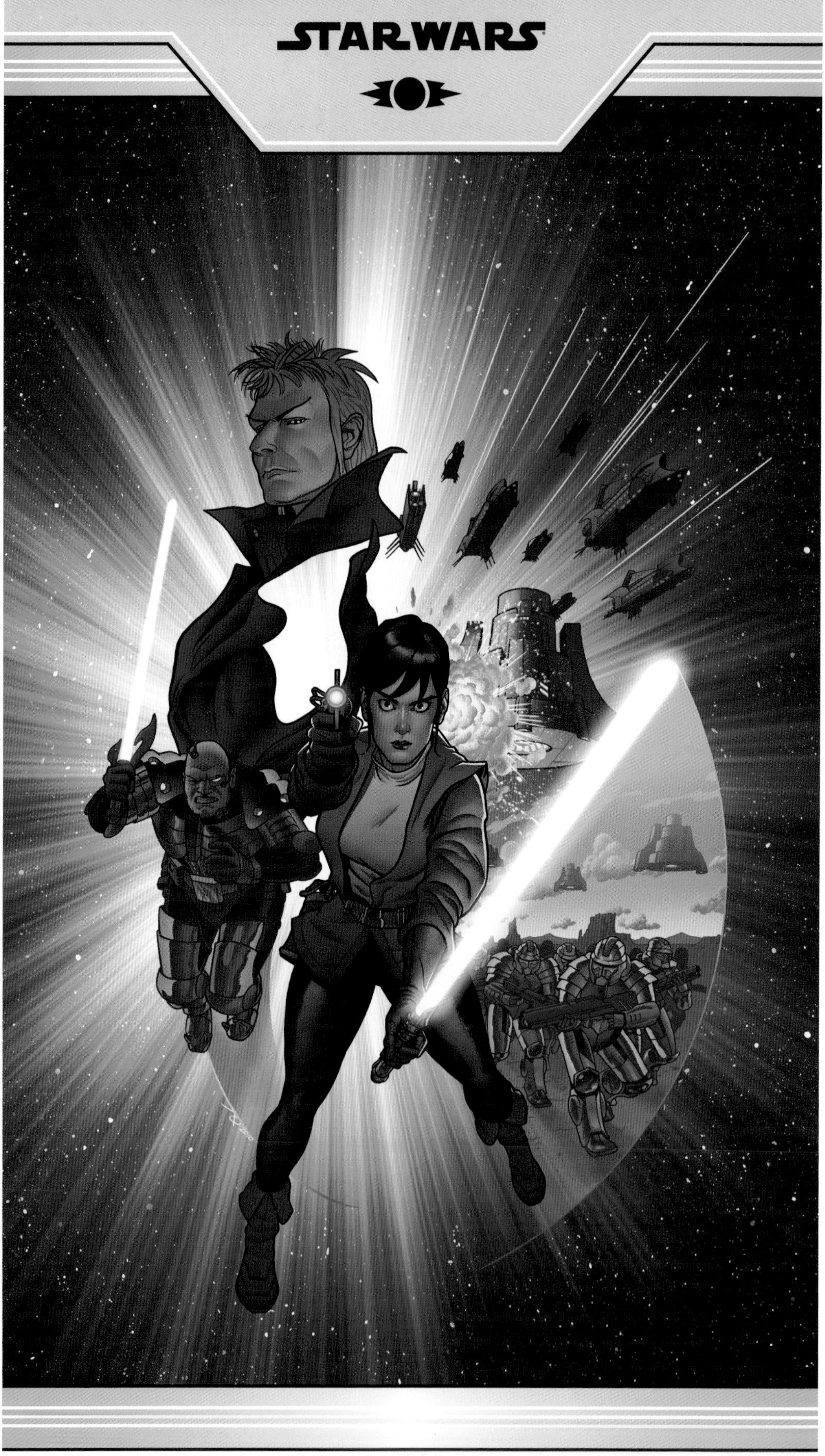
STAR WARS

ILLUSTRATION BY JOE QUINONES

STAR WARS®
KNIGHT ERRANT

VOLUME ONE
AFLAME

Script
JOHN JACKSON MILLER

Pencils
FEDERICO DALLOCCHIO
IVAN RODRIGUEZ

Inks
FEDERICO DALLOCCHIO
IVAN RODRIGUEZ
BELARDINO BRABO
MARCIO LOEZER

Colors
MICHAEL ATIYEH

Letters
MICHAEL HEISLER

Cover Art
JOE QUINONES

DARK HORSE BOOKS

THE OLD REPUBLIC
(25,000–1,000 years before the Battle of Yavin)

The Old Republic was the legendary government that united a galaxy under the rule of the senate. In this era, the Jedi are numerous, and serve as guardians of peace and justice. The *Tales of the Jedi* comics series takes place in this era, chronicling the immense wars fought by the Jedi of old, and the ancient sith.

This story takes place approximately 1,032 years before the Battle of Yavin.

President and Publisher
MIKE RICHARDSON

Collection Designer
AIMEE DANIELSON-GERMANY

Editor
DAVE MARSHALL

Assistant Editors
FREDDYE LINS
BRENDAN WRIGHT

NEIL HANKERSON Executive Vice President TOM WEDDLE Chief Financial Officer RANDY STRADLEY Vice President of Publishing MICHAEL MARTENS Vice President of Book Trade Sales ANITA NELSON Vice President of Business Affairs MICHA HERSHMAN Vice President of Marketing DAVID SCROGGY Vice President of Product Development DALE LAFOUNTAIN Vice President of Information Technology DARLENE VOGEL Senior Director of Print, Design, and Production KEN LIZZI General Counsel DAVEY ESTRADA Editorial Director SCOTT ALLIE Senior Managing Editor CHRIS WARNER Senior Books Editor DIANA SCHUTZ Executive Editor CARY GRAZZINI Director of Print and Development LIA RIBACCHI Art Director CARA NIECE Director of Scheduling

Special thanks to Jann Moorhead, David Anderman, Troy Alders, Leland Chee, Sue Rostoni, and Carol Roeder at Lucas Licensing.

This volume collects issues #1–#5 of the Dark Horse comic-book series *Star Wars: Knight Errant—Aflame*.

Published by
Dark Horse Books
A division of Dark Horse Comics, Inc.
10956 SE Main Street
Milwaukie, OR 97222

DarkHorse.com
StarWars.com

To find a comics shop in your area, call the Comic Shop Locator Service toll-free at 1-888-266-4226

First edition: August 2011
ISBN 978-1-59582-708-1

1 3 5 7 9 10 8 6 4 2
Printed at Midas Printing International, Ltd., Huizhou, China

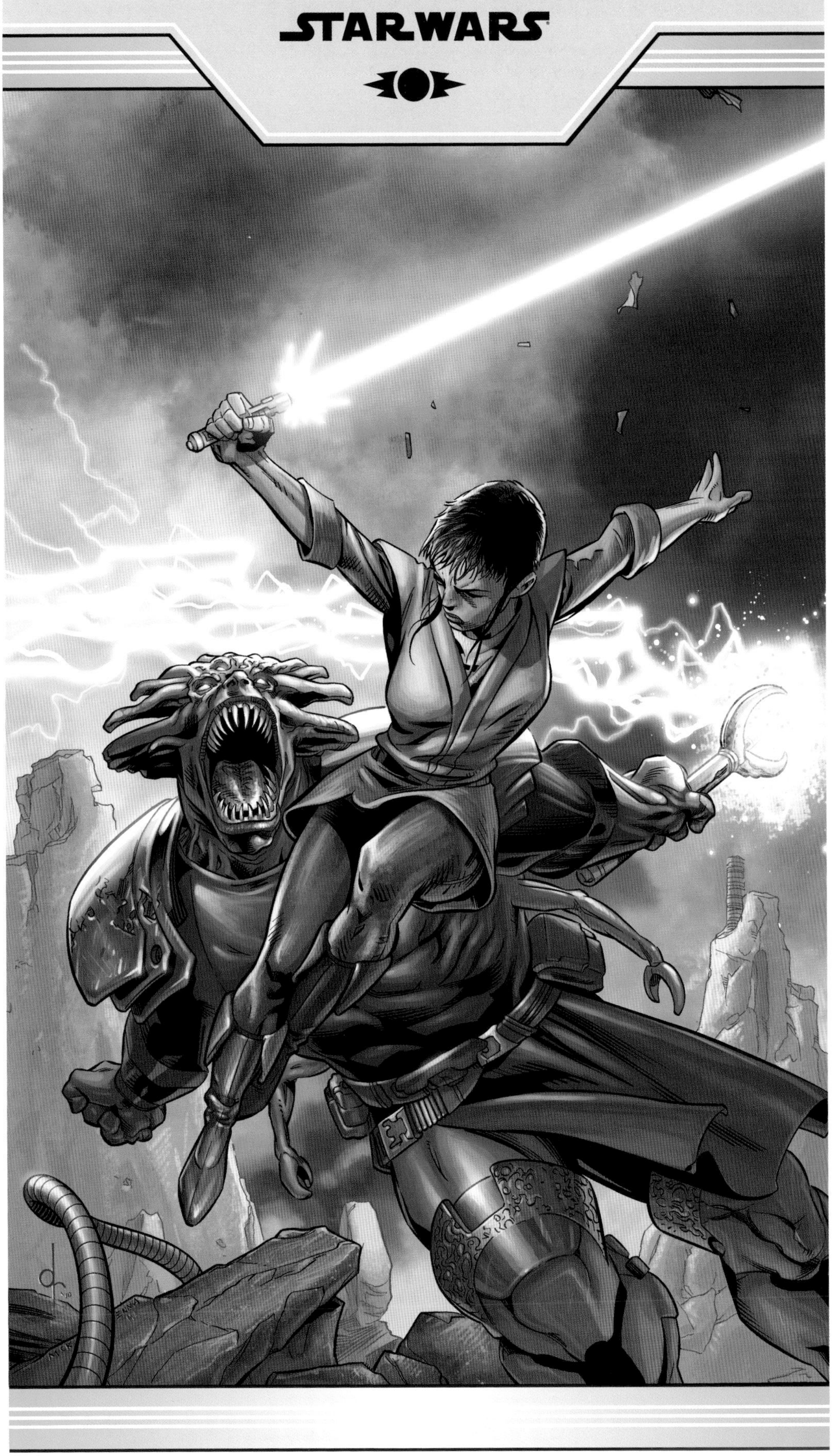
STAR WARS

ILLUSTRATION BY DAVE ROSS WITH MARK MCKENNA AND MICHAEL ATIYEH

AFLAME

It is a dark age for the Republic. A thousand years before Obi-Wan Kenobi met Anakin Skywalker, their Jedi forebears struggle in vain against a rampaging Sith menace. The Republic abandons vast swaths of territory, deactivating many of the communications relays that once bound the galaxy.

But the Sith have other enemies—themselves. Sith Lords battle each other for the right to finish off the Republic. Far behind Sith lines, on Chelloa, Lord Daiman makes a discovery he hopes will help him rise above the other petty princelings once and for all. The Republic is in peril.

Learning of the danger, the charismatic Jedi Master Vannar Treece leads a group of volunteers on what many expect will be a one-way mission. Treece, a veteran campaigner, is more confident. But he cannot plan for everything—and, alone in Sith space, that is usually fatal . . .

This story takes place approximately 1,032 years before the Battle of Yavin.

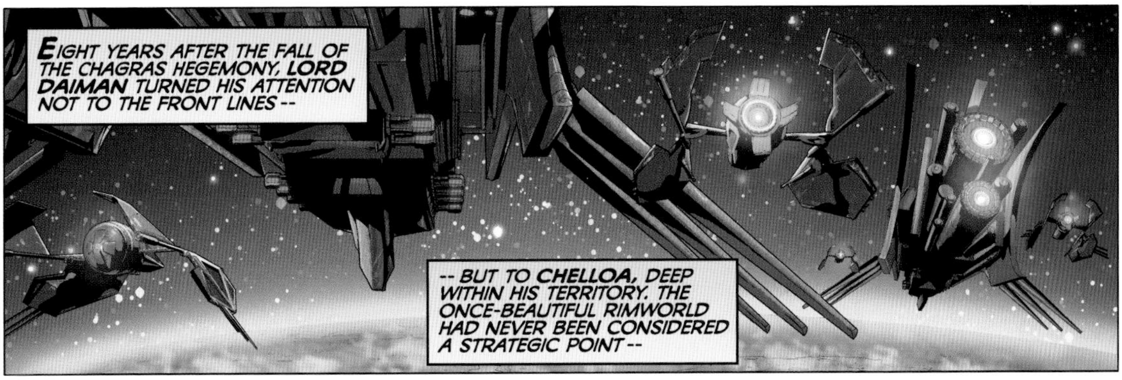
EIGHT YEARS AFTER THE FALL OF THE CHAGRAS HEGEMONY, LORD DAIMAN TURNED HIS ATTENTION NOT TO THE FRONT LINES --
-- BUT TO CHELLOA, DEEP WITHIN HIS TERRITORY. THE ONCE-BEAUTIFUL RIMWORLD HAD NEVER BEEN CONSIDERED A STRATEGIC POINT --

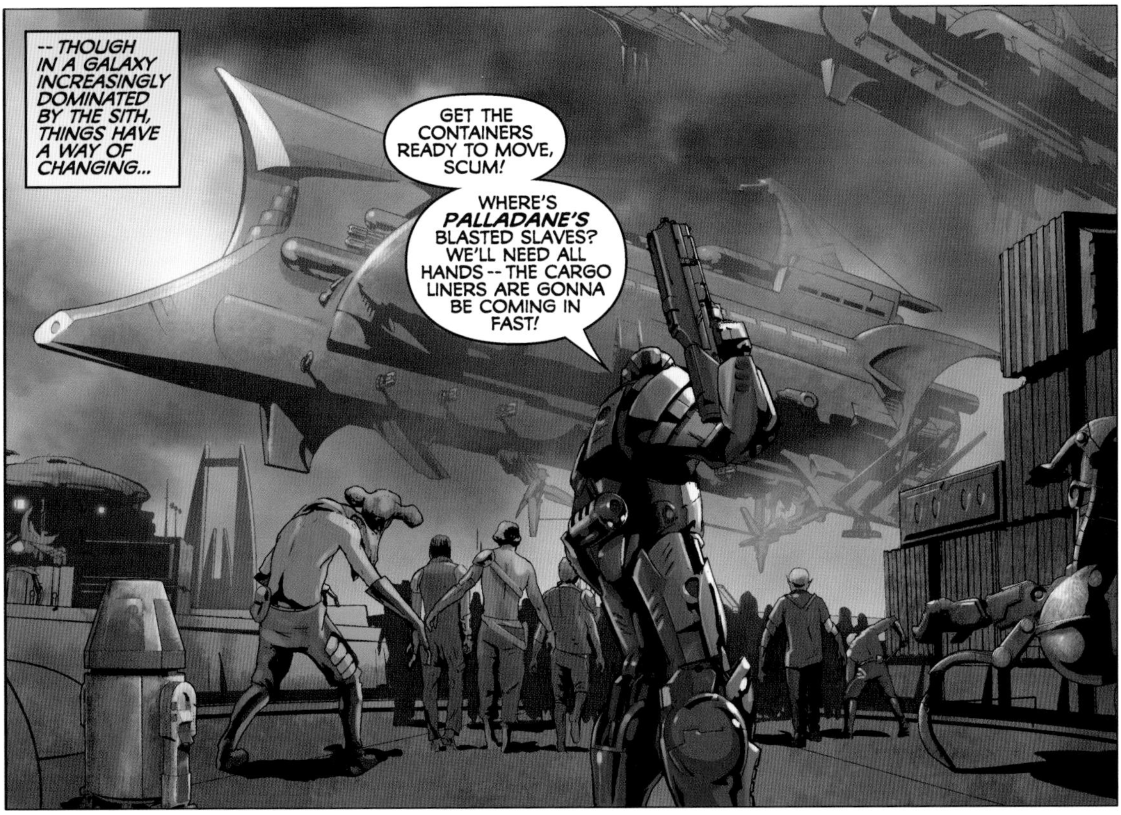
-- THOUGH IN A GALAXY INCREASINGLY DOMINATED BY THE SITH, THINGS HAVE A WAY OF CHANGING...
GET THE CONTAINERS READY TO MOVE, SCUM!
WHERE'S PALLADANE'S BLASTED SLAVES? WE'LL NEED ALL HANDS -- THE CARGO LINERS ARE GONNA BE COMING IN FAST!

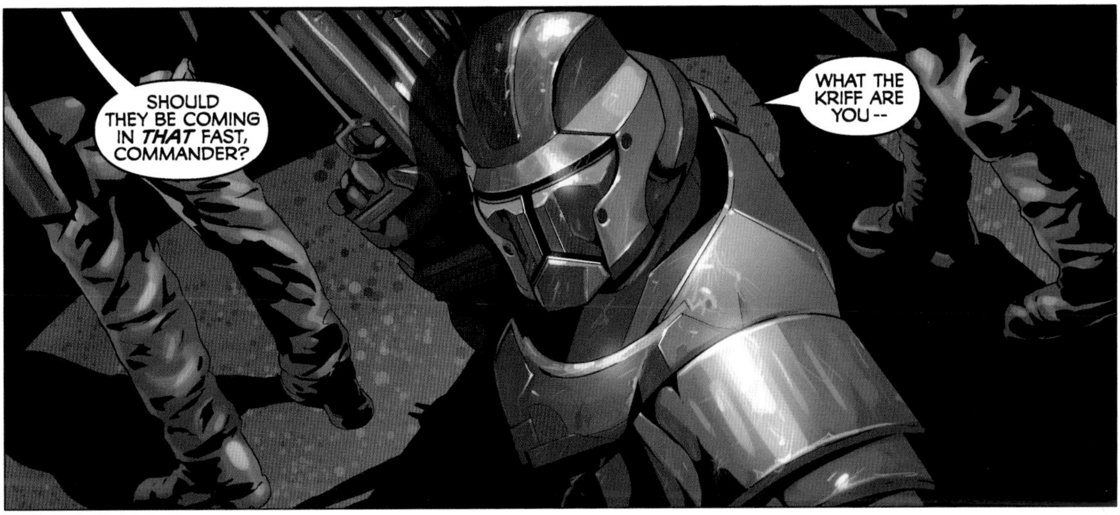
SHOULD THEY BE COMING IN THAT FAST, COMMANDER?
WHAT THE KRIFF ARE YOU --

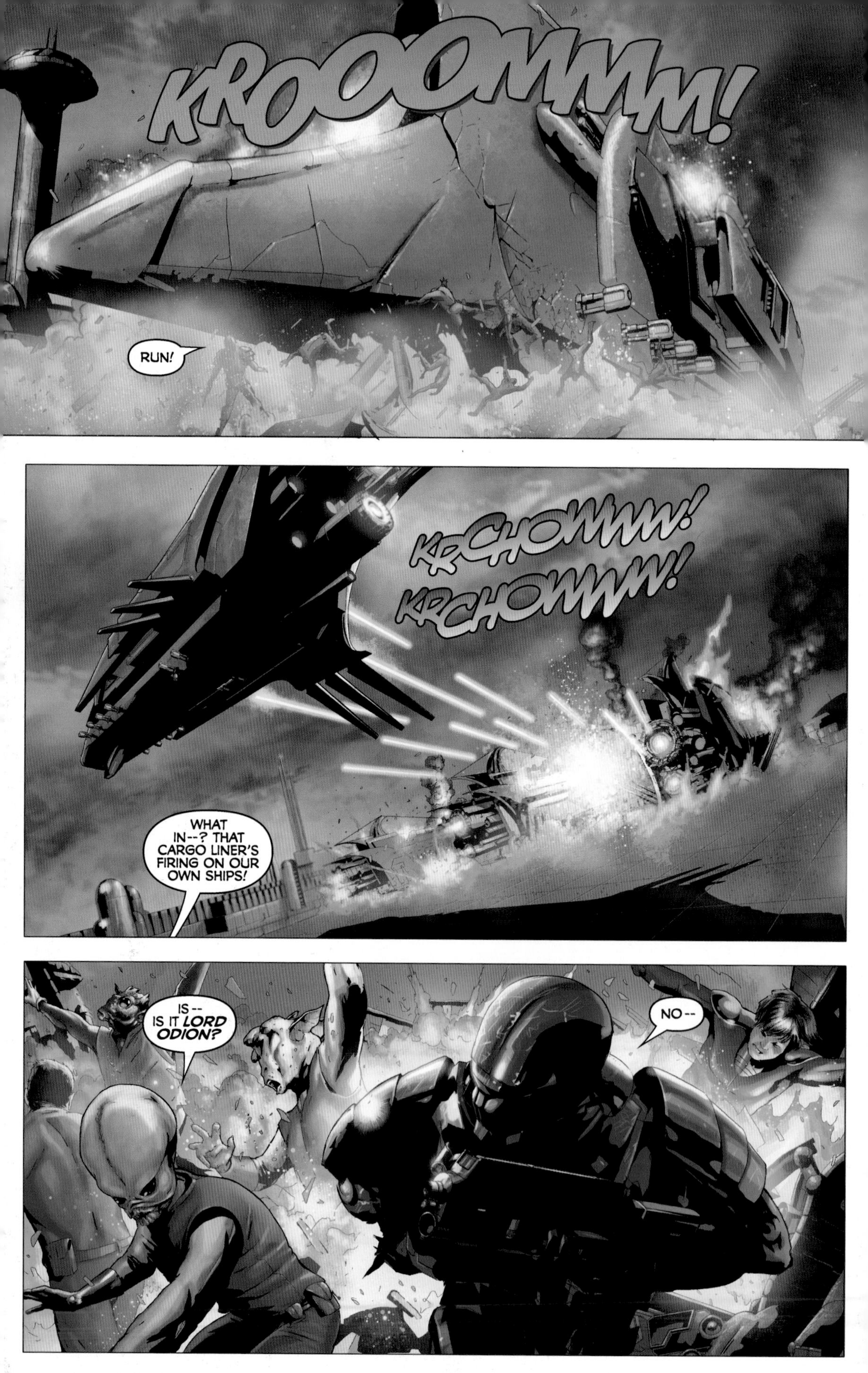
KROOOMMM!
RUN!
KRCHOMMM!
KRCHOMMM!
WHAT IN--? THAT CARGO LINER'S FIRING ON OUR OWN SHIPS!
IS -- IS IT *LORD ODION?*
NO --

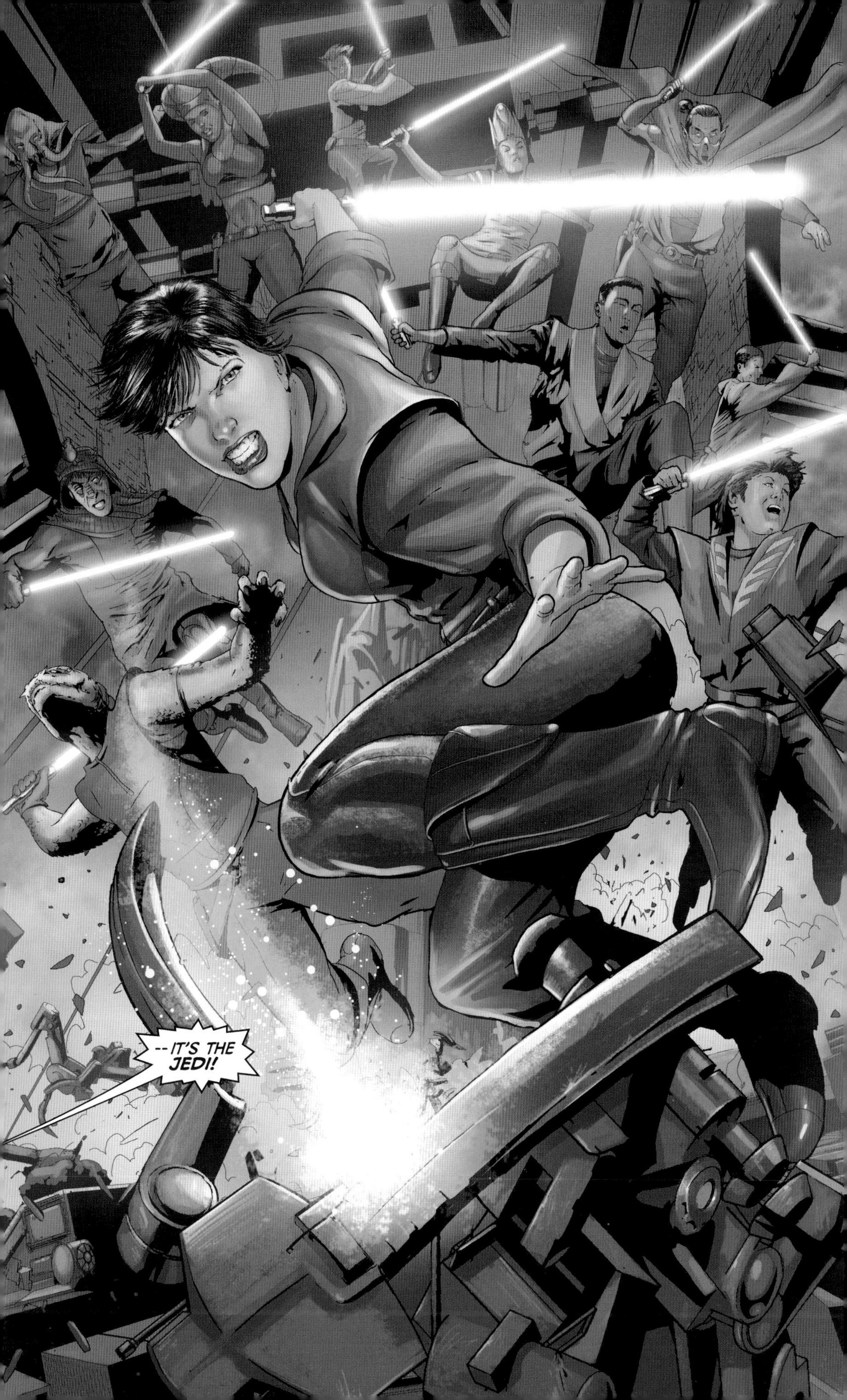
--IT'S THE JEDI!

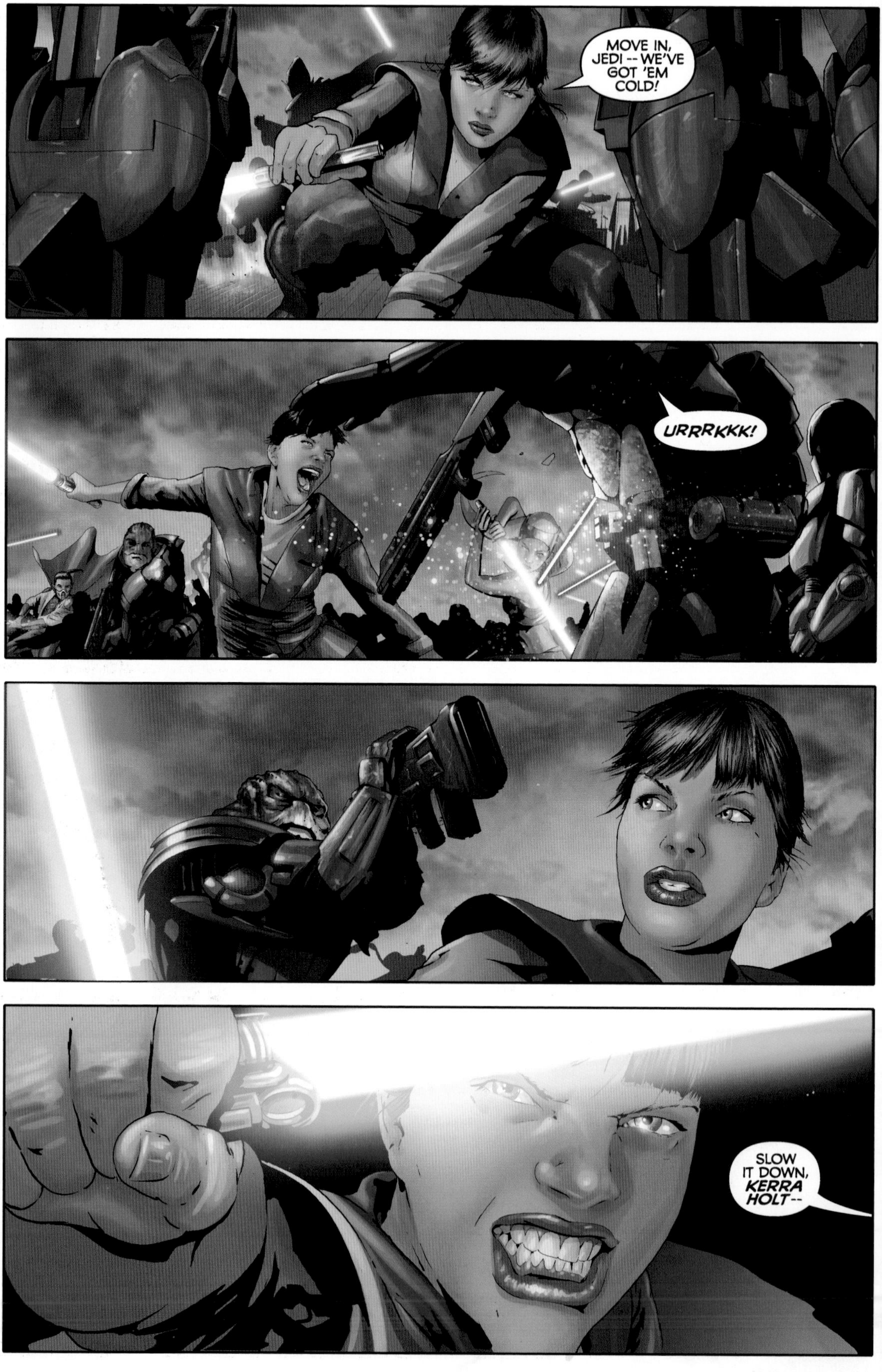
MOVE IN, JEDI -- WE'VE GOT 'EM COLD!
URRRKKK!
SLOW IT DOWN, KERRA HOLT--

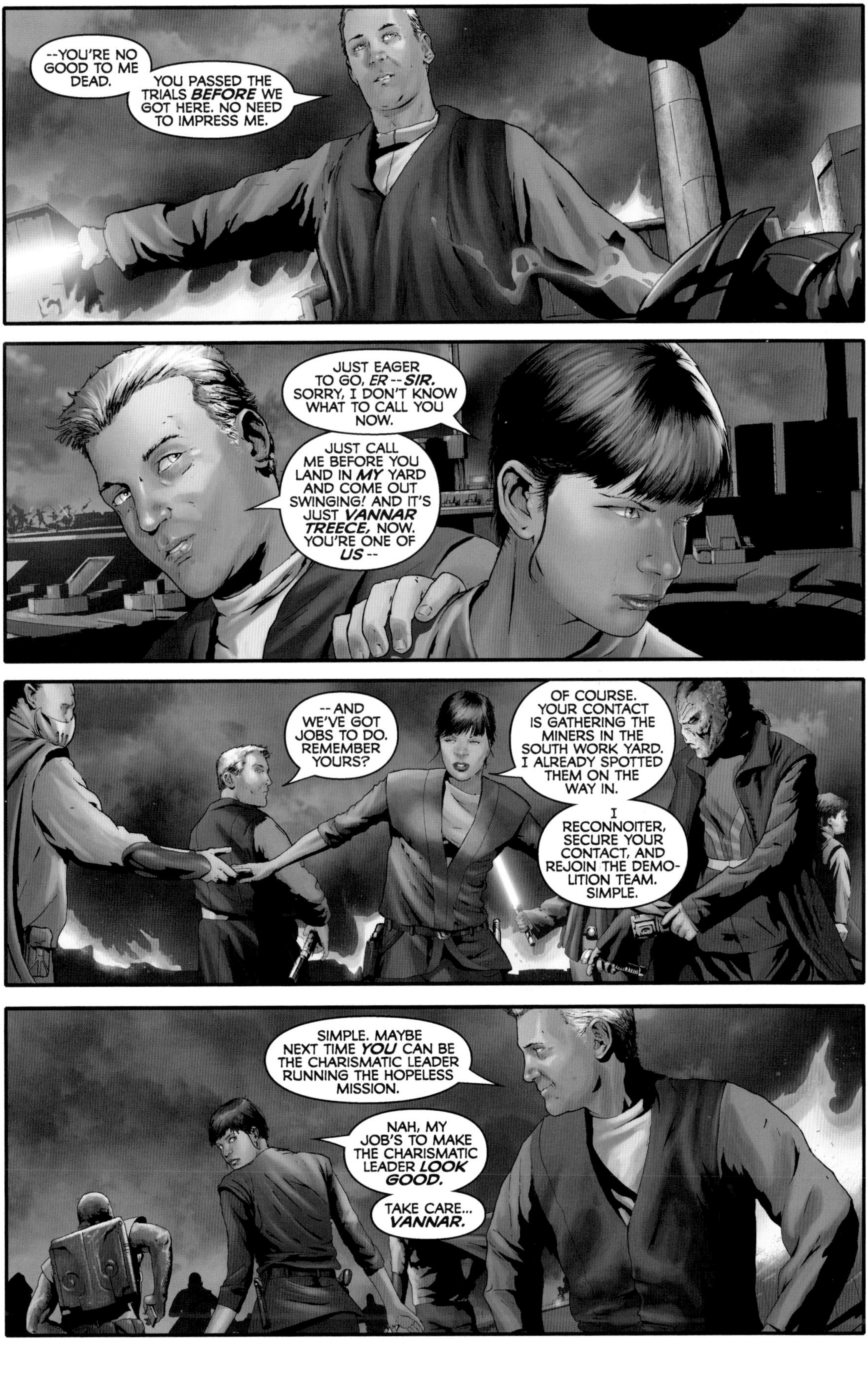
--YOU'RE NO GOOD TO ME DEAD.
YOU PASSED THE TRIALS BEFORE WE GOT HERE. NO NEED TO IMPRESS ME.
JUST EAGER TO GO, ER--SIR. SORRY, I DON'T KNOW WHAT TO CALL YOU NOW.
JUST CALL ME BEFORE YOU LAND IN MY YARD AND COME OUT SWINGING! AND IT'S JUST VANNAR TREECE, NOW. YOU'RE ONE OF US--
--AND WE'VE GOT JOBS TO DO. REMEMBER YOURS?
OF COURSE. YOUR CONTACT IS GATHERING THE MINERS IN THE SOUTH WORK YARD. I ALREADY SPOTTED THEM ON THE WAY IN.
I RECONNOITER, SECURE YOUR CONTACT, AND REJOIN THE DEMOLITION TEAM. SIMPLE.
SIMPLE. MAYBE NEXT TIME YOU CAN BE THE CHARISMATIC LEADER RUNNING THE HOPELESS MISSION.
NAH, MY JOB'S TO MAKE THE CHARISMATIC LEADER LOOK GOOD.
TAKE CARE... VANNAR.

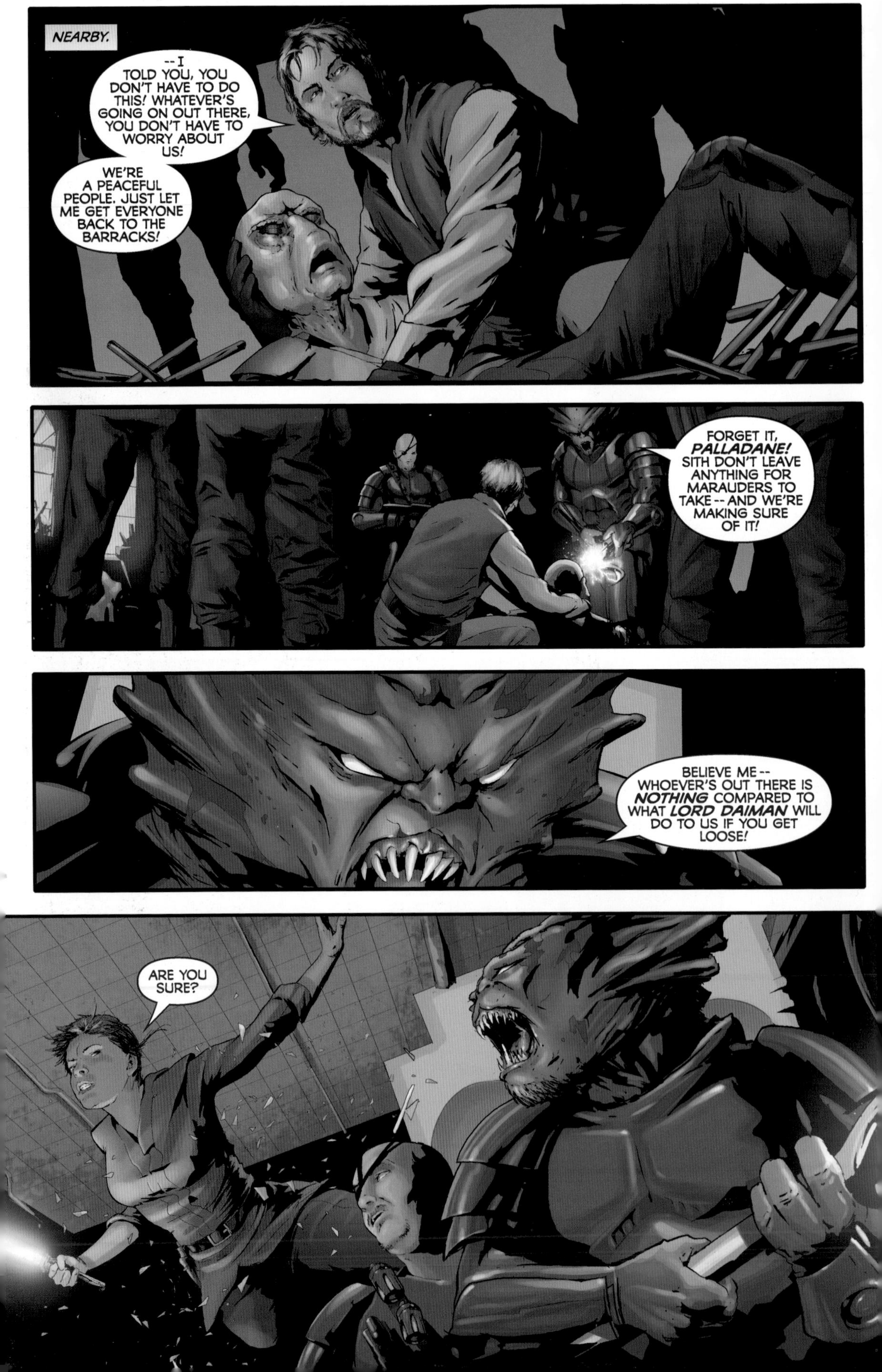
NEARBY.
--I TOLD YOU, YOU DON'T HAVE TO DO THIS! WHATEVER'S GOING ON OUT THERE, YOU DON'T HAVE TO WORRY ABOUT US!
WE'RE A PEACEFUL PEOPLE. JUST LET ME GET EVERYONE BACK TO THE BARRACKS!
FORGET IT, *PALLADANE!* SITH DON'T LEAVE ANYTHING FOR MARAUDERS TO TAKE -- AND WE'RE MAKING SURE OF IT!
BELIEVE ME -- WHOEVER'S OUT THERE IS *NOTHING* COMPARED TO WHAT *LORD DAIMAN* WILL DO TO US IF YOU GET LOOSE!
ARE YOU SURE?

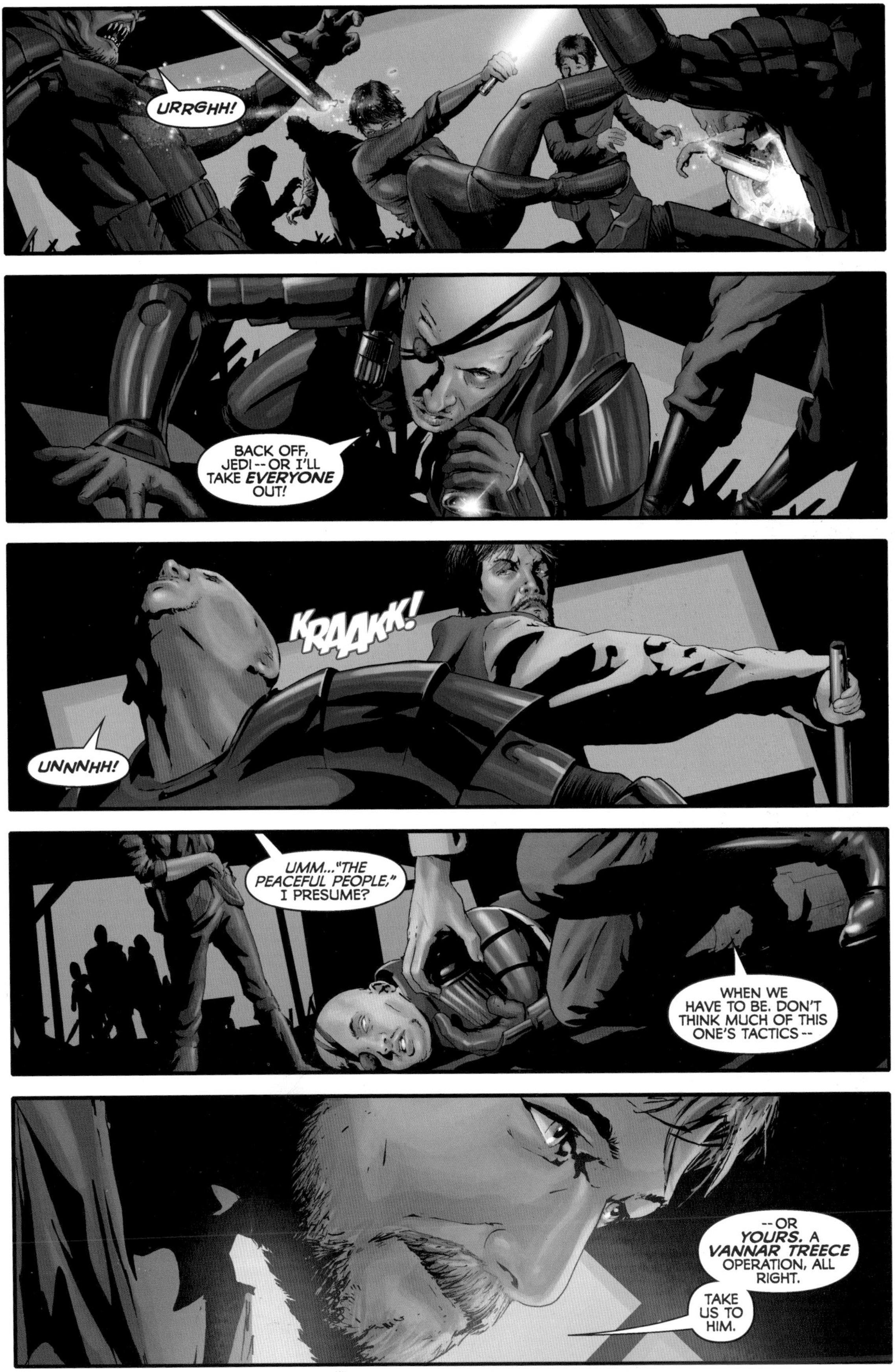
URRGHH!
BACK OFF, JEDI--OR I'LL TAKE EVERYONE OUT!
KRAAKK!
UNNNHH!
UMM..."THE PEACEFUL PEOPLE," I PRESUME?
WHEN WE HAVE TO BE. DON'T THINK MUCH OF THIS ONE'S TACTICS--
--OR YOURS. A VANNAR TREECE OPERATION, ALL RIGHT.
TAKE US TO HIM.

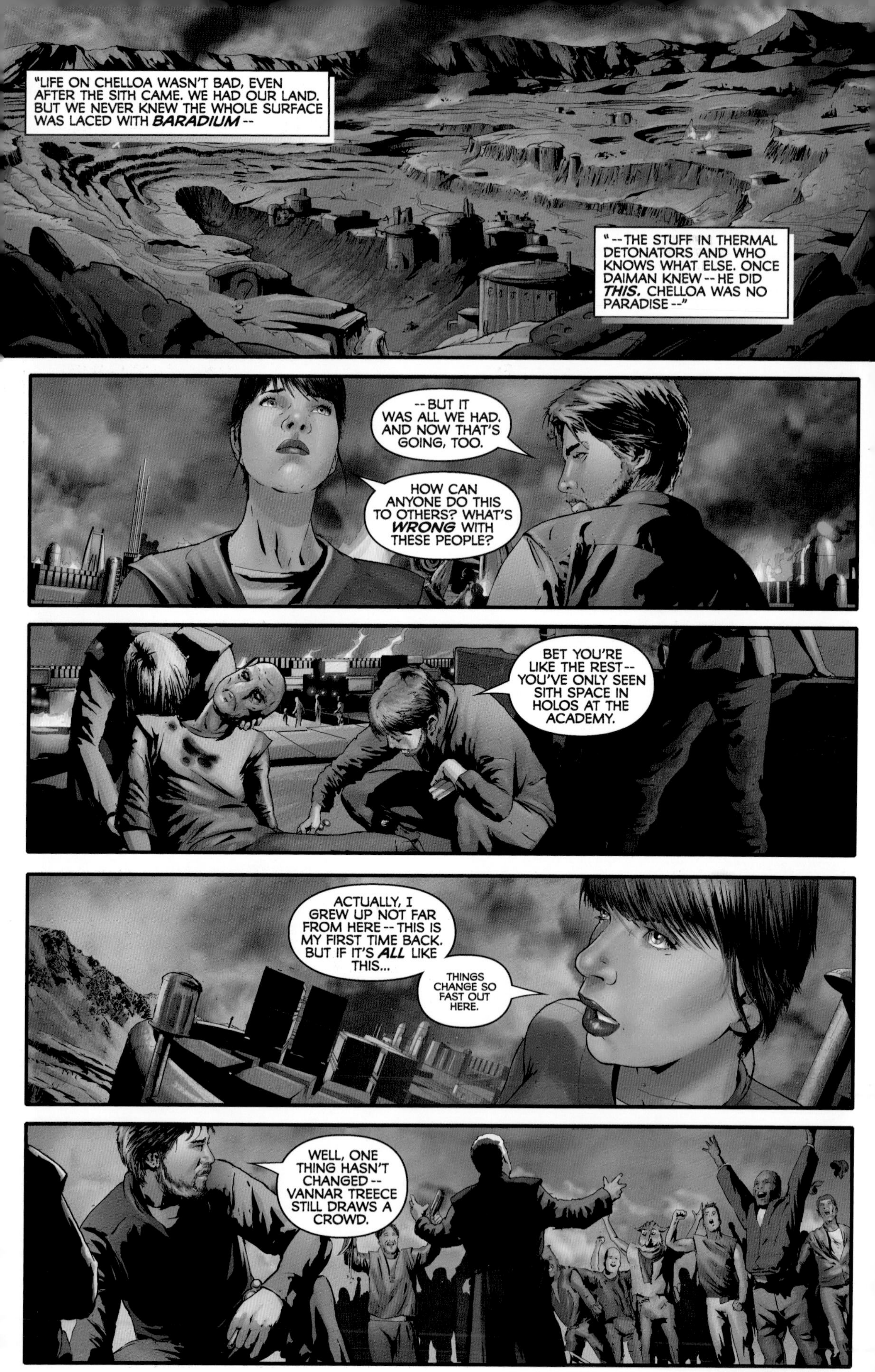
"LIFE ON CHELLOA WASN'T BAD, EVEN AFTER THE SITH CAME. WE HAD OUR LAND. BUT WE NEVER KNEW THE WHOLE SURFACE WAS LACED WITH ***BARADIUM*** --
"--THE STUFF IN THERMAL DETONATORS AND WHO KNOWS WHAT ELSE. ONCE DAIMAN KNEW--HE DID ***THIS.*** CHELLOA WAS NO PARADISE--"
--BUT IT WAS ALL WE HAD. AND NOW THAT'S GOING, TOO.
HOW CAN ANYONE DO THIS TO OTHERS? WHAT'S ***WRONG*** WITH THESE PEOPLE?
BET YOU'RE LIKE THE REST--YOU'VE ONLY SEEN SITH SPACE IN HOLOS AT THE ACADEMY.
ACTUALLY, I GREW UP NOT FAR FROM HERE--THIS IS MY FIRST TIME BACK. BUT IF IT'S ***ALL*** LIKE THIS...
THINGS CHANGE SO FAST OUT HERE.
WELL, ONE THING HASN'T CHANGED--VANNAR TREECE STILL DRAWS A CROWD.

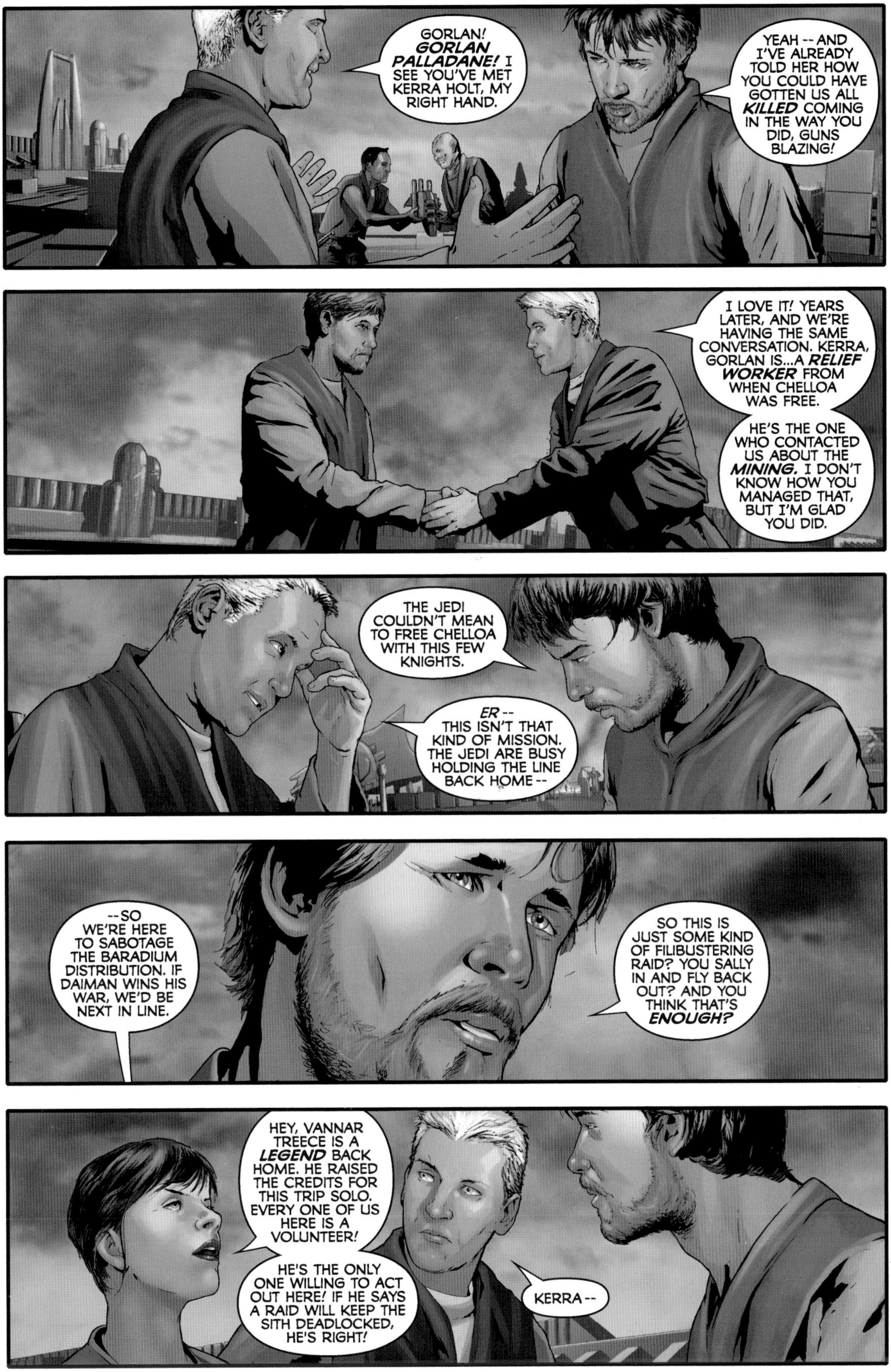
GORLAN! GORLAN PALLADANE! I SEE YOU'VE MET KERRA HOLT, MY RIGHT HAND.
YEAH -- AND I'VE ALREADY TOLD HER HOW YOU COULD HAVE GOTTEN US ALL KILLED COMING IN THE WAY YOU DID, GUNS BLAZING!
I LOVE IT! YEARS LATER, AND WE'RE HAVING THE SAME CONVERSATION. KERRA, GORLAN IS...A RELIEF WORKER FROM WHEN CHELLOA WAS FREE.
HE'S THE ONE WHO CONTACTED US ABOUT THE MINING. I DON'T KNOW HOW YOU MANAGED THAT, BUT I'M GLAD YOU DID.
THE JEDI COULDN'T MEAN TO FREE CHELLOA WITH THIS FEW KNIGHTS.
ER -- THIS ISN'T THAT KIND OF MISSION. THE JEDI ARE BUSY HOLDING THE LINE BACK HOME --
--SO WE'RE HERE TO SABOTAGE THE BARADIUM DISTRIBUTION. IF DAIMAN WINS HIS WAR, WE'D BE NEXT IN LINE.
SO THIS IS JUST SOME KIND OF FILIBUSTERING RAID? YOU SALLY IN AND FLY BACK OUT? AND YOU THINK THAT'S ENOUGH?
HEY, VANNAR TREECE IS A LEGEND BACK HOME. HE RAISED THE CREDITS FOR THIS TRIP SOLO. EVERY ONE OF US HERE IS A VOLUNTEER!
HE'S THE ONLY ONE WILLING TO ACT OUT HERE! IF HE SAYS A RAID WILL KEEP THE SITH DEADLOCKED, HE'S RIGHT!
KERRA --

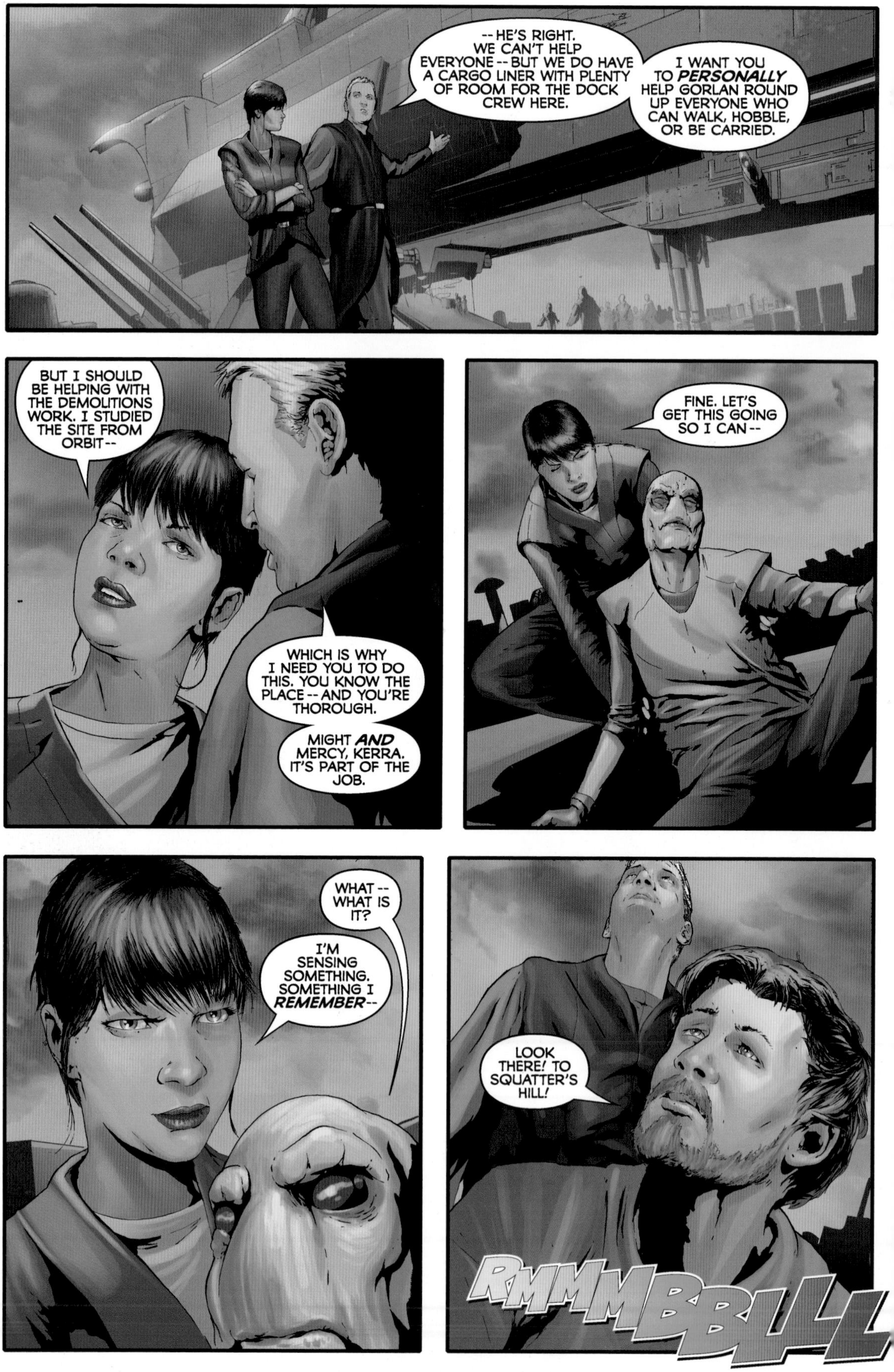
-- HE'S RIGHT. WE CAN'T HELP EVERYONE -- BUT WE DO HAVE A CARGO LINER WITH PLENTY OF ROOM FOR THE DOCK CREW HERE.
I WANT YOU TO *PERSONALLY* HELP GORLAN ROUND UP EVERYONE WHO CAN WALK, HOBBLE, OR BE CARRIED.
BUT I SHOULD BE HELPING WITH THE DEMOLITIONS WORK. I STUDIED THE SITE FROM ORBIT --
WHICH IS WHY I NEED YOU TO DO THIS. YOU KNOW THE PLACE -- AND YOU'RE THOROUGH.
MIGHT *AND* MERCY, KERRA. IT'S PART OF THE JOB.
FINE. LET'S GET THIS GOING SO I CAN --
WHAT -- WHAT IS IT?
I'M SENSING SOMETHING. SOMETHING I *REMEMBER* --
LOOK THERE! TO SQUATTER'S HILL!
RMMMBBLLL

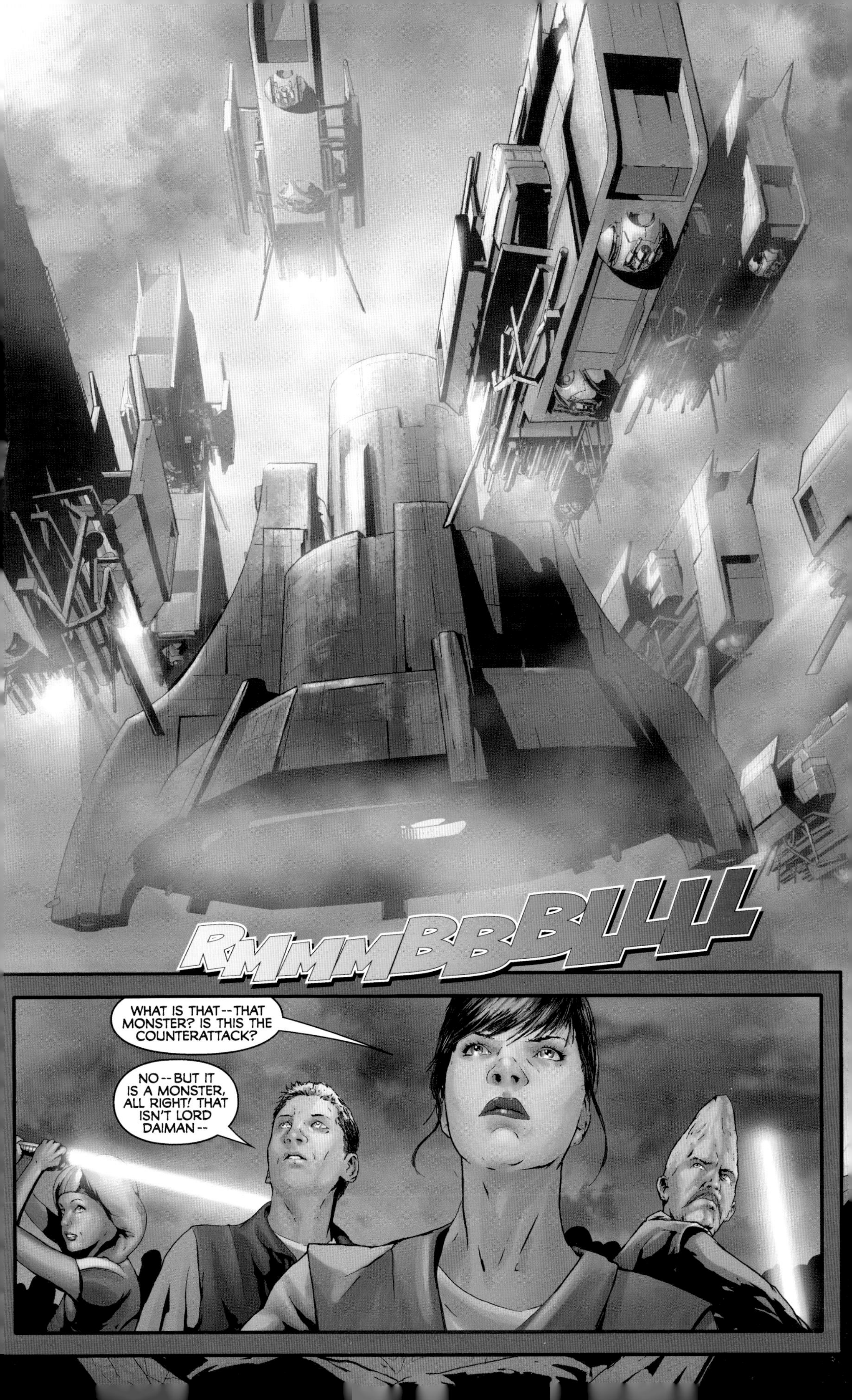
RMMMBBBLLLL
WHAT IS THAT--THAT MONSTER? IS THIS THE COUNTERATTACK?
NO--BUT IT IS A MONSTER, ALL RIGHT! THAT ISN'T LORD DAIMAN--

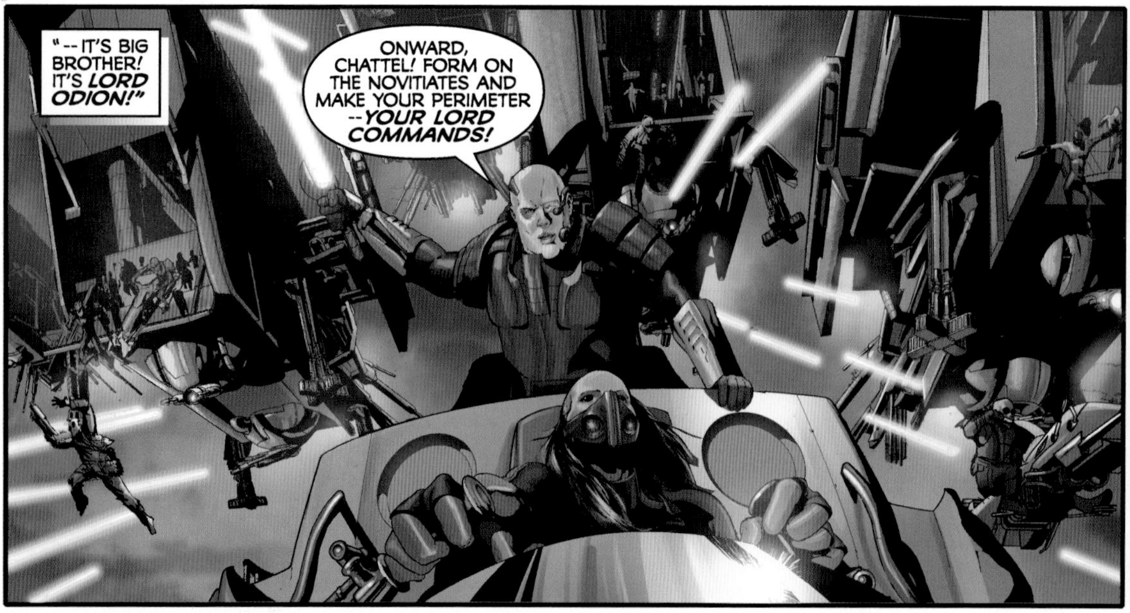
"--IT'S BIG BROTHER! IT'S LORD ODION!"
ONWARD, CHATTEL! FORM ON THE NOVITIATES AND MAKE YOUR PERIMETER --YOUR LORD COMMANDS!

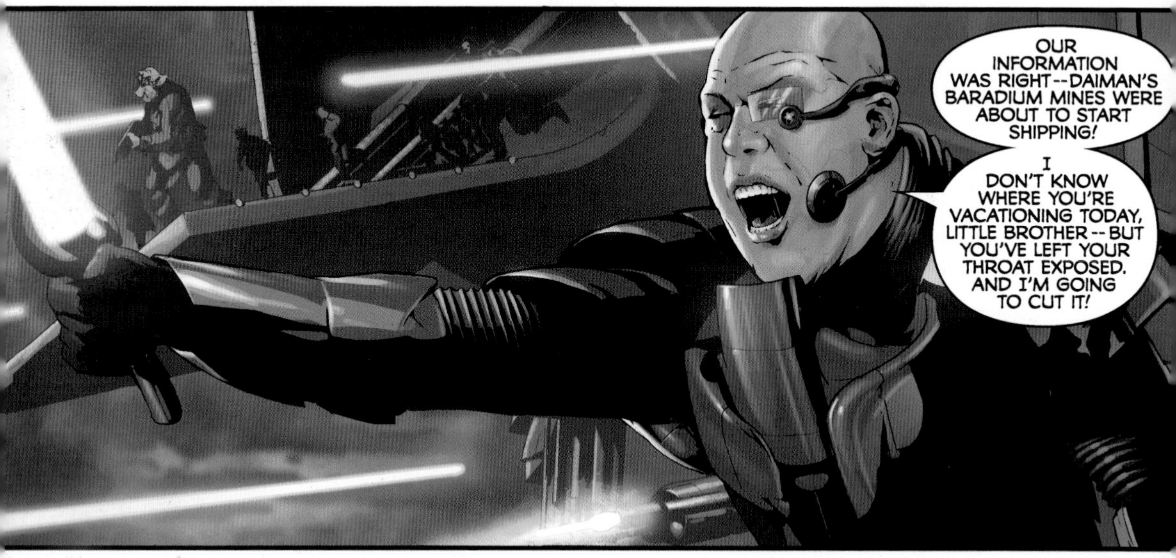
OUR INFORMATION WAS RIGHT--DAIMAN'S BARADIUM MINES WERE ABOUT TO START SHIPPING!
I DON'T KNOW WHERE YOU'RE VACATIONING TODAY, LITTLE BROTHER--BUT YOU'VE LEFT YOUR THROAT EXPOSED. AND I'M GOING TO CUT IT!

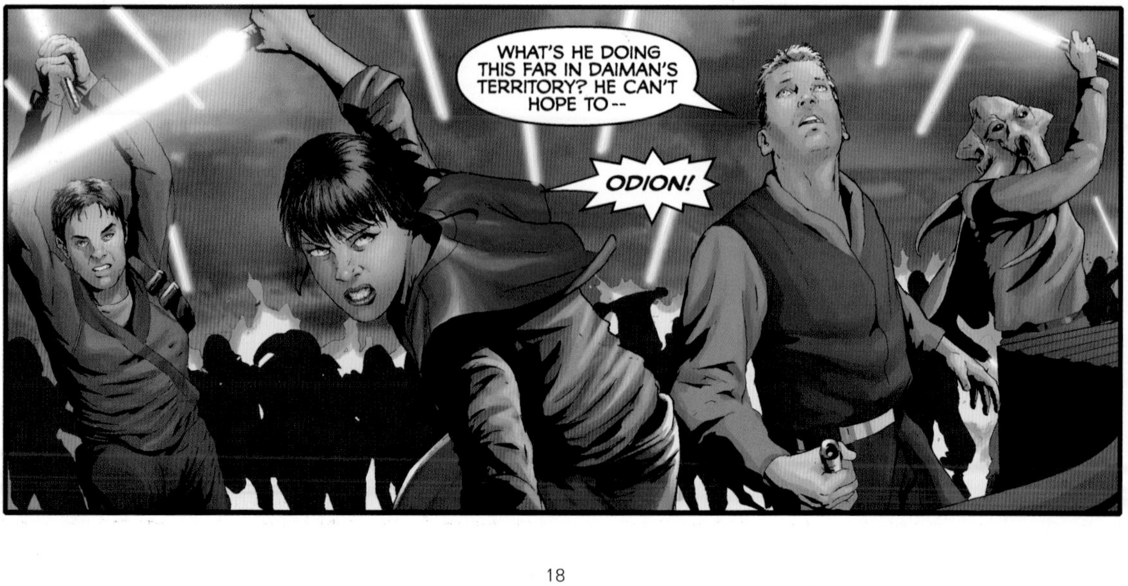
WHAT'S HE DOING THIS FAR IN DAIMAN'S TERRITORY? HE CAN'T HOPE TO--
ODION!

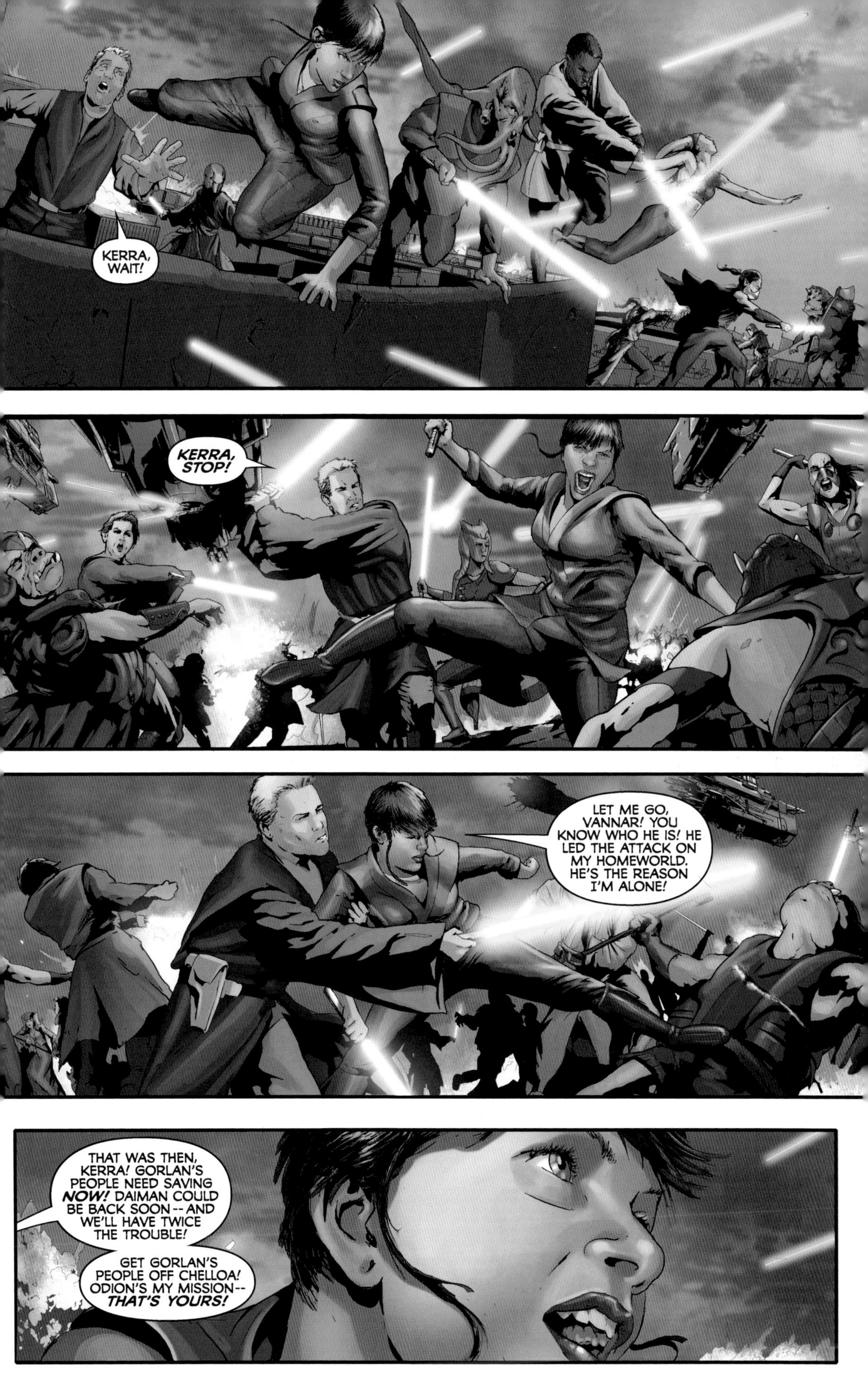
KERRA, WAIT!
KERRA, STOP!
LET ME GO, VANNAR! YOU KNOW WHO HE IS! HE LED THE ATTACK ON MY HOMEWORLD. HE'S THE REASON I'M ALONE!
THAT WAS THEN, KERRA! GORLAN'S PEOPLE NEED SAVING NOW! DAIMAN COULD BE BACK SOON--AND WE'LL HAVE TWICE THE TROUBLE!
GET GORLAN'S PEOPLE OFF CHELLOA! ODION'S MY MISSION--THAT'S YOURS!

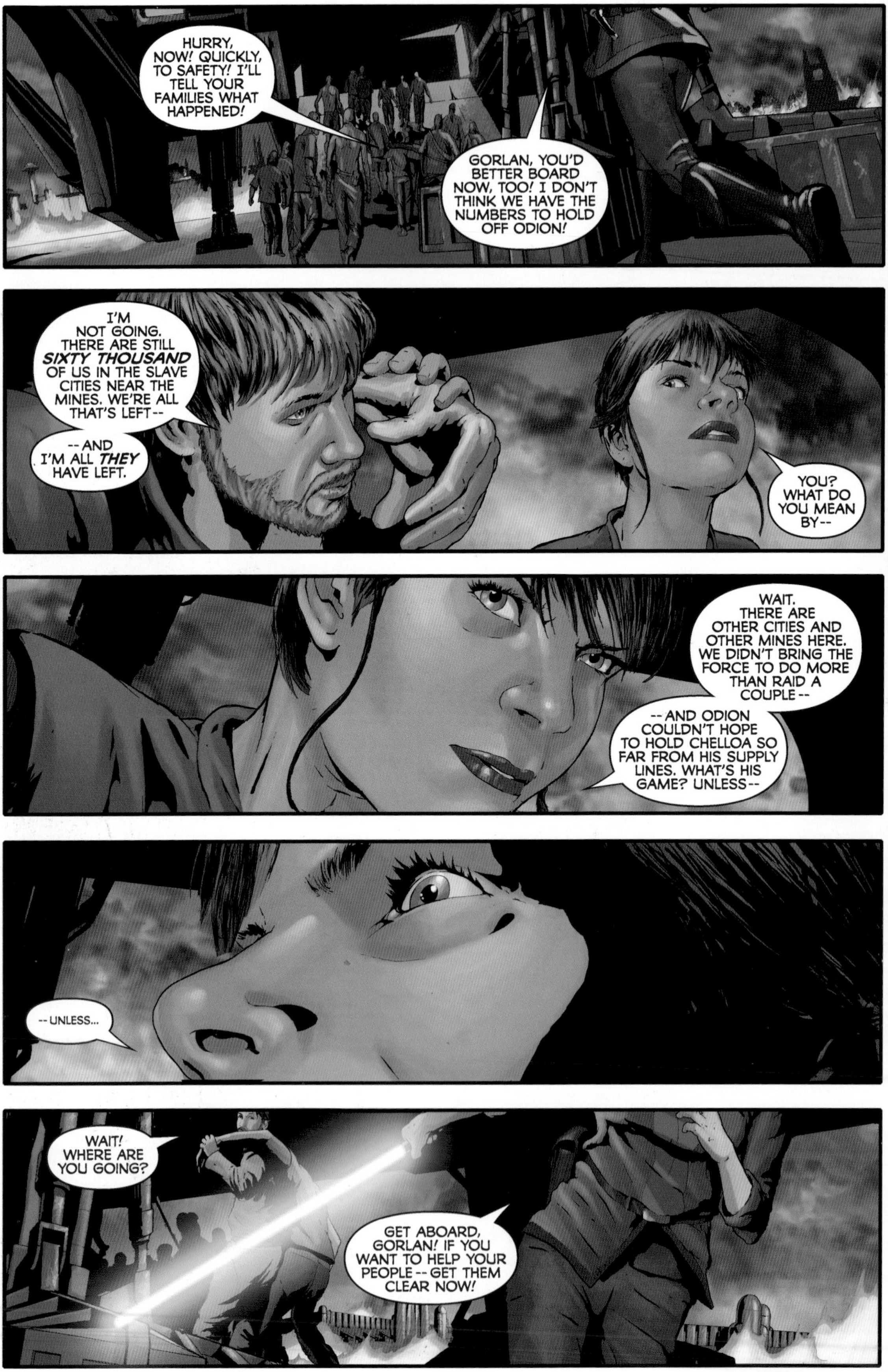
HURRY, NOW! QUICKLY, TO SAFETY! I'LL TELL YOUR FAMILIES WHAT HAPPENED!
GORLAN, YOU'D BETTER BOARD NOW, TOO! I DON'T THINK WE HAVE THE NUMBERS TO HOLD OFF ODION!
I'M NOT GOING. THERE ARE STILL SIXTY THOUSAND OF US IN THE SLAVE CITIES NEAR THE MINES. WE'RE ALL THAT'S LEFT--
--AND I'M ALL THEY HAVE LEFT.
YOU? WHAT DO YOU MEAN BY--
WAIT. THERE ARE OTHER CITIES AND OTHER MINES HERE. WE DIDN'T BRING THE FORCE TO DO MORE THAN RAID A COUPLE--
--AND ODION COULDN'T HOPE TO HOLD CHELLOA SO FAR FROM HIS SUPPLY LINES. WHAT'S HIS GAME? UNLESS--
--UNLESS...
WAIT! WHERE ARE YOU GOING?
GET ABOARD, GORLAN! IF YOU WANT TO HELP YOUR PEOPLE--GET THEM CLEAR NOW!

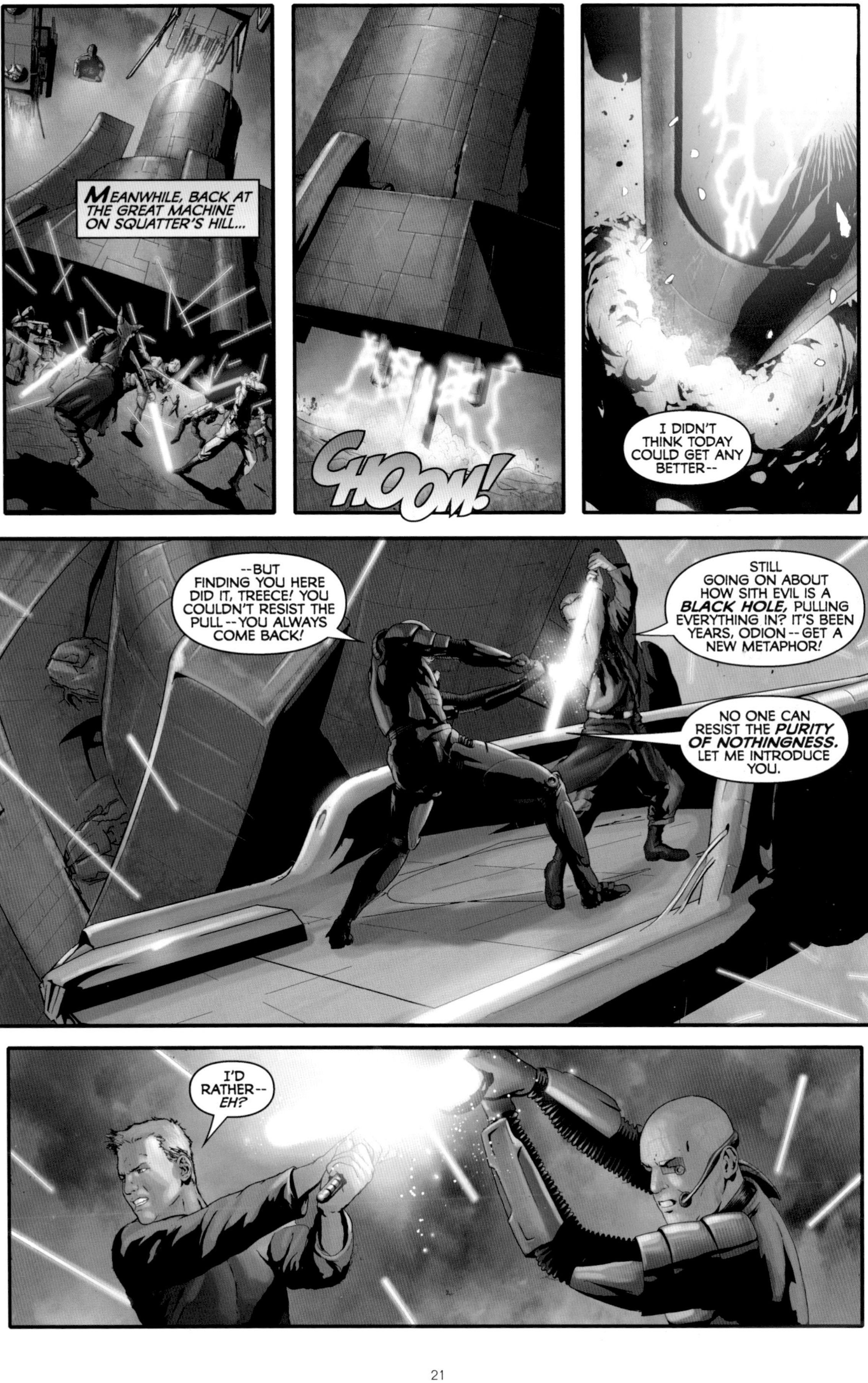
MEANWHILE, BACK AT THE GREAT MACHINE ON SQUATTER'S HILL...
CHOOM!
I DIDN'T THINK TODAY COULD GET ANY BETTER--
--BUT FINDING YOU HERE DID IT, TREECE! YOU COULDN'T RESIST THE PULL--YOU ALWAYS COME BACK!
STILL GOING ON ABOUT HOW SITH EVIL IS A *BLACK HOLE,* PULLING EVERYTHING IN? IT'S BEEN YEARS, ODION--GET A NEW METAPHOR!
NO ONE CAN RESIST THE *PURITY OF NOTHINGNESS.* LET ME INTRODUCE YOU.
I'D RATHER-- *EH?*

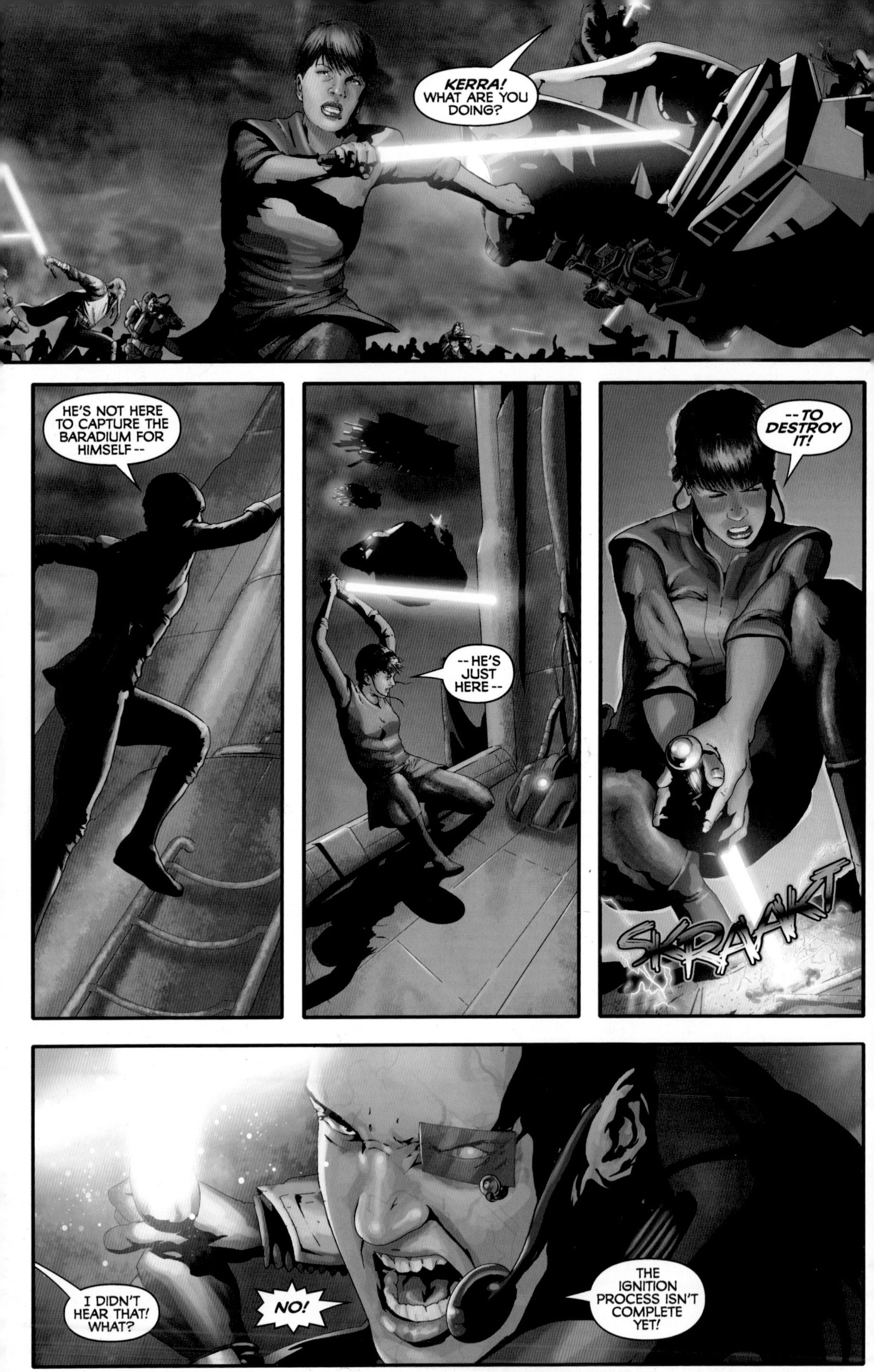
KERRA! WHAT ARE YOU DOING?
HE'S NOT HERE TO CAPTURE THE BARADIUM FOR HIMSELF --
-- HE'S JUST HERE --
-- TO DESTROY IT!
SKRAAKT
I DIDN'T HEAR THAT! WHAT?
NO!
THE IGNITION PROCESS ISN'T COMPLETE YET!

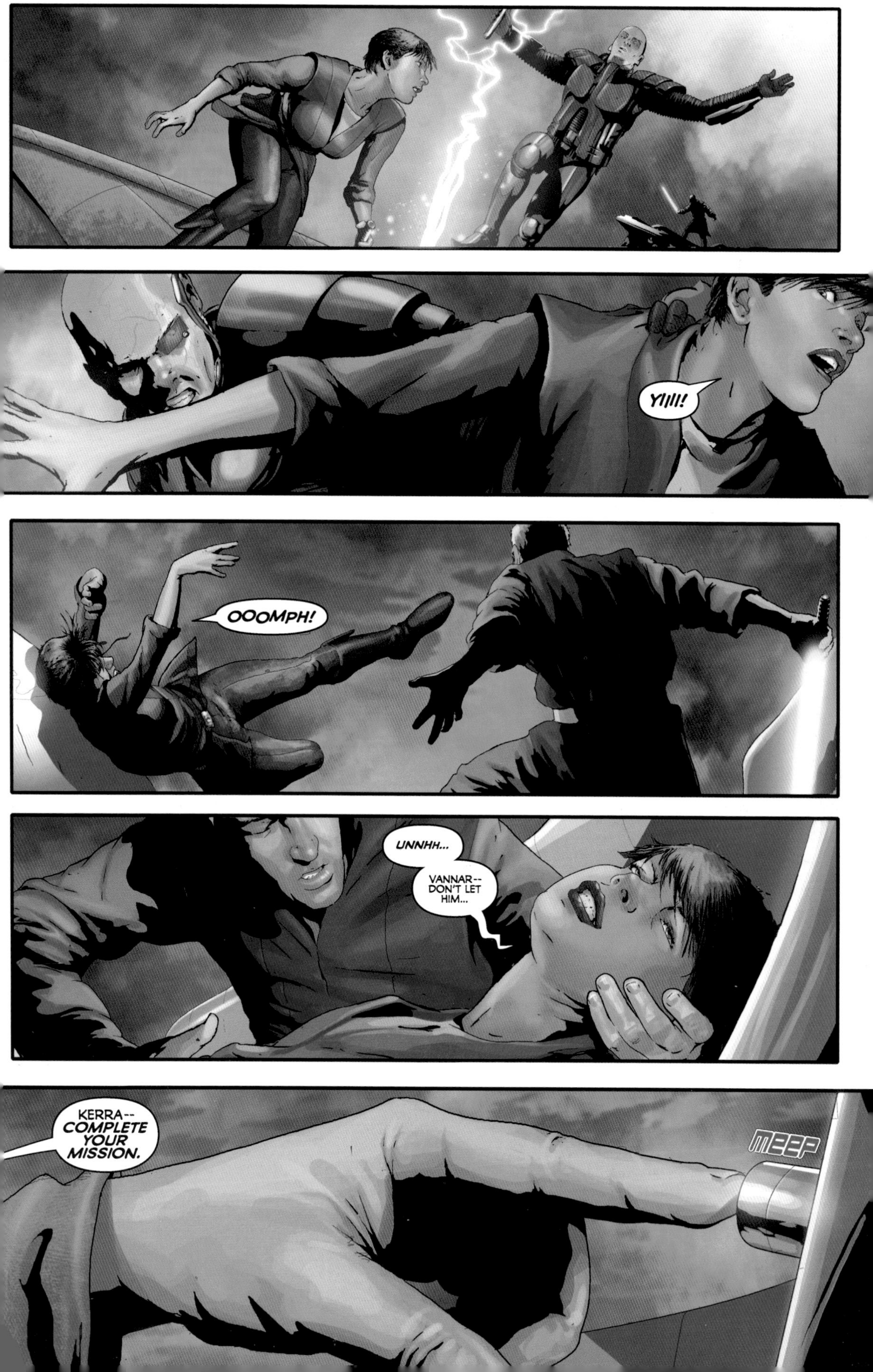
YIIII!
OOOMPH!
UNNHH...
VANNAR-- DON'T LET HIM...
KERRA-- COMPLETE YOUR MISSION.
MEEP

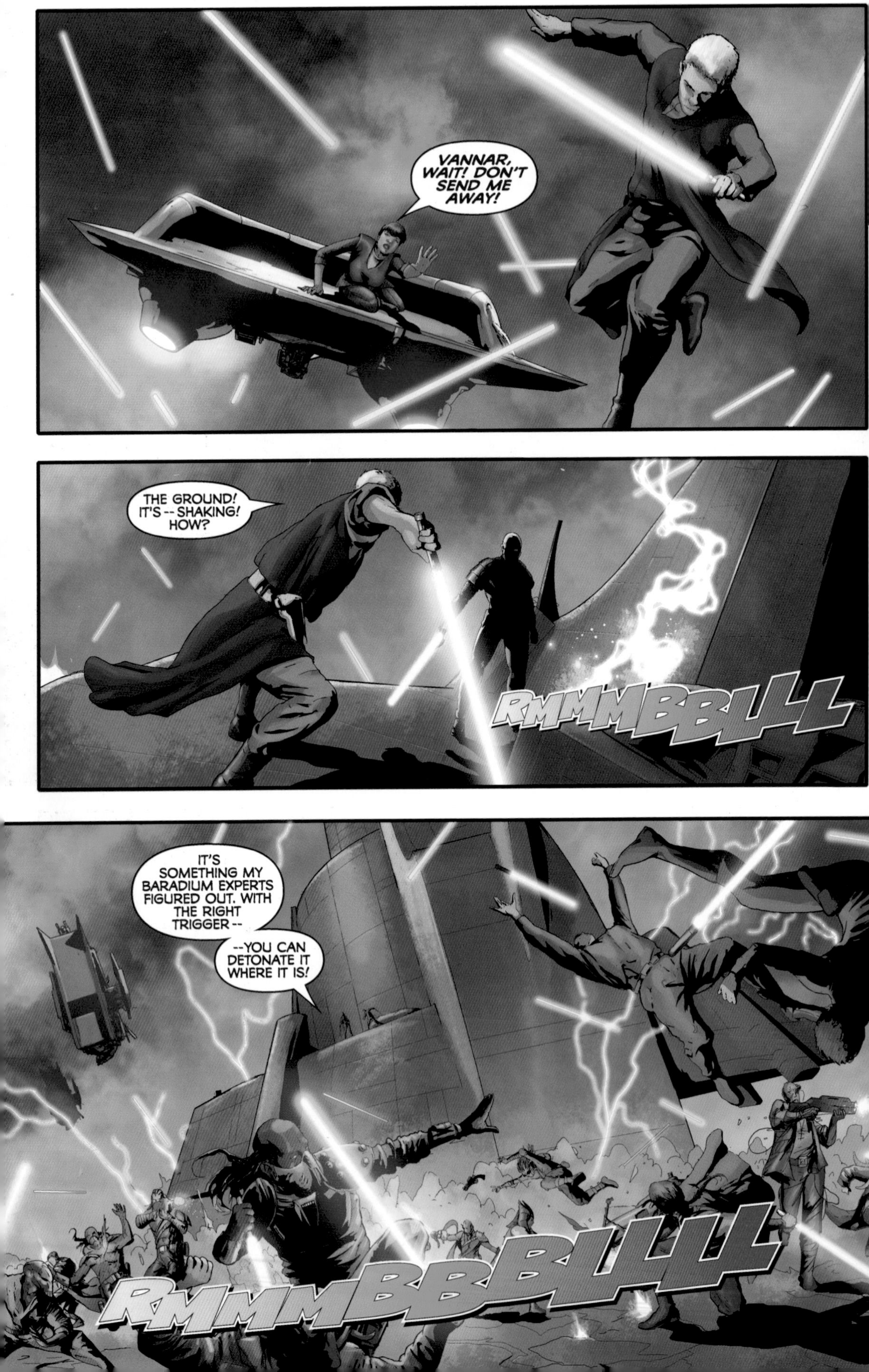
VANNAR, WAIT! DON'T SEND ME AWAY!
THE GROUND! IT'S -- SHAKING! HOW?
RMMMBBBLLL
IT'S SOMETHING MY BARADIUM EXPERTS FIGURED OUT. WITH THE RIGHT TRIGGER --
--YOU CAN DETONATE IT WHERE IT IS!
RMMMBBBLLL

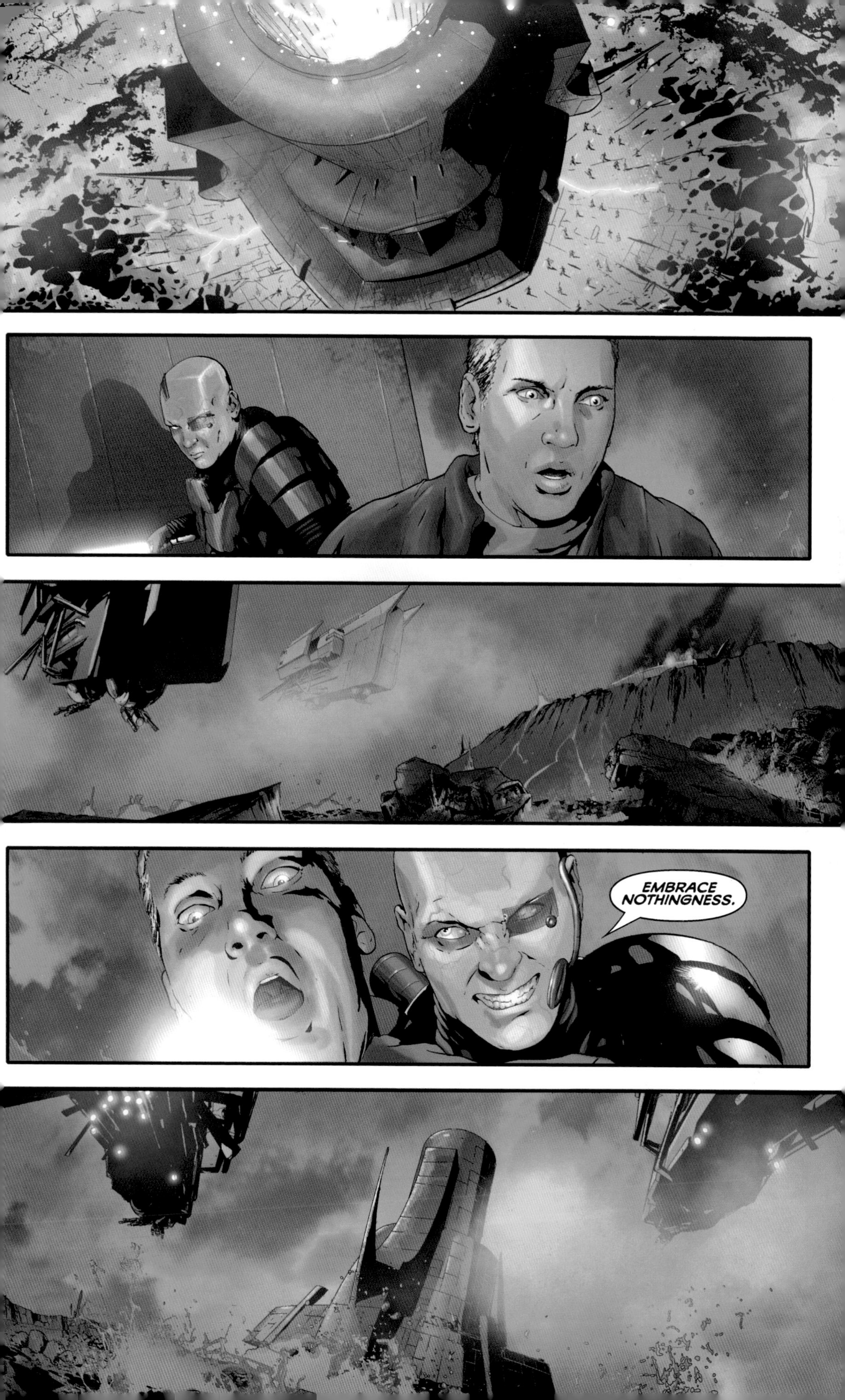
EMBRACE NOTHINGNESS.

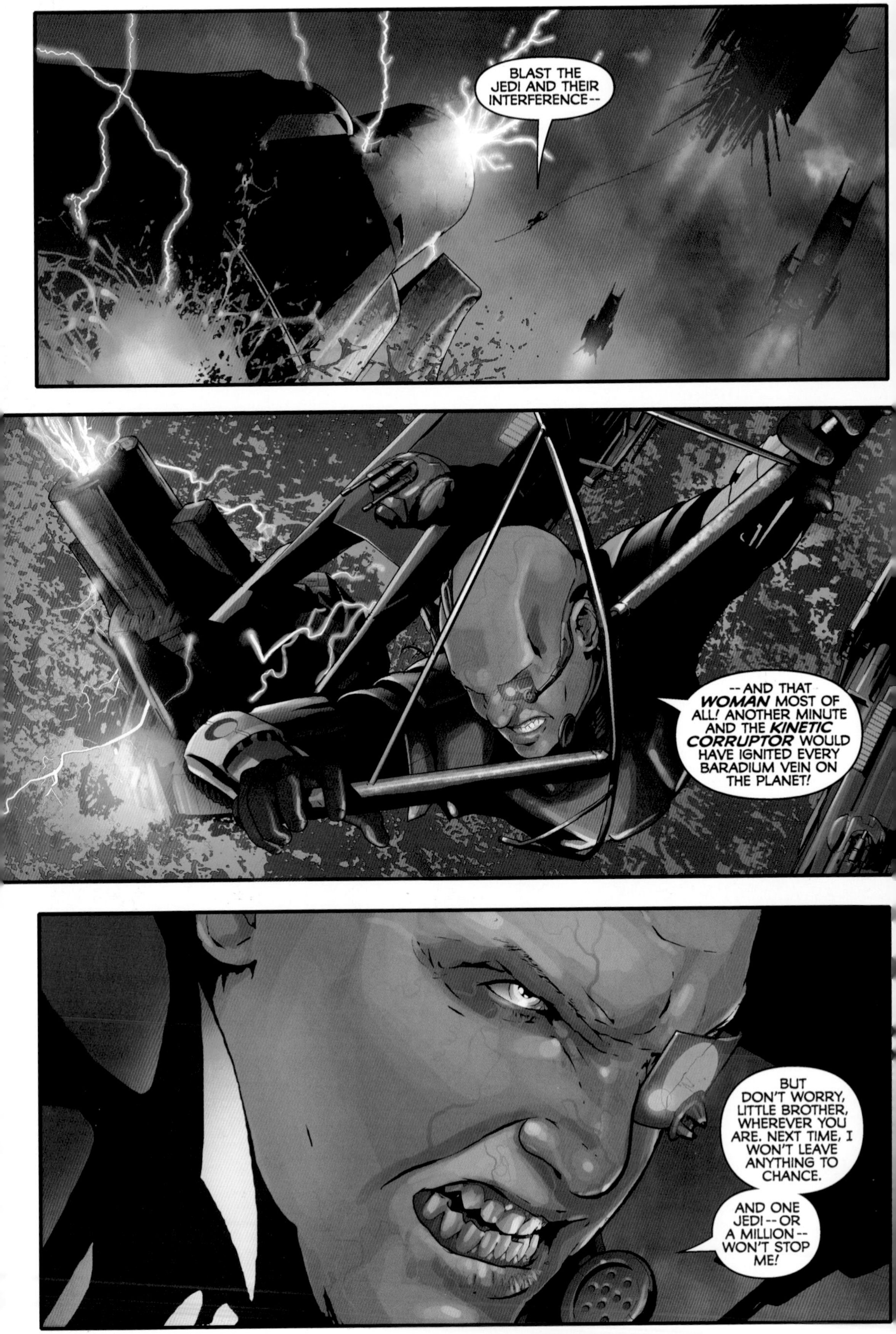
BLAST THE JEDI AND THEIR INTERFERENCE--
--AND THAT WOMAN MOST OF ALL! ANOTHER MINUTE AND THE KINETIC CORRUPTOR WOULD HAVE IGNITED EVERY BARADIUM VEIN ON THE PLANET!
BUT DON'T WORRY, LITTLE BROTHER, WHEREVER YOU ARE. NEXT TIME, I WON'T LEAVE ANYTHING TO CHANCE.
AND ONE JEDI--OR A MILLION--WON'T STOP ME!

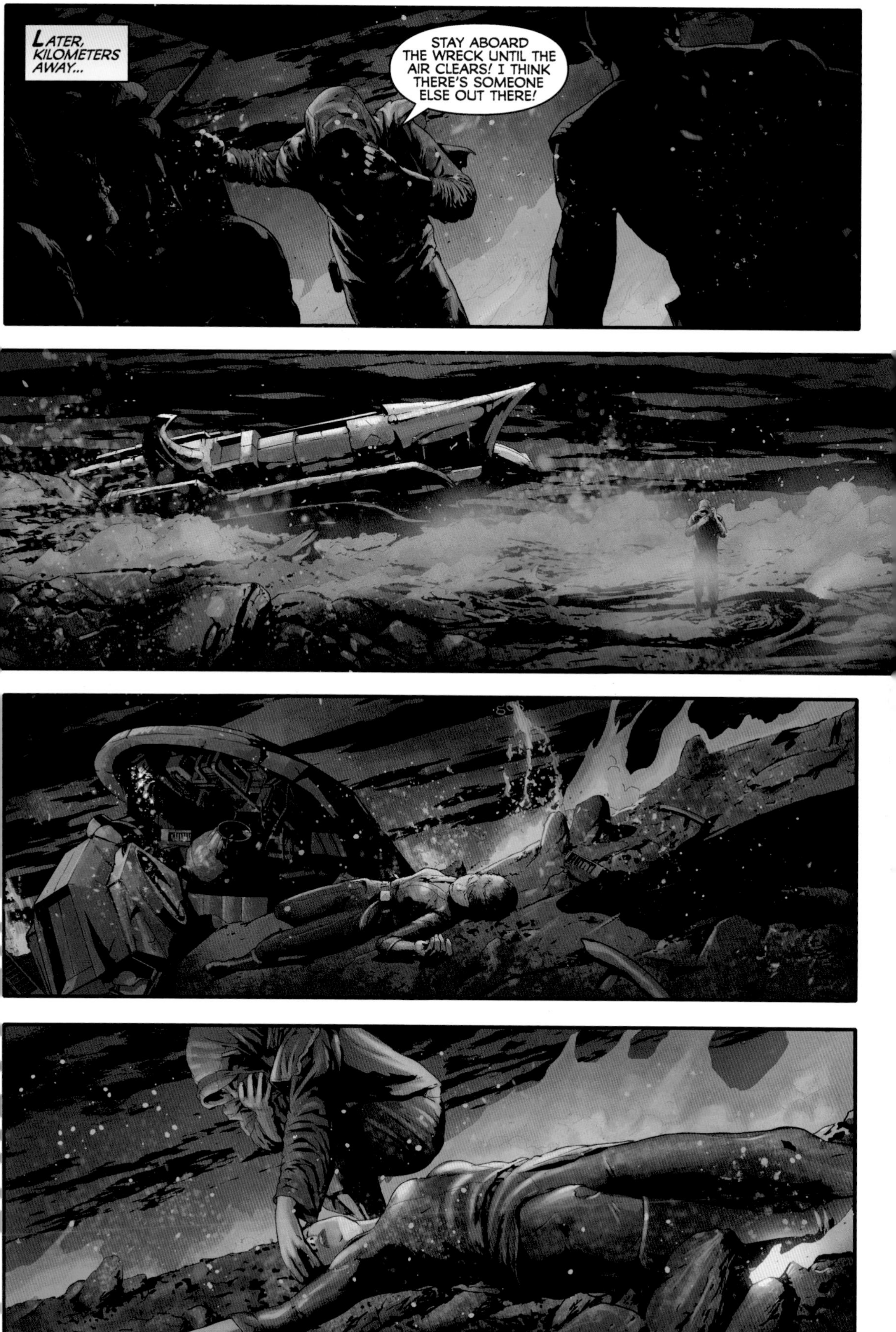
LATER, KILOMETERS AWAY...
STAY ABOARD THE WRECK UNTIL THE AIR CLEARS! I THINK THERE'S SOMEONE ELSE OUT THERE!

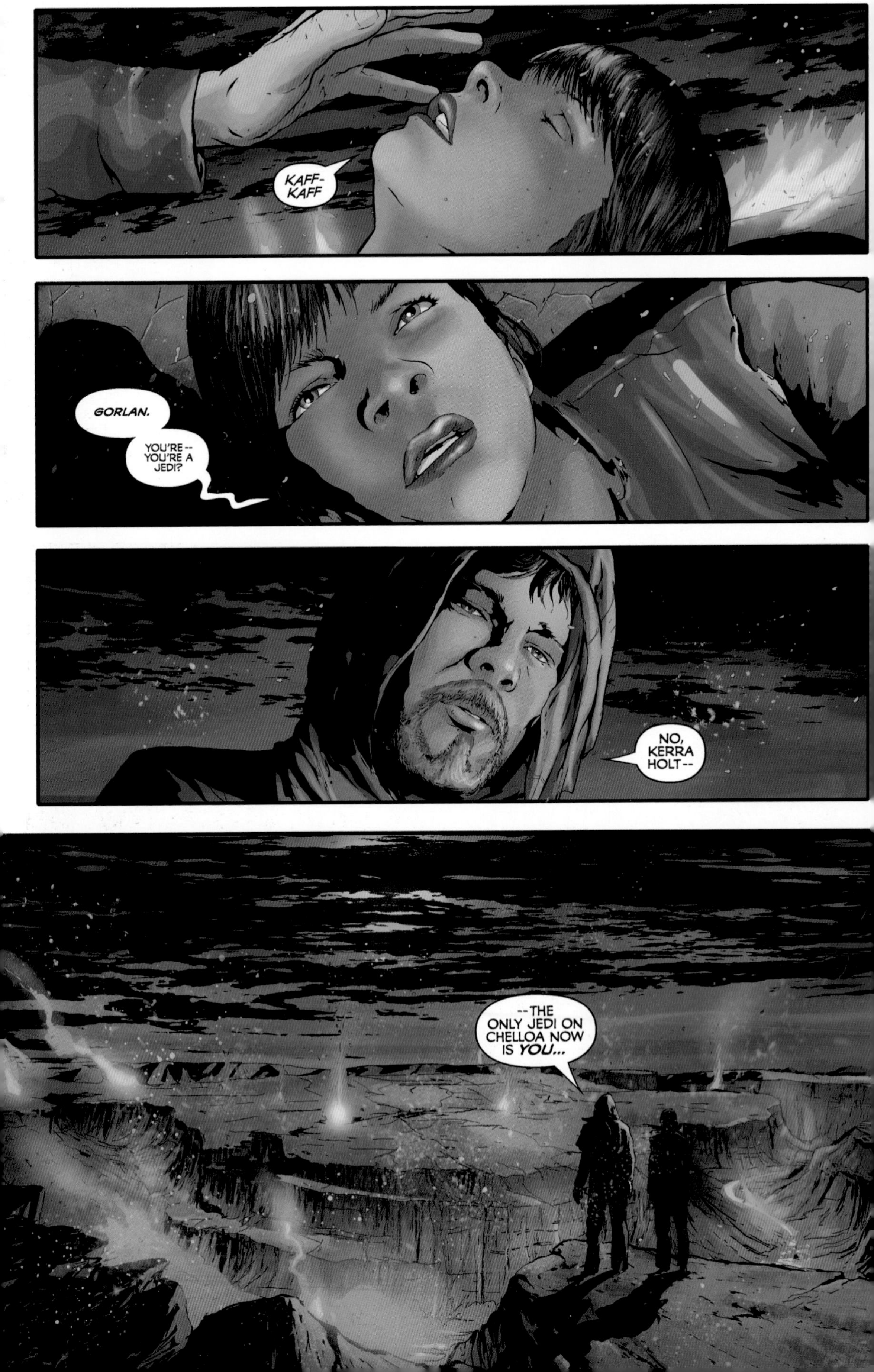
KAFF-KAFF
GORLAN.
YOU'RE--YOU'RE A JEDI?
NO, KERRA HOLT--
--THE ONLY JEDI ON CHELLOA NOW IS *YOU...*

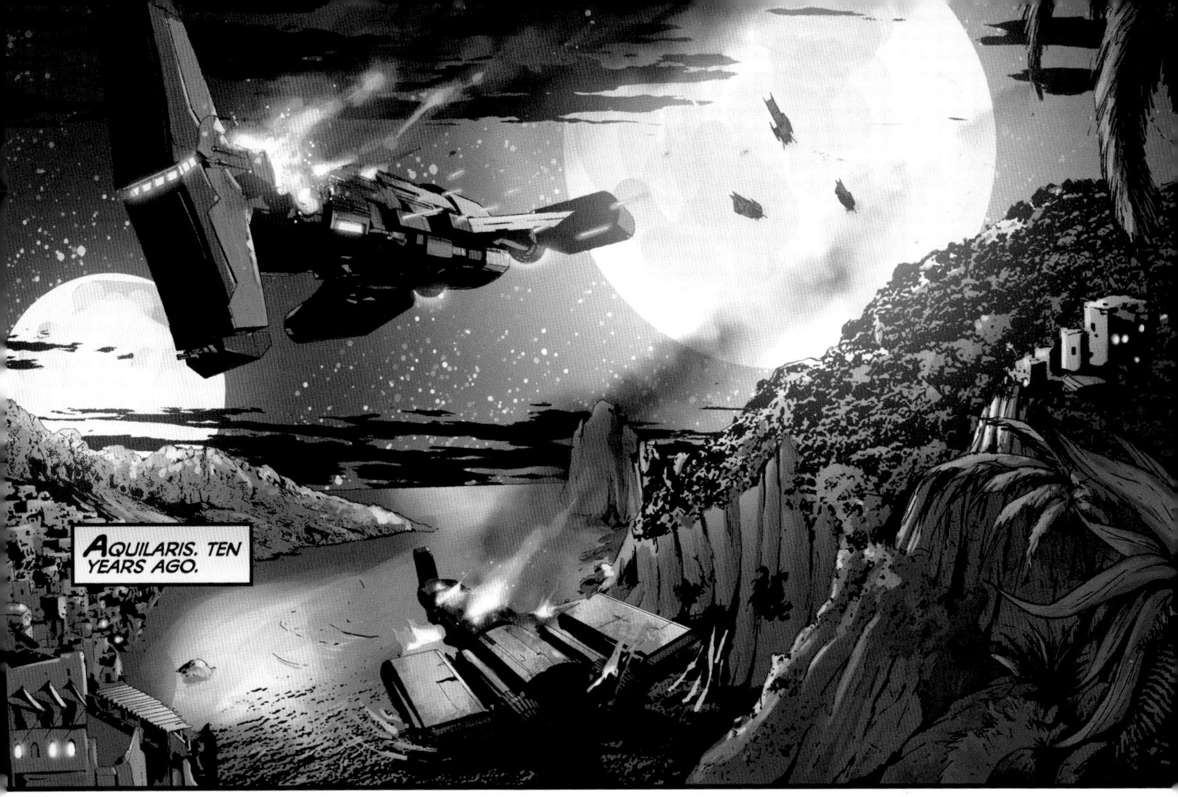
AQUILARIS. TEN YEARS AGO.

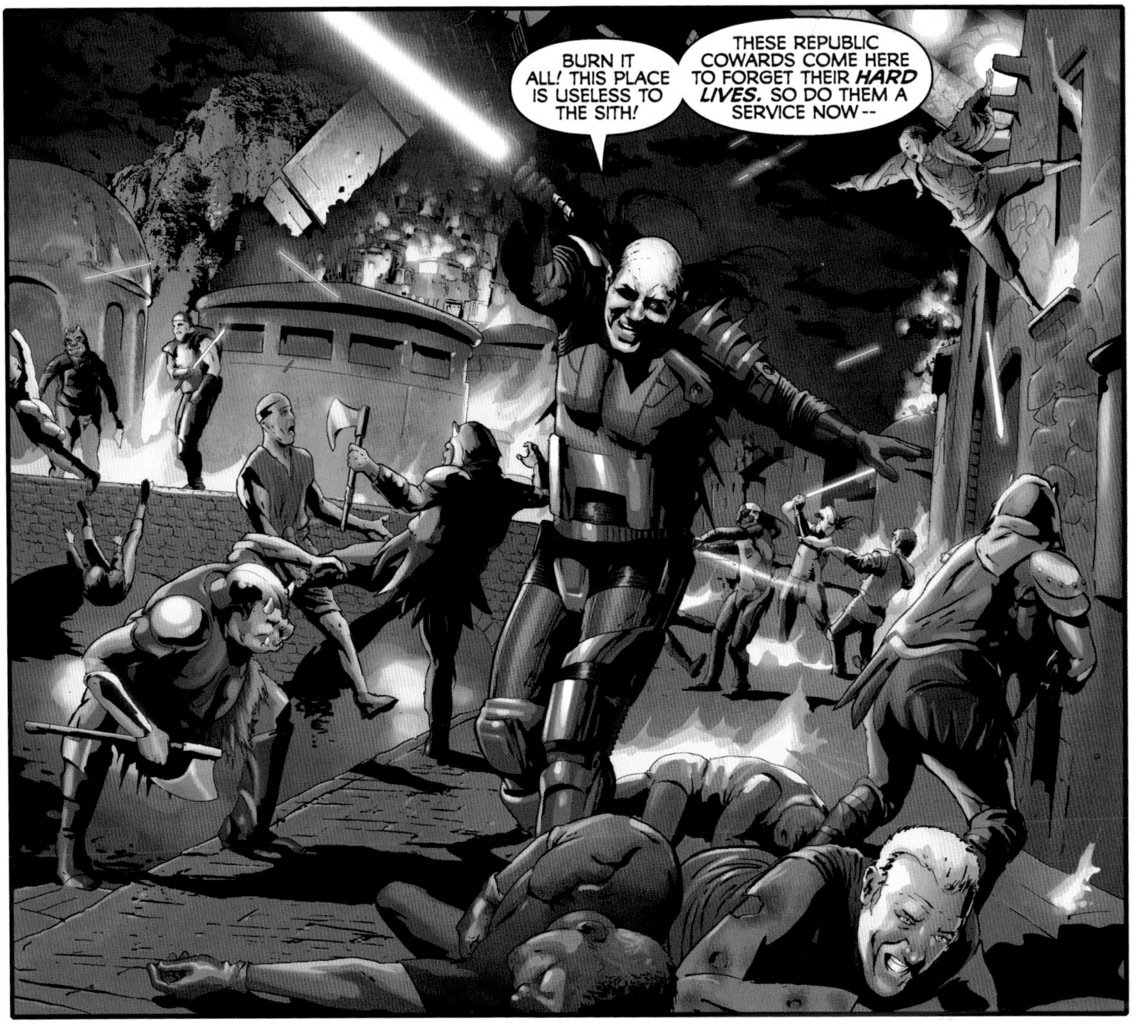
BURN IT ALL! THIS PLACE IS USELESS TO THE SITH!
THESE REPUBLIC COWARDS COME HERE TO FORGET THEIR HARD LIVES. SO DO THEM A SERVICE NOW--

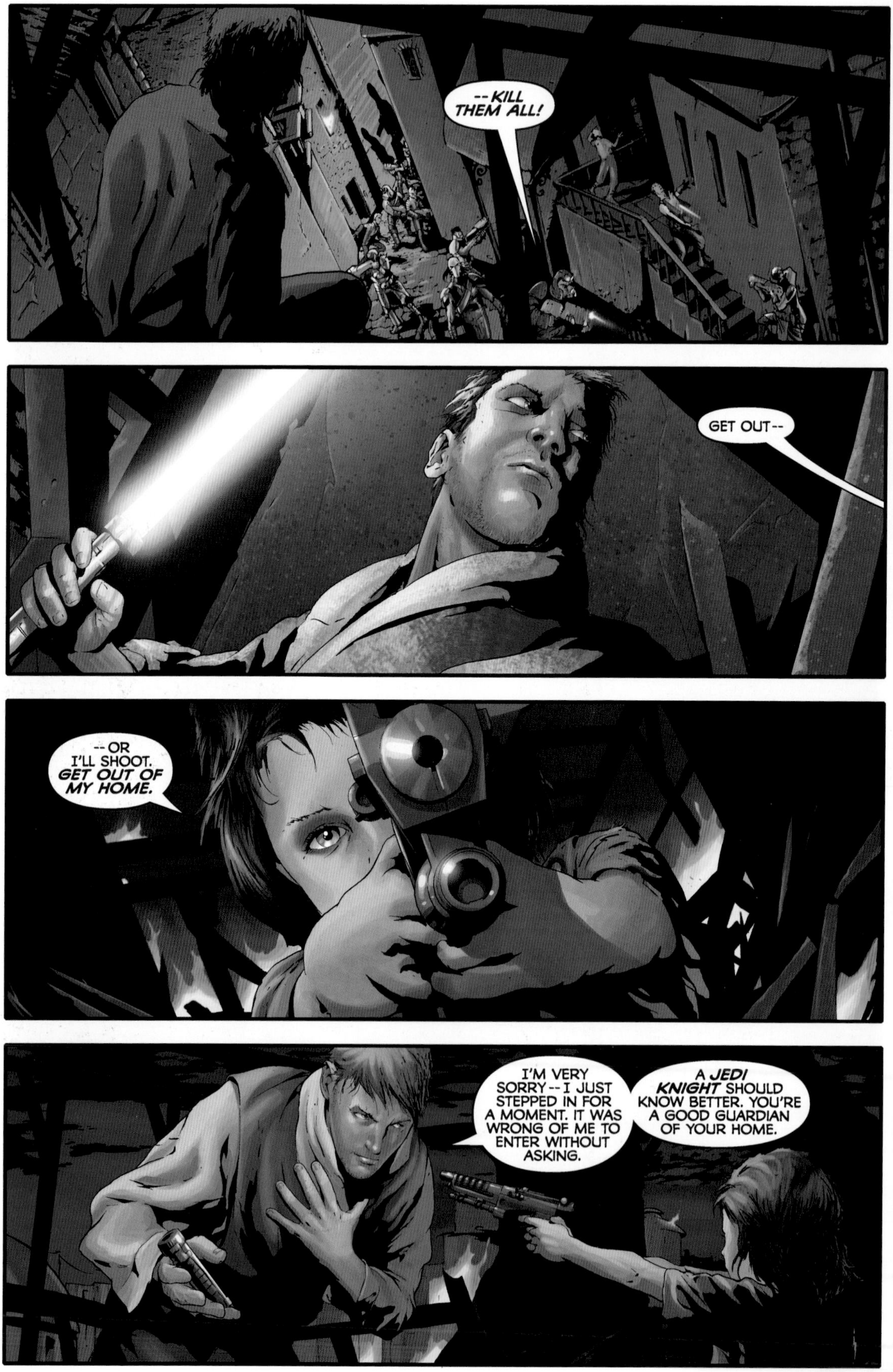
--*KILL THEM ALL!*
GET OUT--
--OR I'LL SHOOT. *GET OUT OF MY HOME.*
I'M VERY SORRY--I JUST STEPPED IN FOR A MOMENT. IT WAS WRONG OF ME TO ENTER WITHOUT ASKING.
A *JEDI KNIGHT* SHOULD KNOW BETTER. YOU'RE A GOOD GUARDIAN OF YOUR HOME.

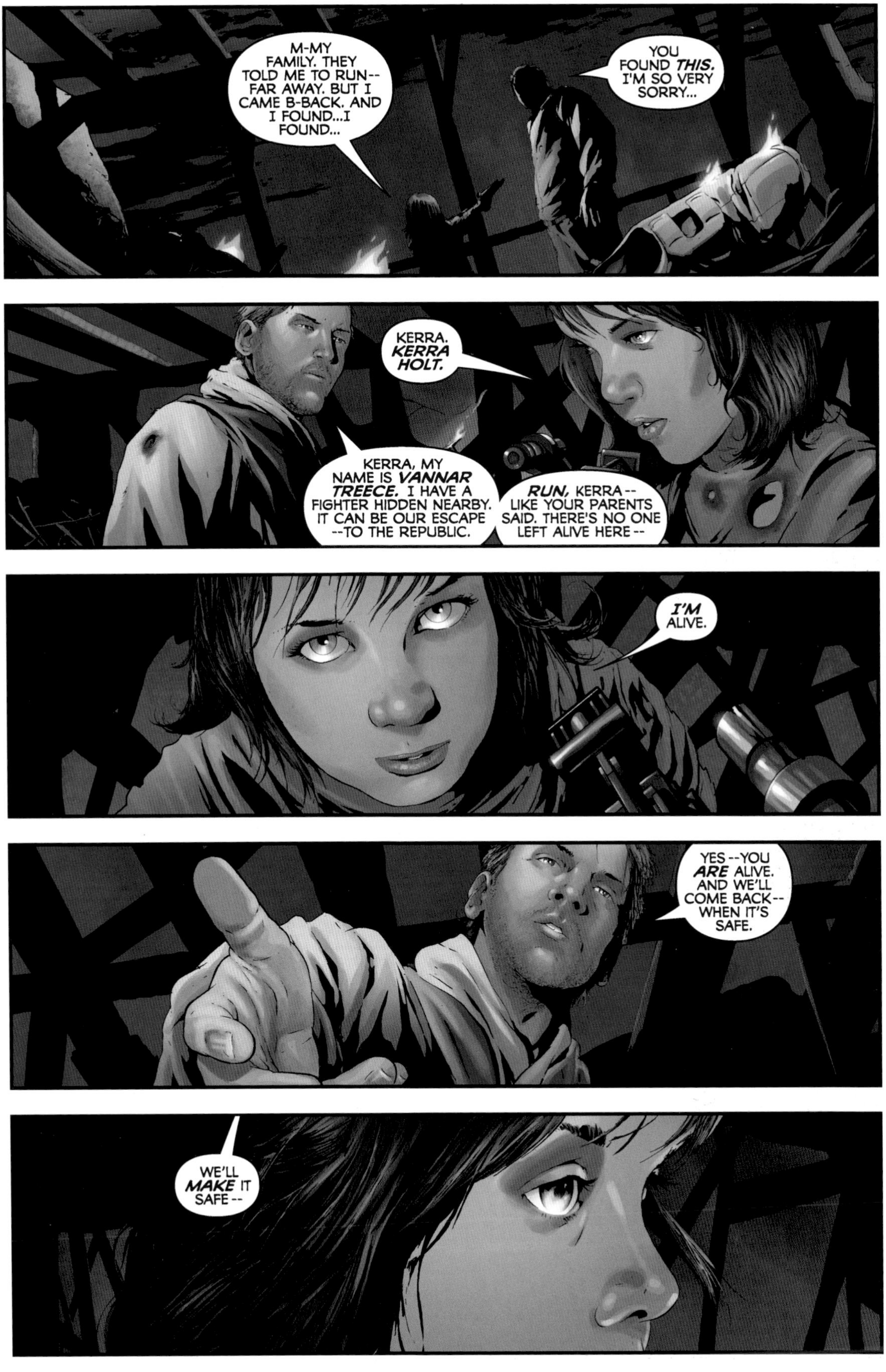
M-MY FAMILY. THEY TOLD ME TO RUN-- FAR AWAY. BUT I CAME B-BACK. AND I FOUND...I FOUND...
YOU FOUND *THIS.* I'M SO VERY SORRY...
KERRA. *KERRA HOLT.*
KERRA, MY NAME IS *VANNAR TREECE.* I HAVE A FIGHTER HIDDEN NEARBY. IT CAN BE OUR ESCAPE --TO THE REPUBLIC.
RUN, KERRA-- LIKE YOUR PARENTS SAID. THERE'S NO ONE LEFT ALIVE HERE--
I'M ALIVE.
YES--YOU *ARE* ALIVE. AND WE'LL COME BACK-- WHEN IT'S SAFE.
WE'LL *MAKE* IT SAFE--

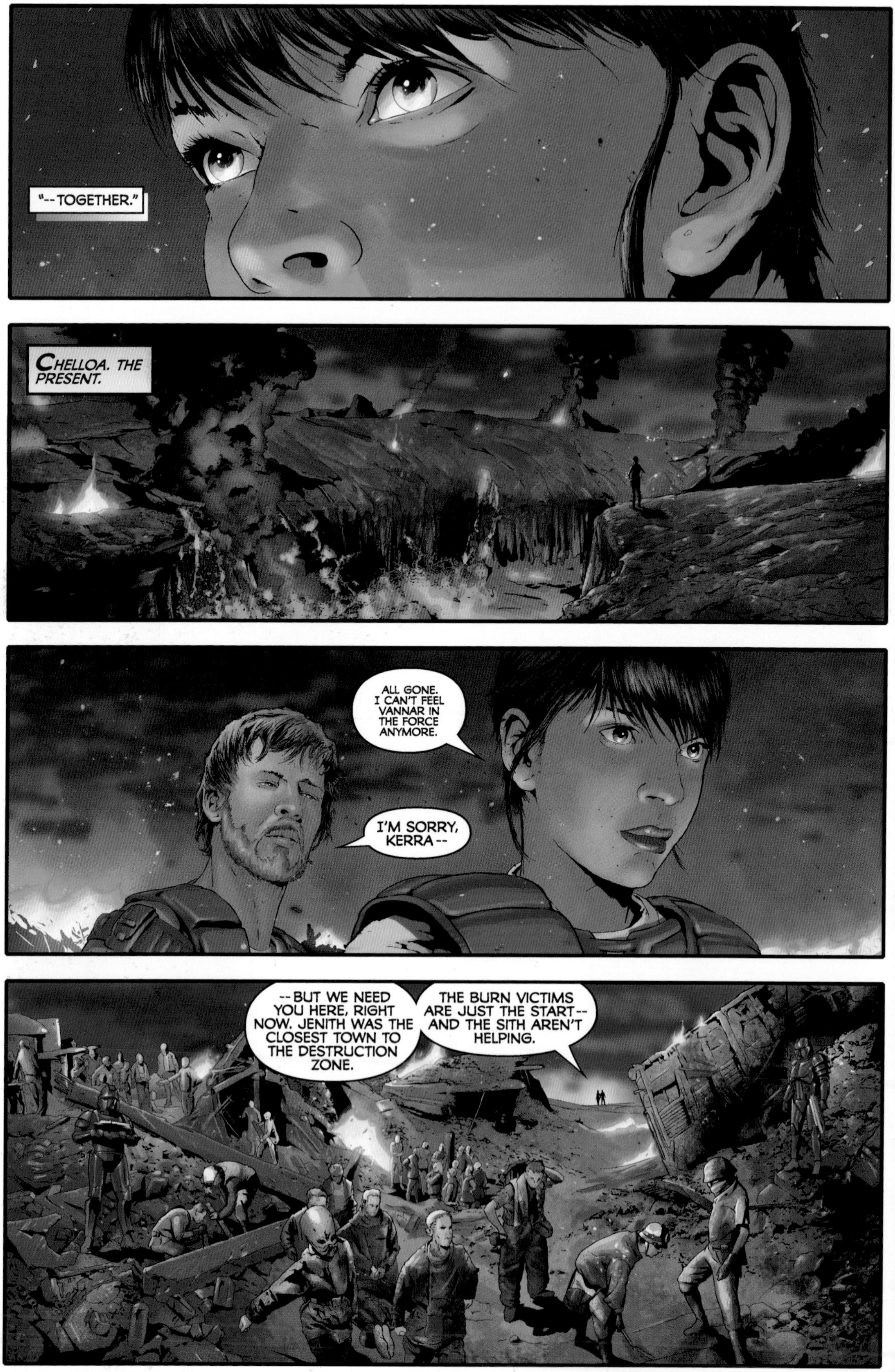
"--TOGETHER."
CHELLOA. THE PRESENT.
ALL GONE. I CAN'T FEEL VANNAR IN THE FORCE ANYMORE.
I'M SORRY, KERRA--
--BUT WE NEED YOU HERE, RIGHT NOW. JENITH WAS THE CLOSEST TOWN TO THE DESTRUCTION ZONE.
THE BURN VICTIMS ARE JUST THE START-- AND THE SITH AREN'T HELPING.

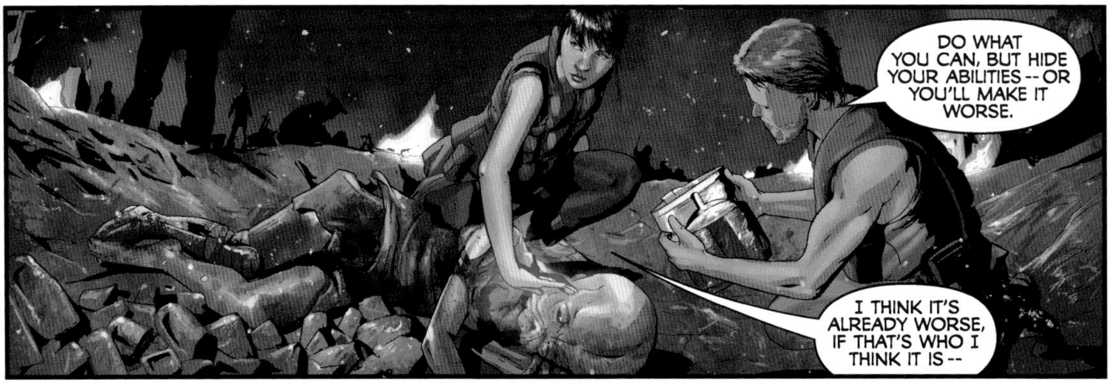
DO WHAT YOU CAN, BUT HIDE YOUR ABILITIES -- OR YOU'LL MAKE IT WORSE.
I THINK IT'S ALREADY WORSE, IF THAT'S WHO I THINK IT IS --

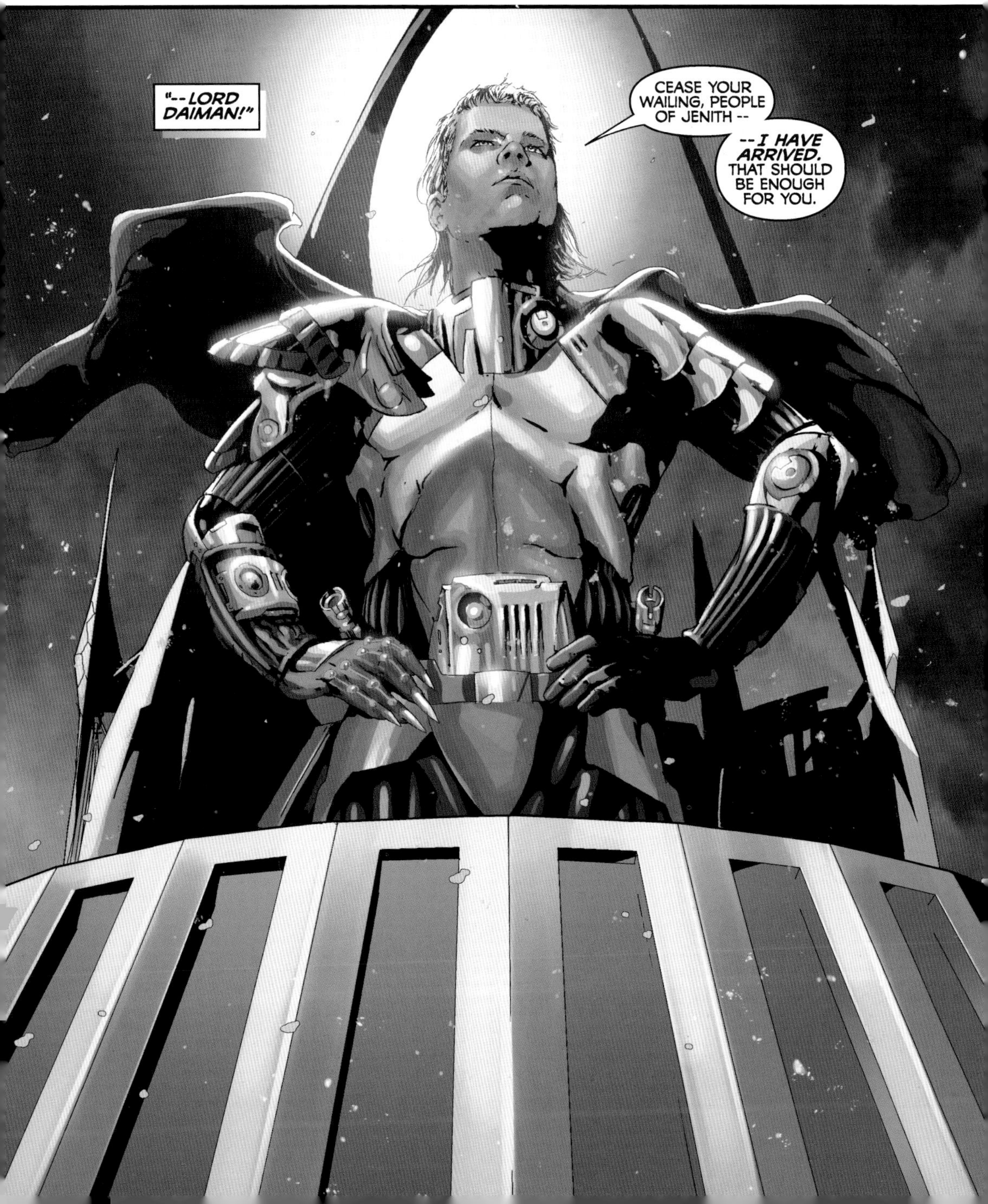
"-- LORD DAIMAN!"
CEASE YOUR WAILING, PEOPLE OF JENITH --
-- I HAVE ARRIVED. THAT SHOULD BE ENOUGH FOR YOU.

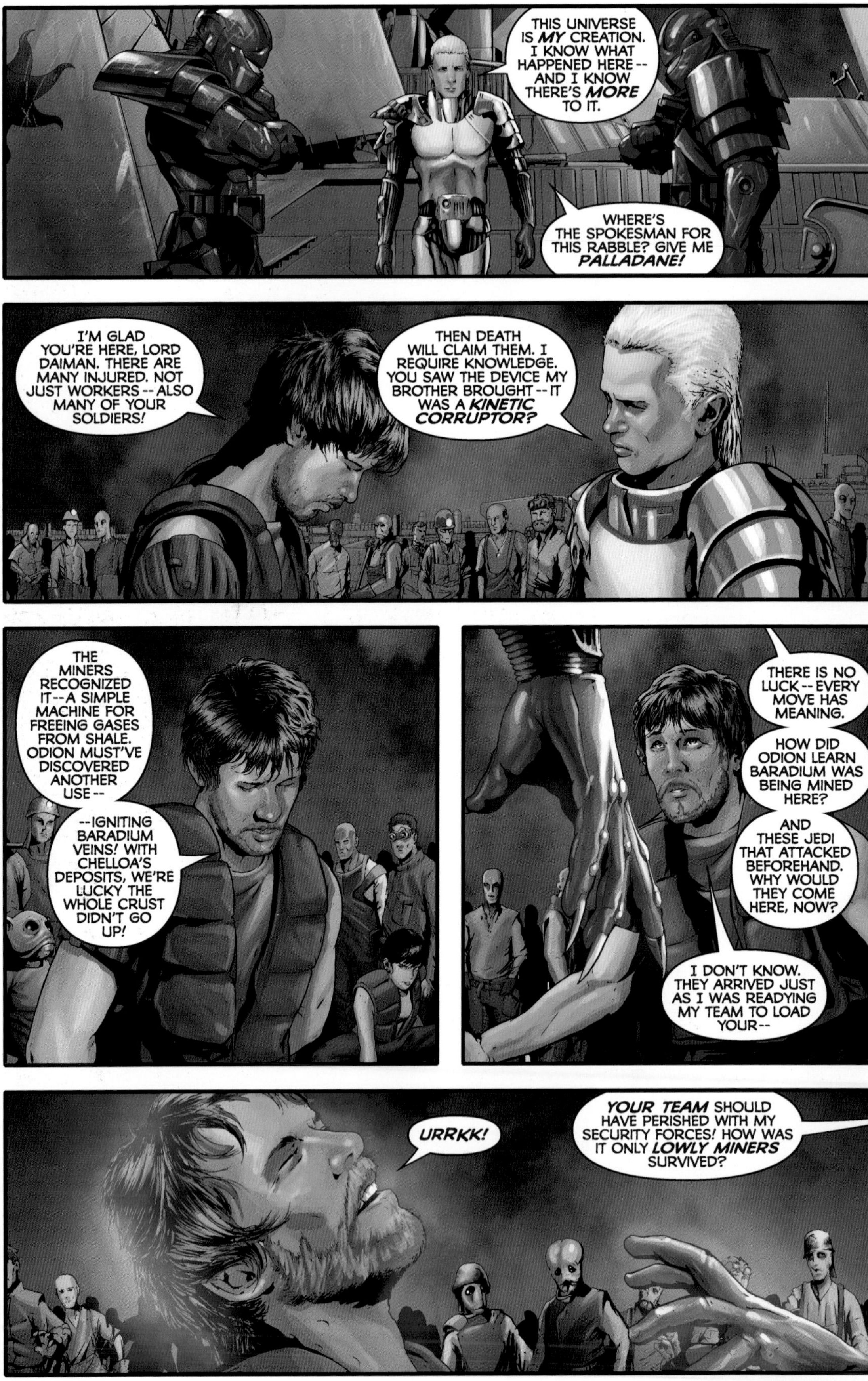
THIS UNIVERSE IS *MY* CREATION. I KNOW WHAT HAPPENED HERE -- AND I KNOW THERE'S *MORE* TO IT.
WHERE'S THE SPOKESMAN FOR THIS RABBLE? GIVE ME *PALLADANE!*
I'M GLAD YOU'RE HERE, LORD DAIMAN. THERE ARE MANY INJURED. NOT JUST WORKERS -- ALSO MANY OF YOUR SOLDIERS!
THEN DEATH WILL CLAIM THEM. I REQUIRE KNOWLEDGE. YOU SAW THE DEVICE MY BROTHER BROUGHT -- IT WAS A *KINETIC CORRUPTOR?*
THE MINERS RECOGNIZED IT -- A SIMPLE MACHINE FOR FREEING GASES FROM SHALE. ODION MUST'VE DISCOVERED ANOTHER USE --
--IGNITING BARADIUM VEINS! WITH CHELLOA'S DEPOSITS, WE'RE LUCKY THE WHOLE CRUST DIDN'T GO UP!
THERE IS NO LUCK -- EVERY MOVE HAS MEANING.
HOW DID ODION LEARN BARADIUM WAS BEING MINED HERE?
AND THESE JEDI THAT ATTACKED BEFOREHAND. WHY WOULD THEY COME HERE, NOW?
I DON'T KNOW. THEY ARRIVED JUST AS I WAS READYING MY TEAM TO LOAD YOUR--
URRKK!
YOUR TEAM SHOULD HAVE PERISHED WITH MY SECURITY FORCES! HOW WAS IT ONLY *LOWLY MINERS* SURVIVED?

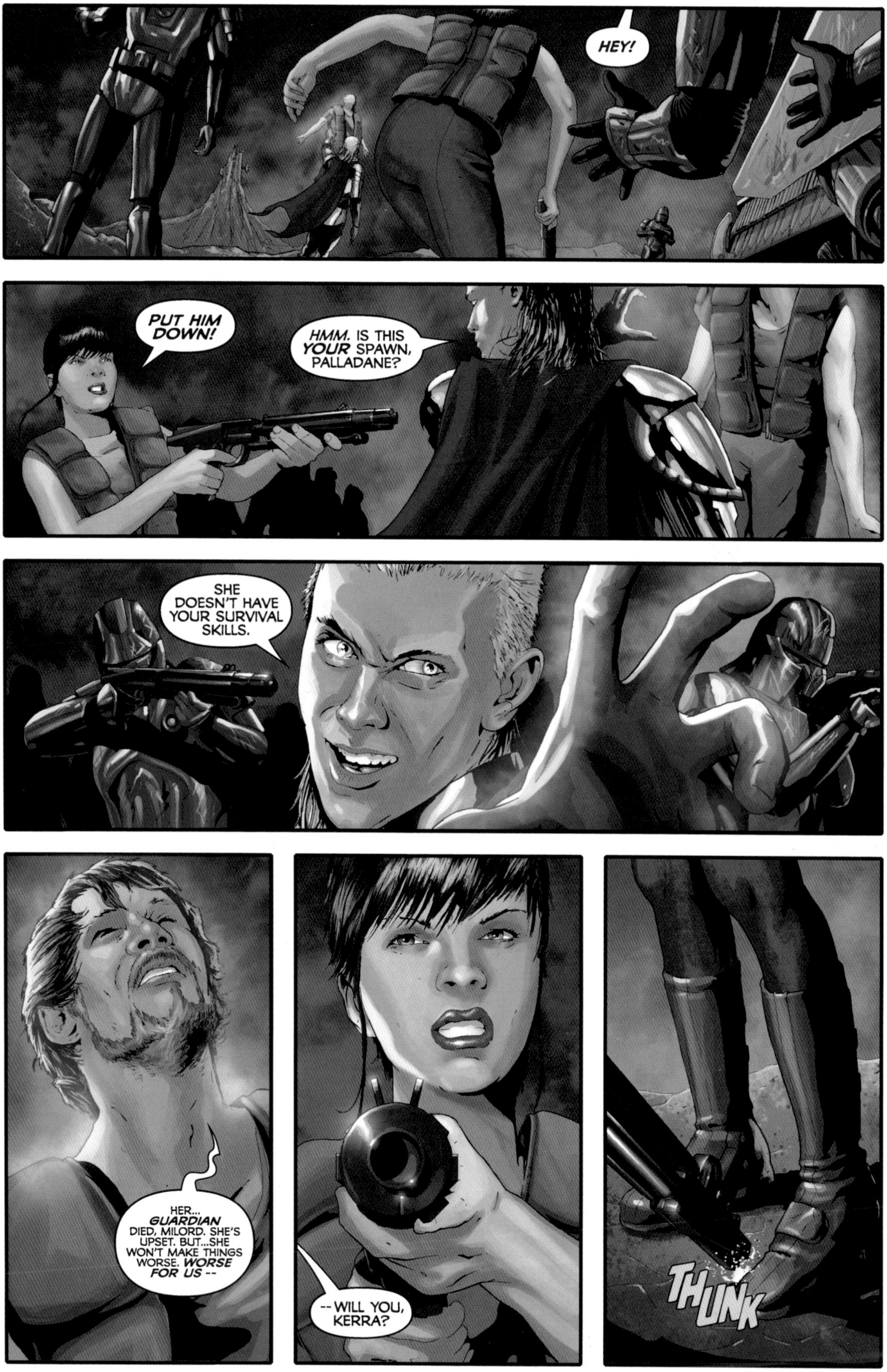
HEY!
PUT HIM DOWN!
HMM. IS THIS YOUR SPAWN, PALLADANE?
SHE DOESN'T HAVE YOUR SURVIVAL SKILLS.
HER... GUARDIAN DIED, MILORD. SHE'S UPSET. BUT...SHE WON'T MAKE THINGS WORSE. WORSE FOR US --
-- WILL YOU, KERRA?
THUNK

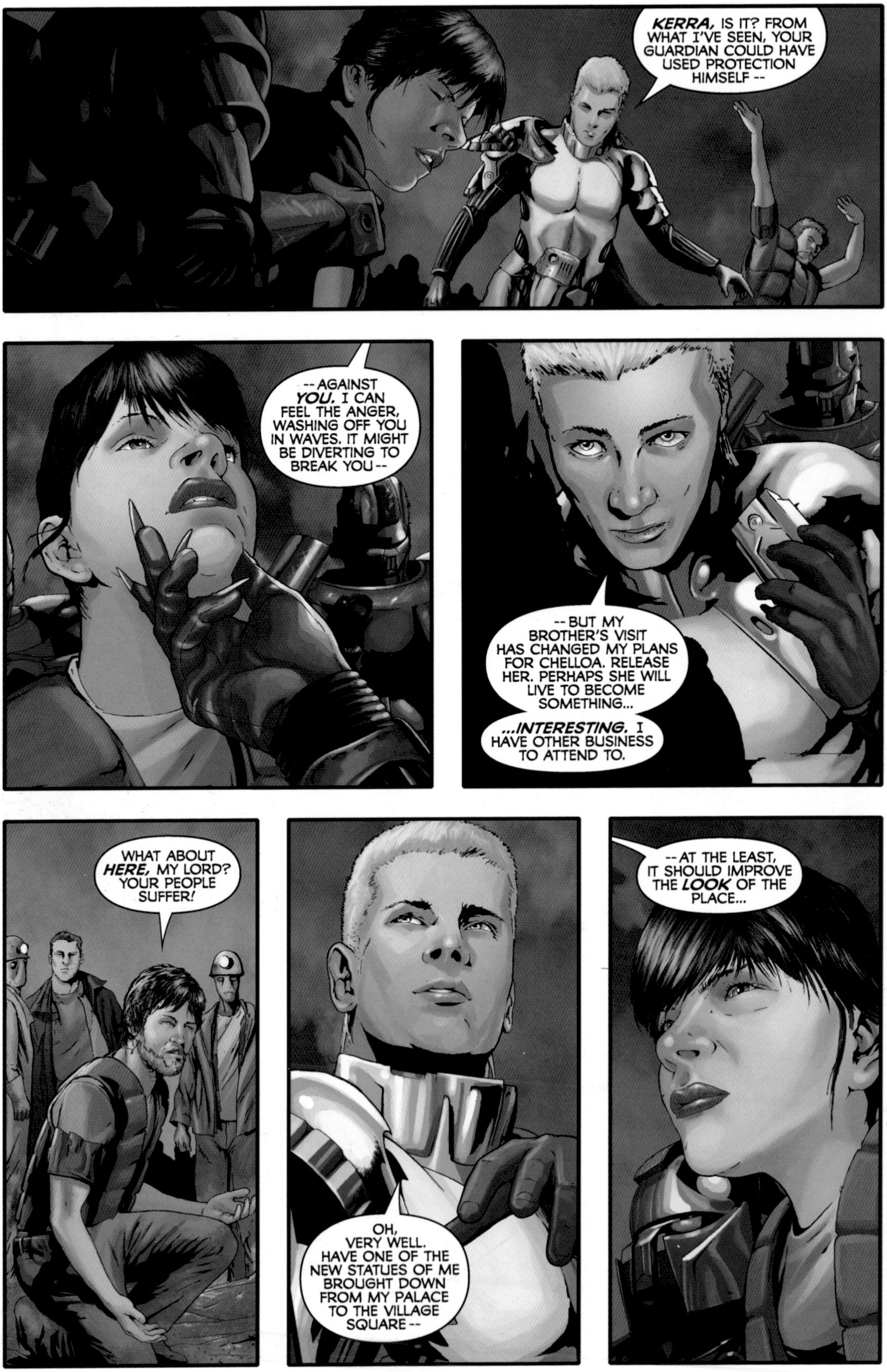
KERRA, IS IT? FROM WHAT I'VE SEEN, YOUR GUARDIAN COULD HAVE USED PROTECTION HIMSELF --
-- AGAINST YOU. I CAN FEEL THE ANGER, WASHING OFF YOU IN WAVES. IT MIGHT BE DIVERTING TO BREAK YOU --
-- BUT MY BROTHER'S VISIT HAS CHANGED MY PLANS FOR CHELLOA. RELEASE HER. PERHAPS SHE WILL LIVE TO BECOME SOMETHING...
...INTERESTING. I HAVE OTHER BUSINESS TO ATTEND TO.
WHAT ABOUT HERE, MY LORD? YOUR PEOPLE SUFFER!
OH, VERY WELL. HAVE ONE OF THE NEW STATUES OF ME BROUGHT DOWN FROM MY PALACE TO THE VILLAGE SQUARE --
-- AT THE LEAST, IT SHOULD IMPROVE THE LOOK OF THE PLACE...

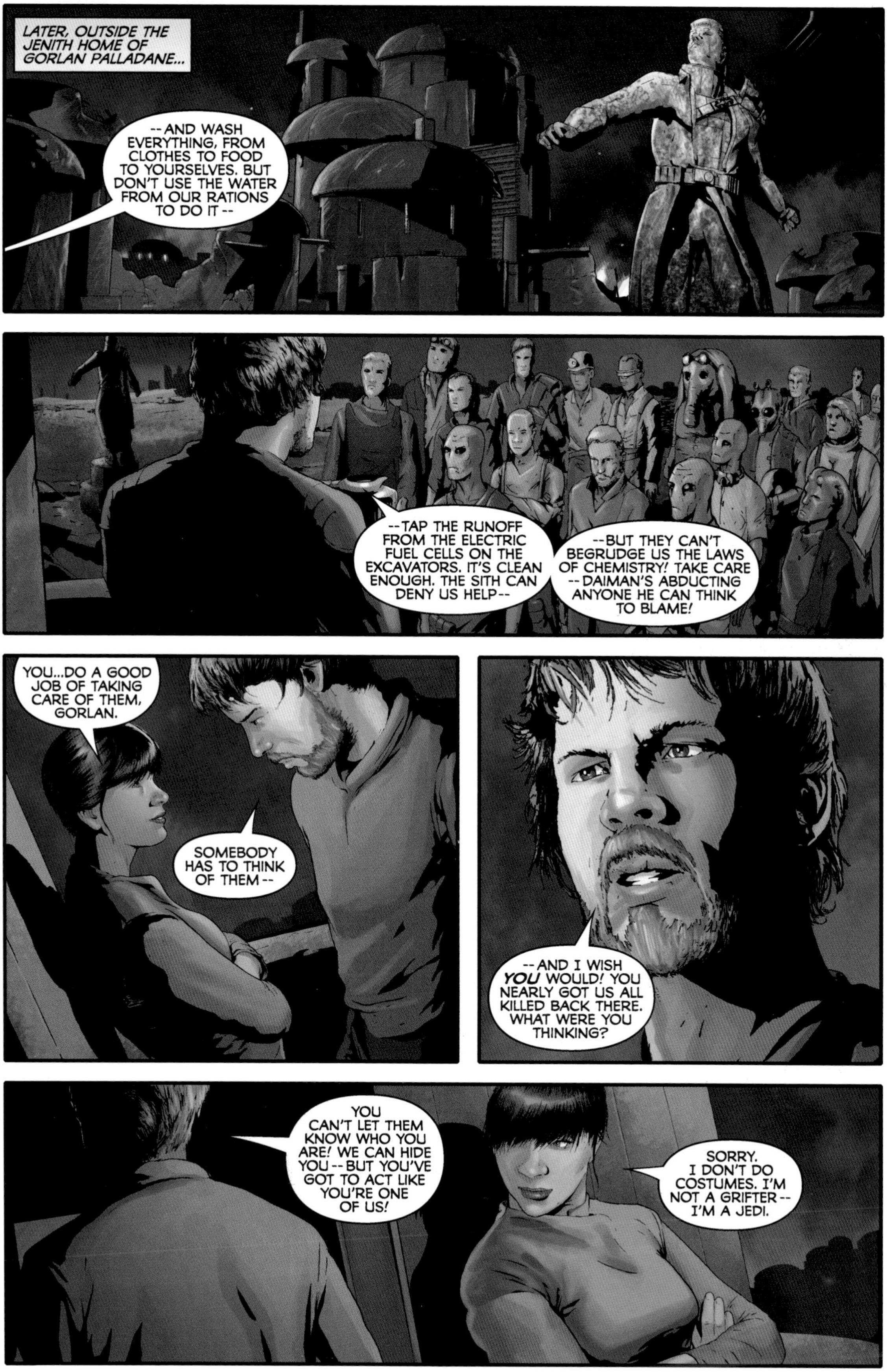
LATER, OUTSIDE THE JENITH HOME OF GORLAN PALLADANE...
--AND WASH EVERYTHING, FROM CLOTHES TO FOOD TO YOURSELVES. BUT DON'T USE THE WATER FROM OUR RATIONS TO DO IT --
--TAP THE RUNOFF FROM THE ELECTRIC FUEL CELLS ON THE EXCAVATORS. IT'S CLEAN ENOUGH. THE SITH CAN DENY US HELP--
--BUT THEY CAN'T BEGRUDGE US THE LAWS OF CHEMISTRY! TAKE CARE --DAIMAN'S ABDUCTING ANYONE HE CAN THINK TO BLAME!
YOU...DO A GOOD JOB OF TAKING CARE OF THEM, GORLAN.
SOMEBODY HAS TO THINK OF THEM --
--AND I WISH *YOU* WOULD! YOU NEARLY GOT US ALL KILLED BACK THERE. WHAT WERE YOU THINKING?
YOU CAN'T LET THEM KNOW WHO YOU ARE! WE CAN HIDE YOU -- BUT YOU'VE GOT TO ACT LIKE YOU'RE ONE OF US!
SORRY. I DON'T DO COSTUMES. I'M NOT A GRIFTER -- I'M A JEDI.

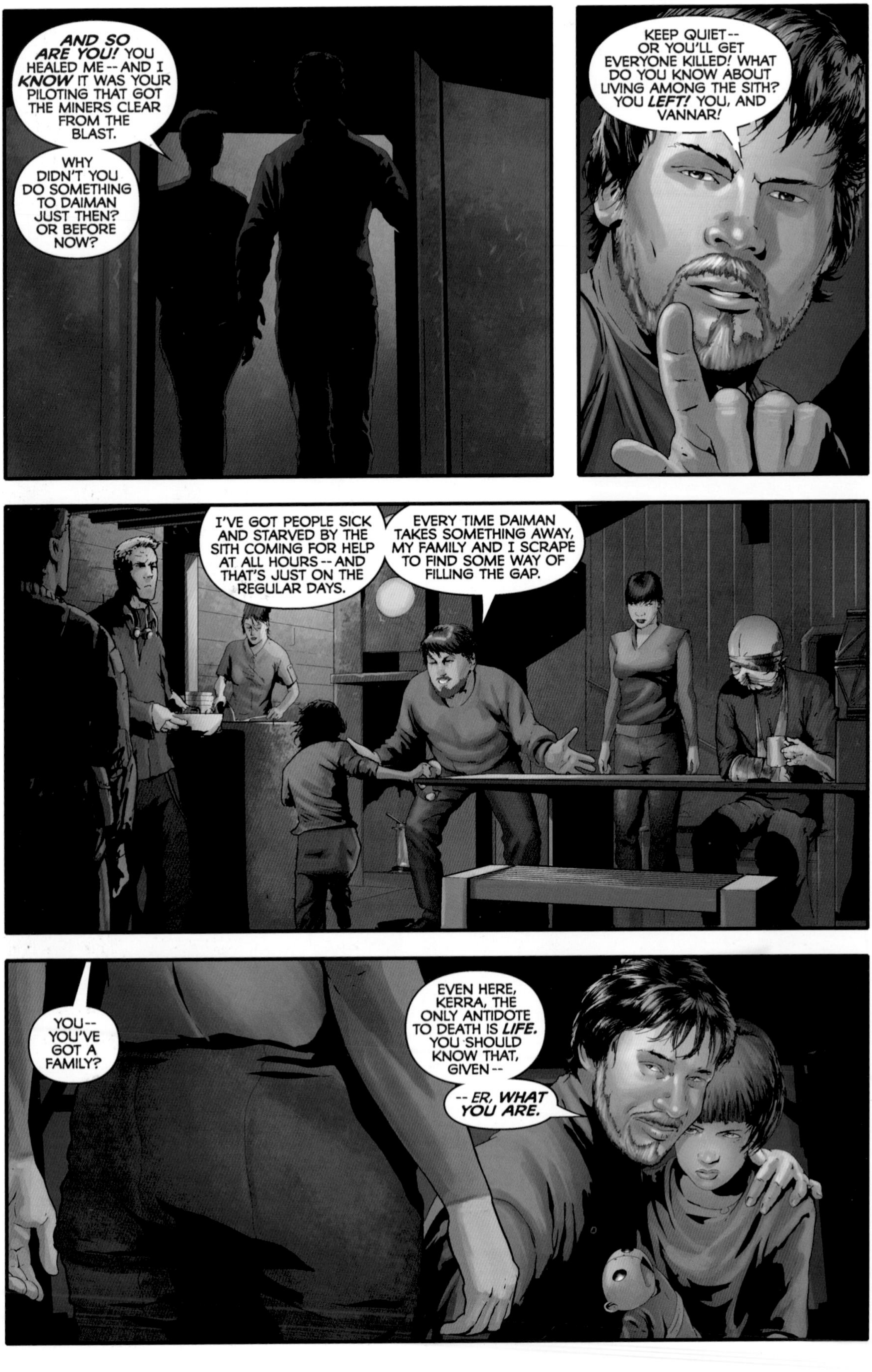
AND SO ARE YOU! YOU HEALED ME -- AND I KNOW IT WAS YOUR PILOTING THAT GOT THE MINERS CLEAR FROM THE BLAST.
WHY DIDN'T YOU DO SOMETHING TO DAIMAN JUST THEN? OR BEFORE NOW?
KEEP QUIET -- OR YOU'LL GET EVERYONE KILLED! WHAT DO YOU KNOW ABOUT LIVING AMONG THE SITH? YOU LEFT! YOU, AND VANNAR!
I'VE GOT PEOPLE SICK AND STARVED BY THE SITH COMING FOR HELP AT ALL HOURS -- AND THAT'S JUST ON THE REGULAR DAYS.
EVERY TIME DAIMAN TAKES SOMETHING AWAY, MY FAMILY AND I SCRAPE TO FIND SOME WAY OF FILLING THE GAP.
YOU -- YOU'VE GOT A FAMILY?
EVEN HERE, KERRA, THE ONLY ANTIDOTE TO DEATH IS LIFE. YOU SHOULD KNOW THAT, GIVEN --
-- ER, WHAT YOU ARE.

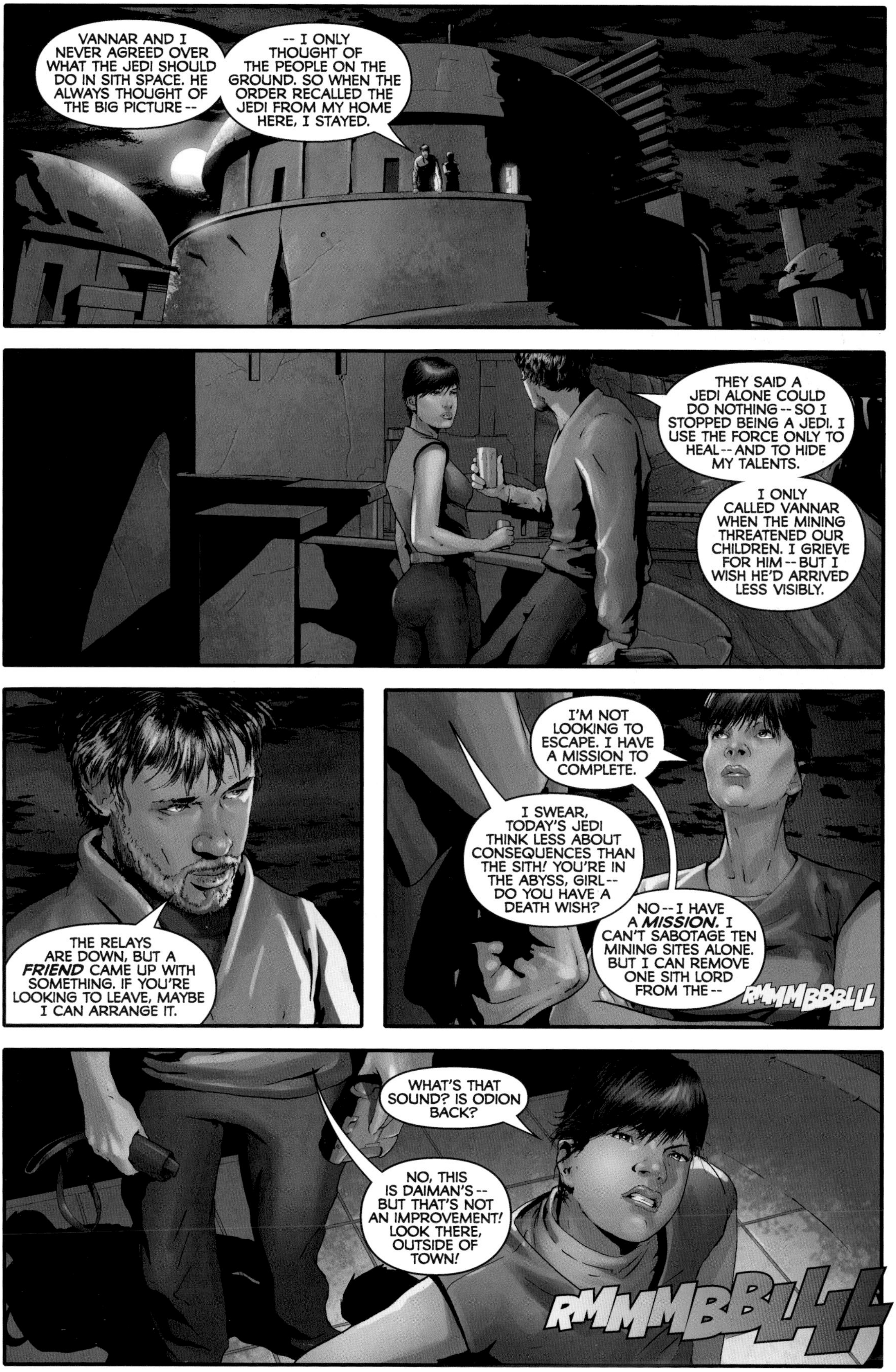
VANNAR AND I NEVER AGREED OVER WHAT THE JEDI SHOULD DO IN SITH SPACE. HE ALWAYS THOUGHT OF THE BIG PICTURE --
-- I ONLY THOUGHT OF THE PEOPLE ON THE GROUND. SO WHEN THE ORDER RECALLED THE JEDI FROM MY HOME HERE, I STAYED.
THEY SAID A JEDI ALONE COULD DO NOTHING -- SO I STOPPED BEING A JEDI. I USE THE FORCE ONLY TO HEAL -- AND TO HIDE MY TALENTS.
I ONLY CALLED VANNAR WHEN THE MINING THREATENED OUR CHILDREN. I GRIEVE FOR HIM -- BUT I WISH HE'D ARRIVED LESS VISIBLY.
THE RELAYS ARE DOWN, BUT A ***FRIEND*** CAME UP WITH SOMETHING. IF YOU'RE LOOKING TO LEAVE, MAYBE I CAN ARRANGE IT.
I'M NOT LOOKING TO ESCAPE. I HAVE A MISSION TO COMPLETE.
I SWEAR, TODAY'S JEDI THINK LESS ABOUT CONSEQUENCES THAN THE SITH! YOU'RE IN THE ABYSS, GIRL -- DO YOU HAVE A DEATH WISH?
NO -- I HAVE A ***MISSION.*** I CAN'T SABOTAGE TEN MINING SITES ALONE. BUT I CAN REMOVE ONE SITH LORD FROM THE --
RMMMBBBLLL
WHAT'S THAT SOUND? IS ODION BACK?
NO, THIS IS DAIMAN'S -- BUT THAT'S NOT AN IMPROVEMENT! LOOK THERE, OUTSIDE OF TOWN!
RMMMBBBLLL

"THERE, WITH THE PERSONNEL *TRANSPORT!* DON'T YOU KNOW WHAT THAT IS?

"THE SITH FRONTIERS CHANGE SO OFTEN. THE SUPPLY LINES HAVE TO KEEP MOVING. SO THEY DEVELOPED *THAT*--

"-- A *MOBILE MUNITIONS COMPLEX!*

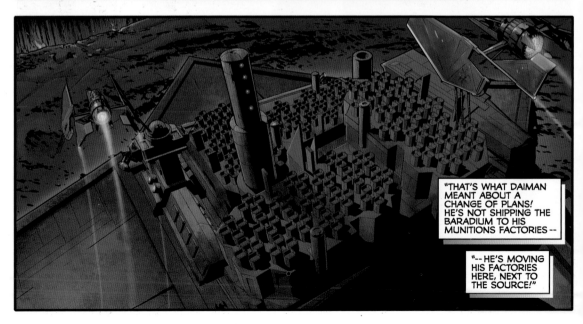

"THAT'S WHAT DAIMAN MEANT ABOUT A CHANGE OF PLANS! HE'S NOT SHIPPING THE BARADIUM TO HIS MUNITIONS FACTORIES --

"-- HE'S MOVING HIS FACTORIES HERE, NEXT TO THE SOURCE!"

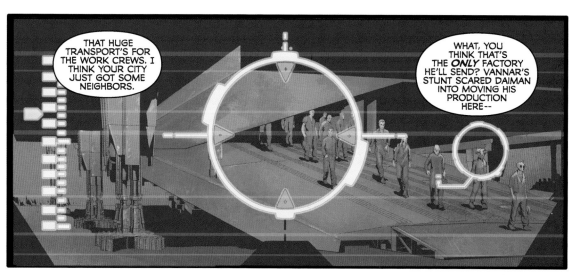

THAT HUGE TRANSPORT'S FOR THE WORK CREWS. I THINK YOUR CITY JUST GOT SOME NEIGHBORS.

WHAT, YOU THINK THAT'S THE *ONLY* FACTORY HE'LL SEND? VANNAR'S STUNT SCARED DAIMAN INTO MOVING HIS PRODUCTION HERE--

--WHO'S TO SAY ODION'S ATTACK WON'T FORCE HIM TO EXPLOIT CHELLOA AS FAST AS HE CAN? THE MINES WERE BAD ENOUGH --

--WE'RE ABOUT TO BECOME A TOXIC *ARSENAL!*

IF YOU WANT TO STOP THAT, *JOIN ME.* LOOK, YOU'VE DONE WELL BY YOUR PEOPLE HERE --

-- BUT THERE'S JUST NO WAY TO LIVE UNDER SITH RULE. BETTER TO DIE FIGHTING. ARE YOU WITH ME?

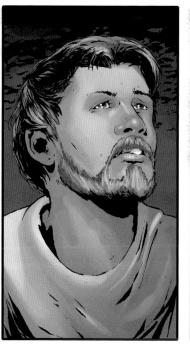

ALONE, THEN.

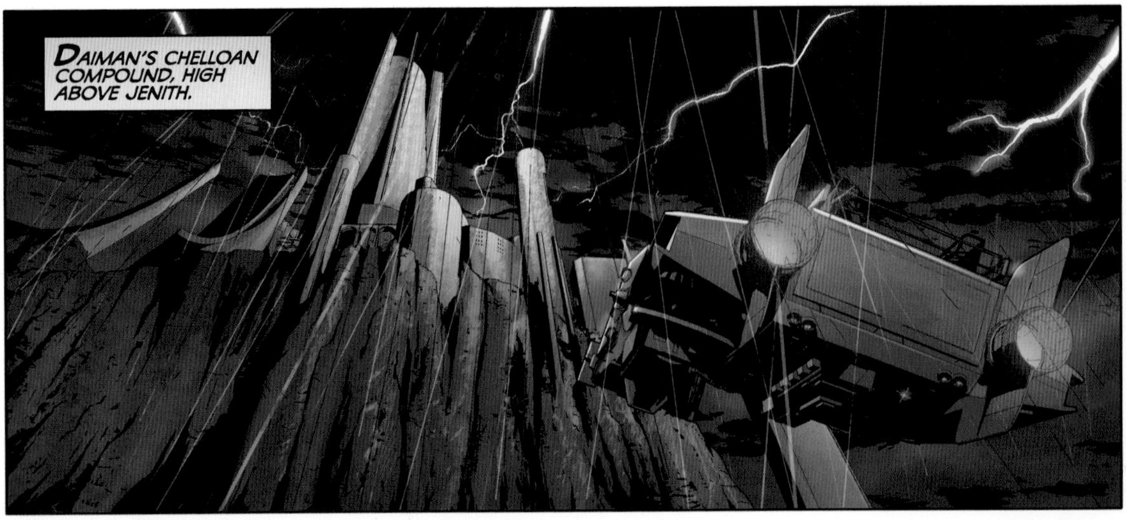
DAIMAN'S CHELLOAN COMPOUND, HIGH ABOVE JENITH.

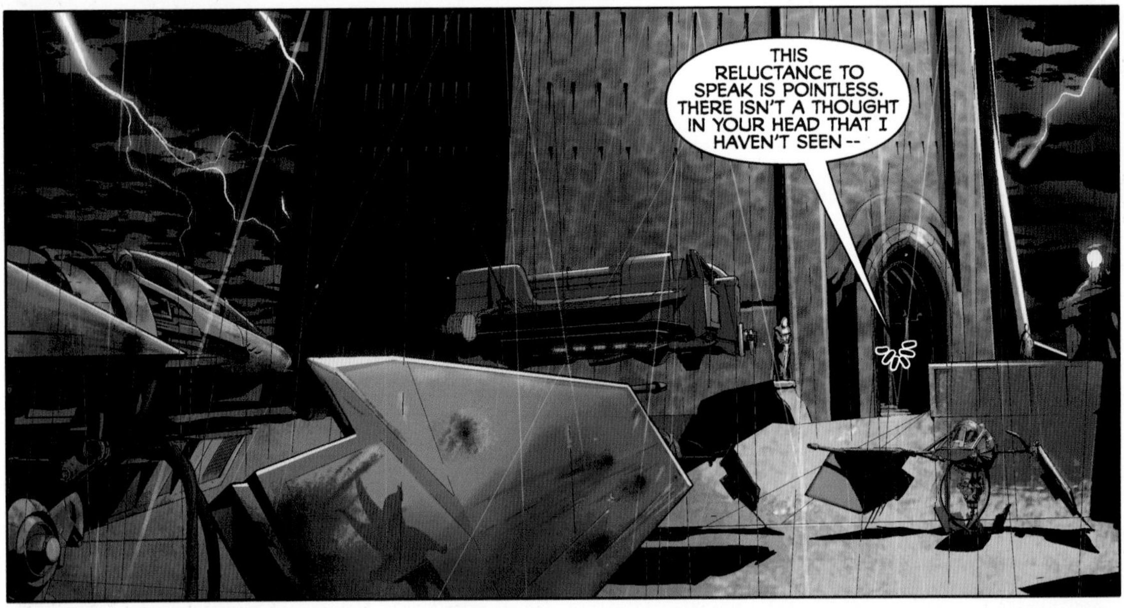
THIS RELUCTANCE TO SPEAK IS POINTLESS. THERE ISN'T A THOUGHT IN YOUR HEAD THAT I HAVEN'T SEEN--

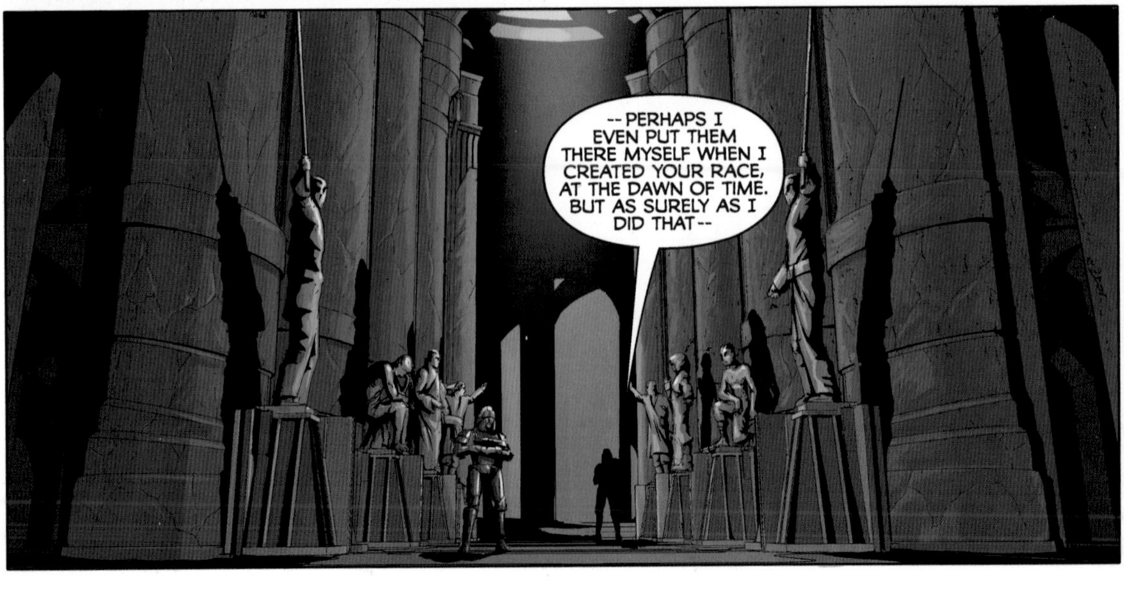
--PERHAPS I EVEN PUT THEM THERE MYSELF WHEN I CREATED YOUR RACE, AT THE DAWN OF TIME. BUT AS SURELY AS I DID THAT--

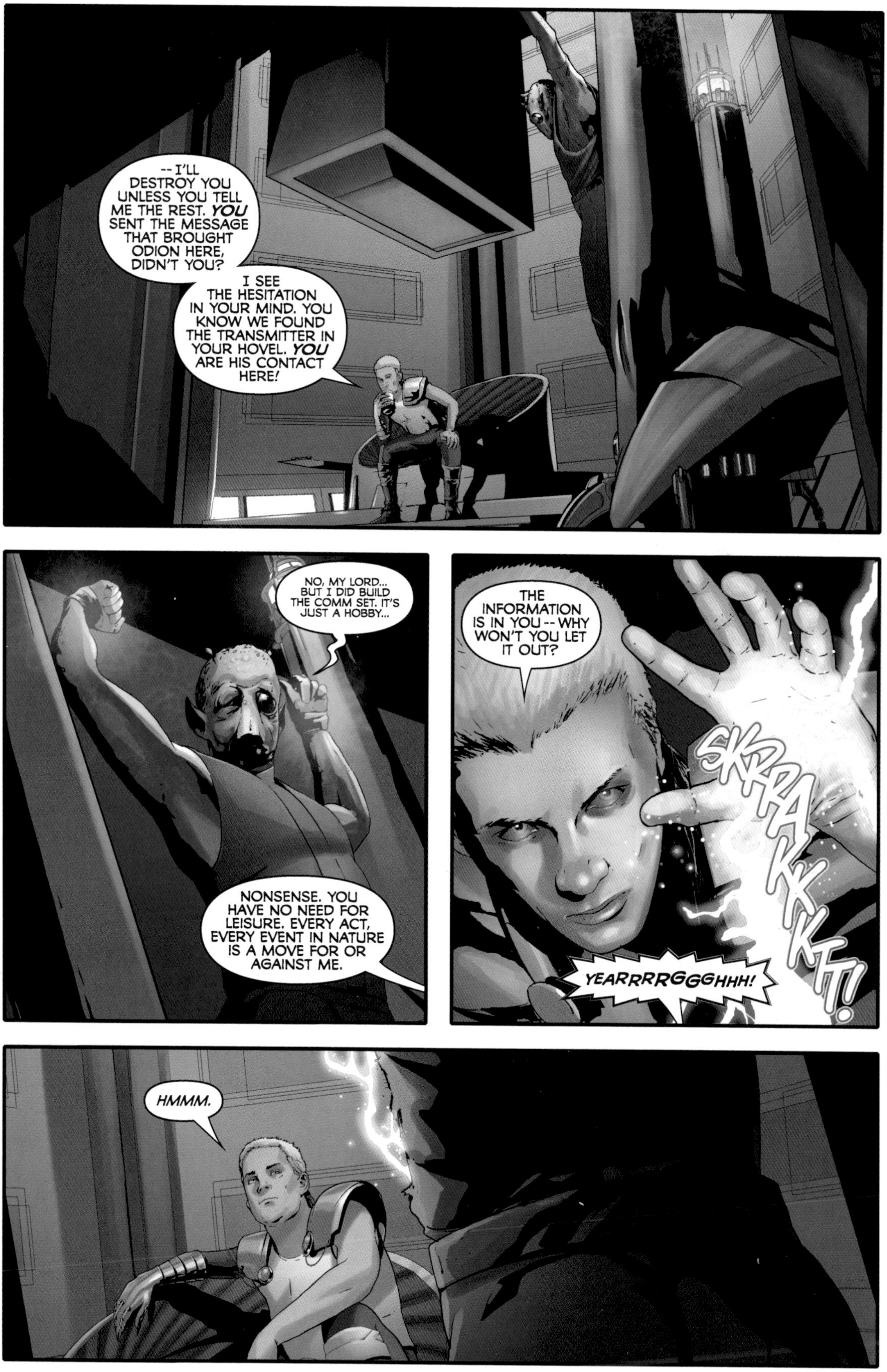
--I'LL DESTROY YOU UNLESS YOU TELL ME THE REST. YOU SENT THE MESSAGE THAT BROUGHT ODION HERE, DIDN'T YOU?
I SEE THE HESITATION IN YOUR MIND. YOU KNOW WE FOUND THE TRANSMITTER IN YOUR HOVEL. YOU ARE HIS CONTACT HERE!
NO, MY LORD... BUT I DID BUILD THE COMM SET. IT'S JUST A HOBBY...
NONSENSE. YOU HAVE NO NEED FOR LEISURE. EVERY ACT, EVERY EVENT IN NATURE IS A MOVE FOR OR AGAINST ME.
THE INFORMATION IS IN YOU--WHY WON'T YOU LET IT OUT?
SKRAKKKTT!
YEARRRRGGGHHH!
HMMM.

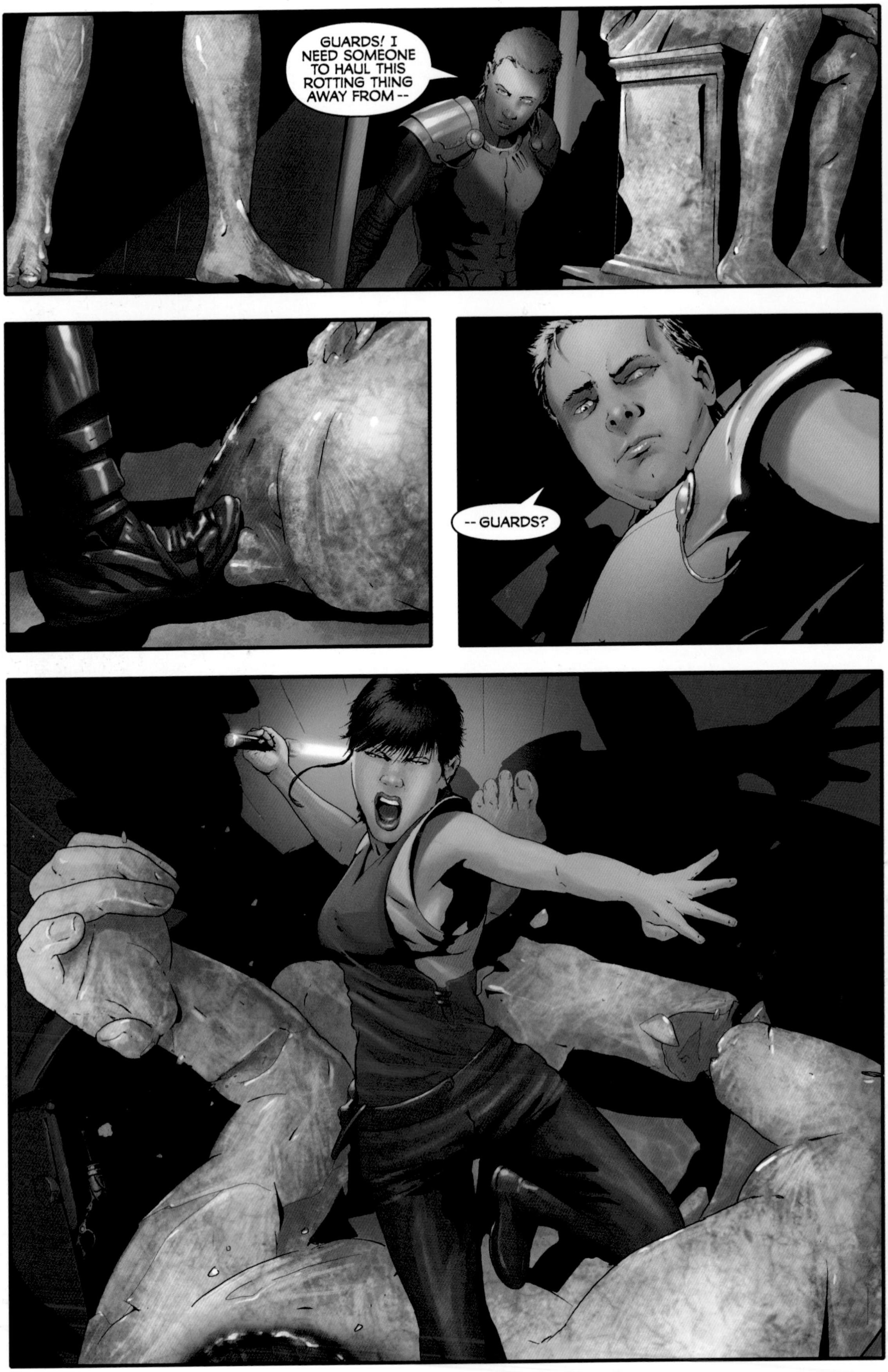
GUARDS! I NEED SOMEONE TO HAUL THIS ROTTING THING AWAY FROM --
-- GUARDS?

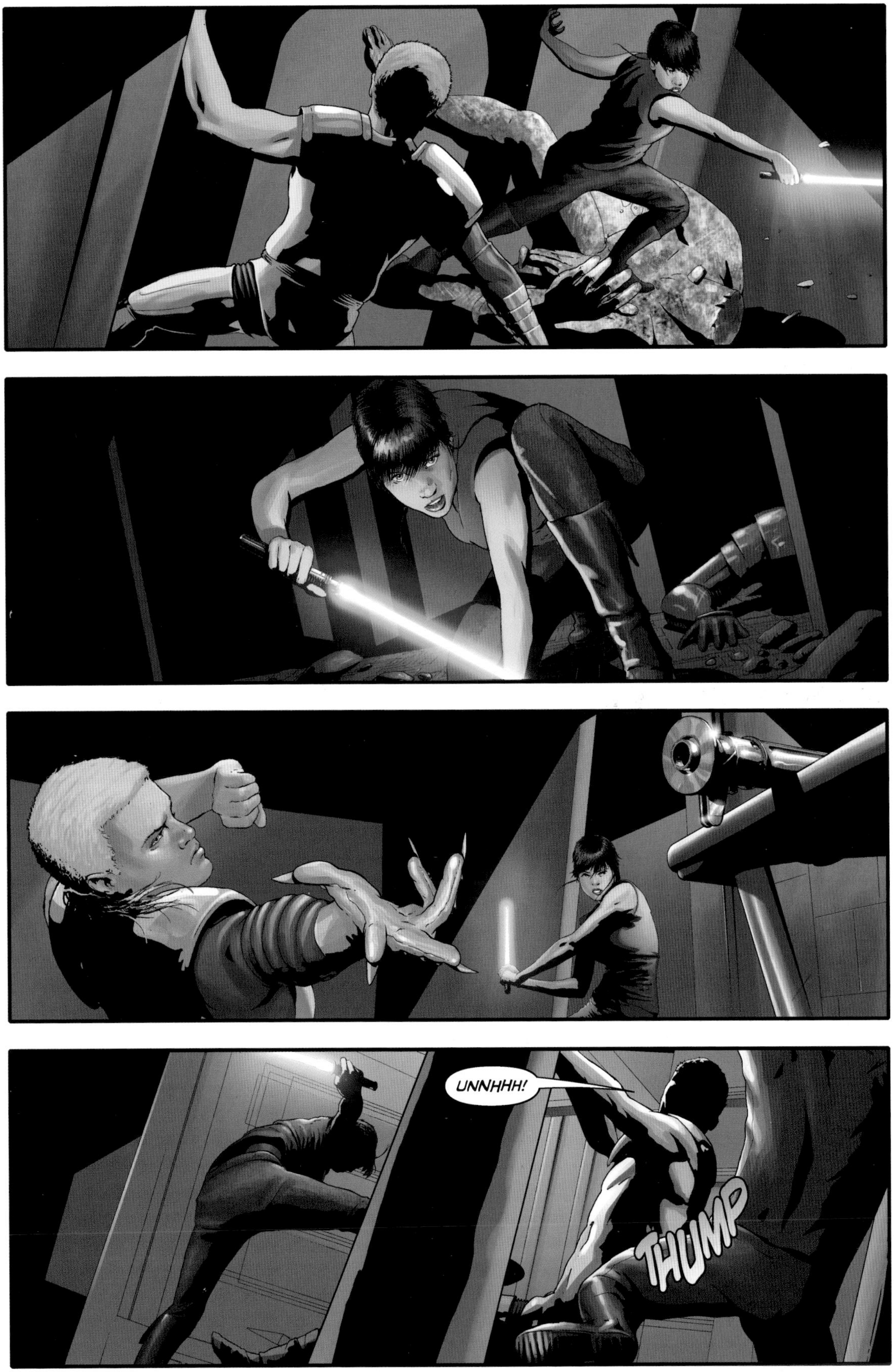
UNNHHH!
THUMP

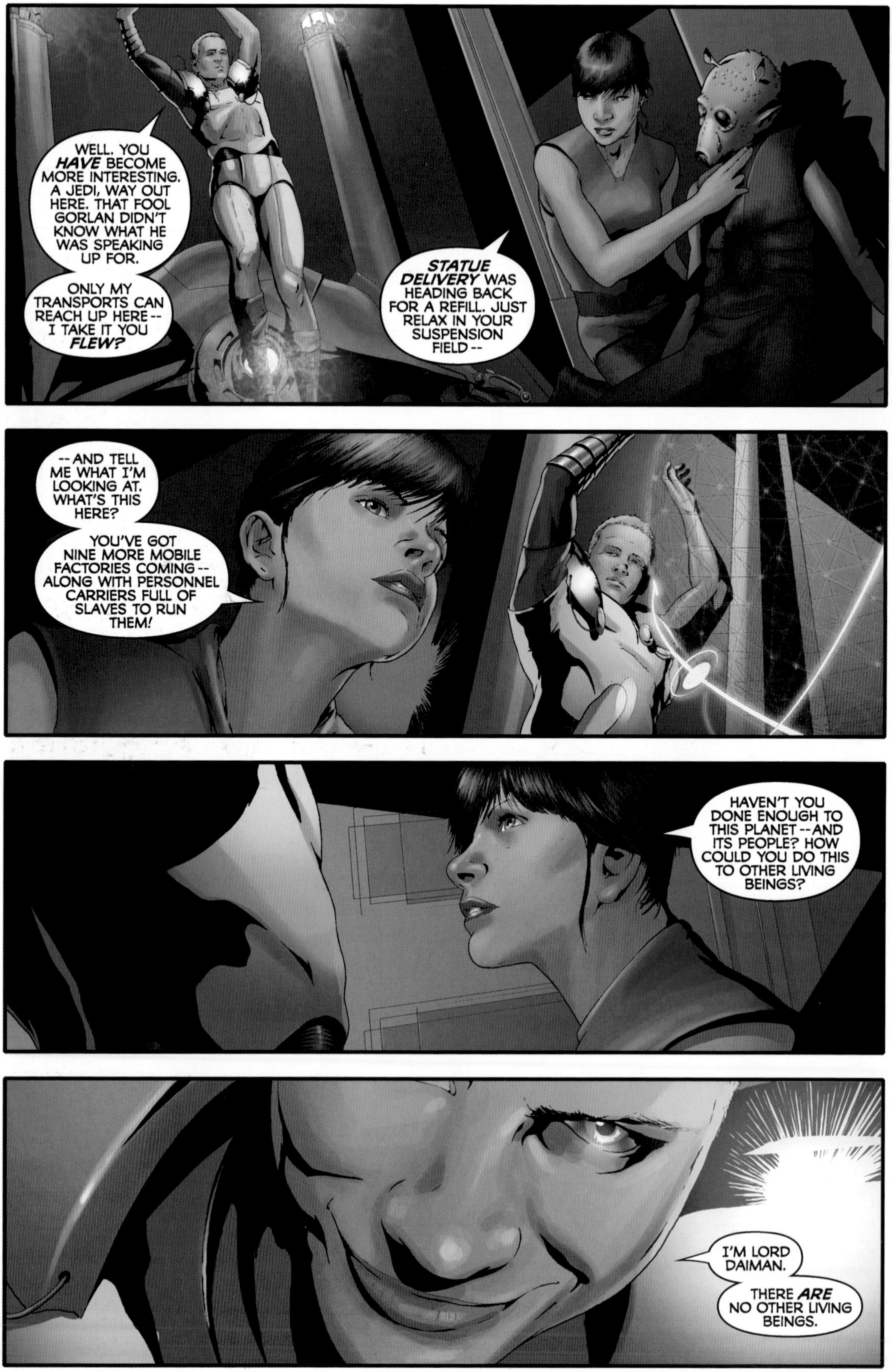

WELL. YOU *HAVE* BECOME MORE INTERESTING. A JEDI, WAY OUT HERE. THAT FOOL GORLAN DIDN'T KNOW WHAT HE WAS SPEAKING UP FOR.
ONLY MY TRANSPORTS CAN REACH UP HERE -- I TAKE IT YOU *FLEW?*
STATUE DELIVERY WAS HEADING BACK FOR A REFILL. JUST RELAX IN YOUR SUSPENSION FIELD --
-- AND TELL ME WHAT I'M LOOKING AT. WHAT'S THIS HERE?
YOU'VE GOT NINE MORE MOBILE FACTORIES COMING -- ALONG WITH PERSONNEL CARRIERS FULL OF SLAVES TO RUN THEM!
HAVEN'T YOU DONE ENOUGH TO THIS PLANET -- AND ITS PEOPLE? HOW COULD YOU DO THIS TO OTHER LIVING BEINGS?
I'M LORD DAIMAN.
THERE *ARE* NO OTHER LIVING BEINGS.

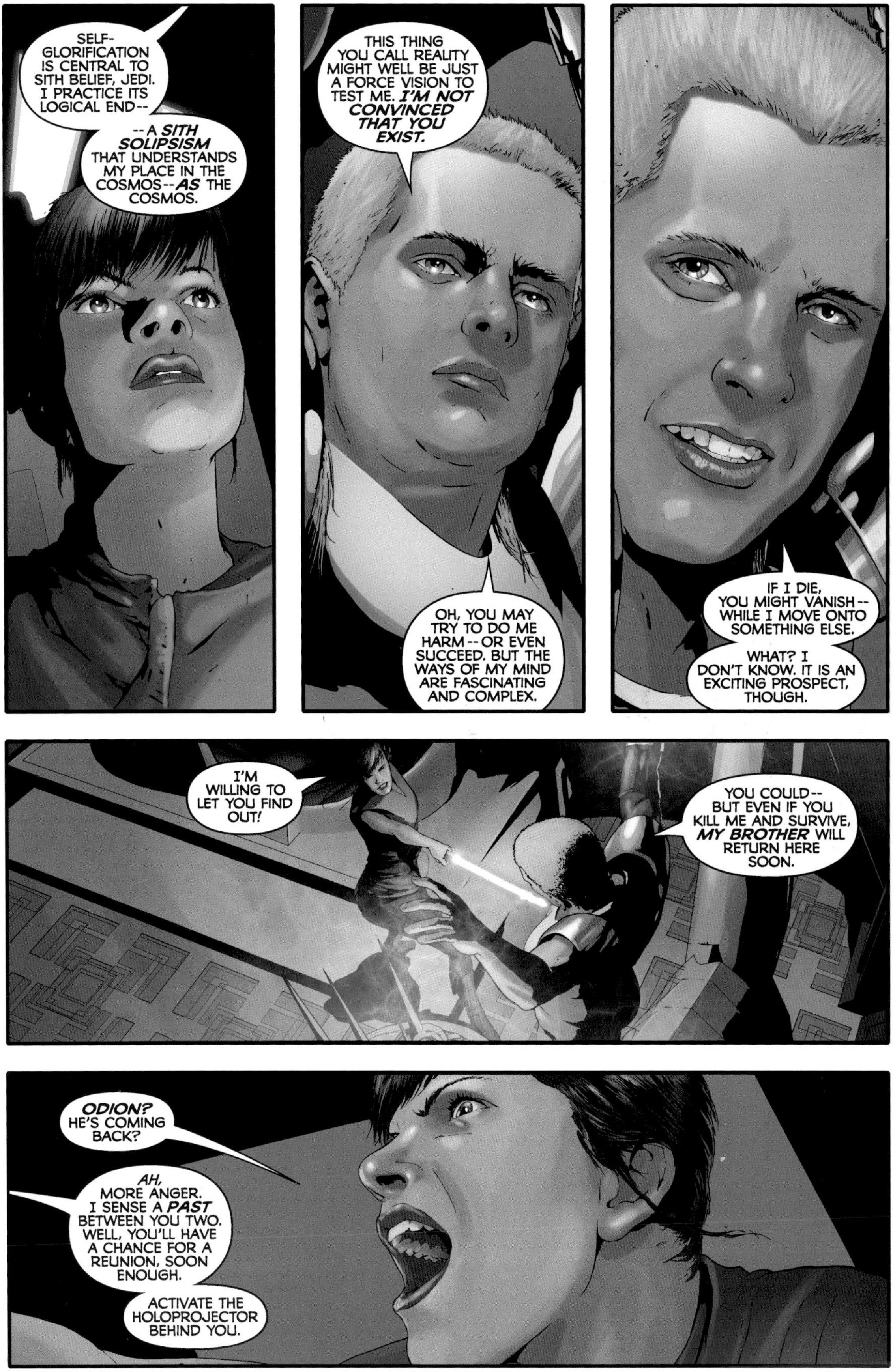
SELF-GLORIFICATION IS CENTRAL TO SITH BELIEF, JEDI. I PRACTICE ITS LOGICAL END--
--A *SITH SOLIPSISM* THAT UNDERSTANDS MY PLACE IN THE COSMOS--*AS* THE COSMOS.
THIS THING YOU CALL REALITY MIGHT WELL BE JUST A FORCE VISION TO TEST ME. *I'M NOT CONVINCED THAT YOU EXIST.*
OH, YOU MAY TRY TO DO ME HARM--OR EVEN SUCCEED. BUT THE WAYS OF MY MIND ARE FASCINATING AND COMPLEX.
IF I DIE, YOU MIGHT VANISH--WHILE I MOVE ONTO SOMETHING ELSE.
WHAT? I DON'T KNOW. IT IS AN EXCITING PROSPECT, THOUGH.
I'M WILLING TO LET YOU FIND OUT!
YOU COULD--BUT EVEN IF YOU KILL ME AND SURVIVE, *MY BROTHER* WILL RETURN HERE SOON.
ODION? HE'S COMING BACK?
AH, MORE ANGER. I SENSE A *PAST* BETWEEN YOU TWO. WELL, YOU'LL HAVE A CHANCE FOR A REUNION, SOON ENOUGH.
ACTIVATE THE HOLOPROJECTOR BEHIND YOU.

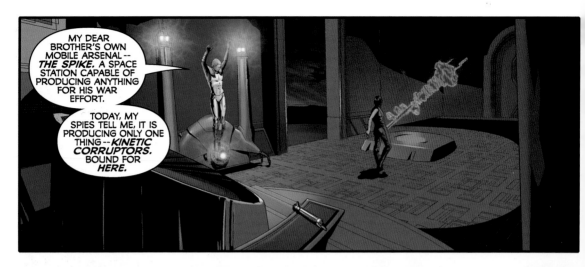

MY DEAR BROTHER'S OWN MOBILE ARSENAL -- *THE SPIKE.* A SPACE STATION CAPABLE OF PRODUCING ANYTHING FOR HIS WAR EFFORT.

TODAY, MY SPIES TELL ME, IT IS PRODUCING ONLY ONE THING -- *KINETIC CORRUPTORS.* BOUND FOR *HERE.*

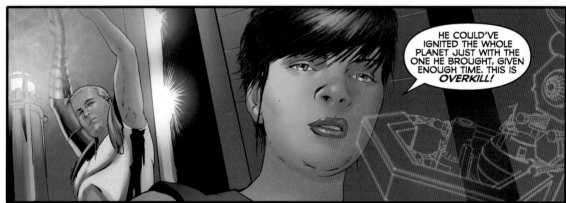

HE COULD'VE IGNITED THE WHOLE PLANET JUST WITH THE ONE HE BROUGHT, GIVEN ENOUGH TIME. THIS IS *OVERKILL!*

MOVE AND COUNTERMOVE. BESIDES, IT'S YOUR JEDI WHO CAUSED THIS. MY FORCES COULD'VE STOPPED ODION FROM ACTIVATING IT --

-- IF THEY HADN'T BEEN BUSY WITH *YOU.* I'M SENDING FIGHTERS TO ATTACK THE ARSENAL NOW, BUT IF ODION RETURNS --

-- *IT'S YOUR FAULT.*

BUT I DON'T THINK YOU'LL LIVE LONG ENOUGH TO WORRY ABOUT ALL OF THAT --

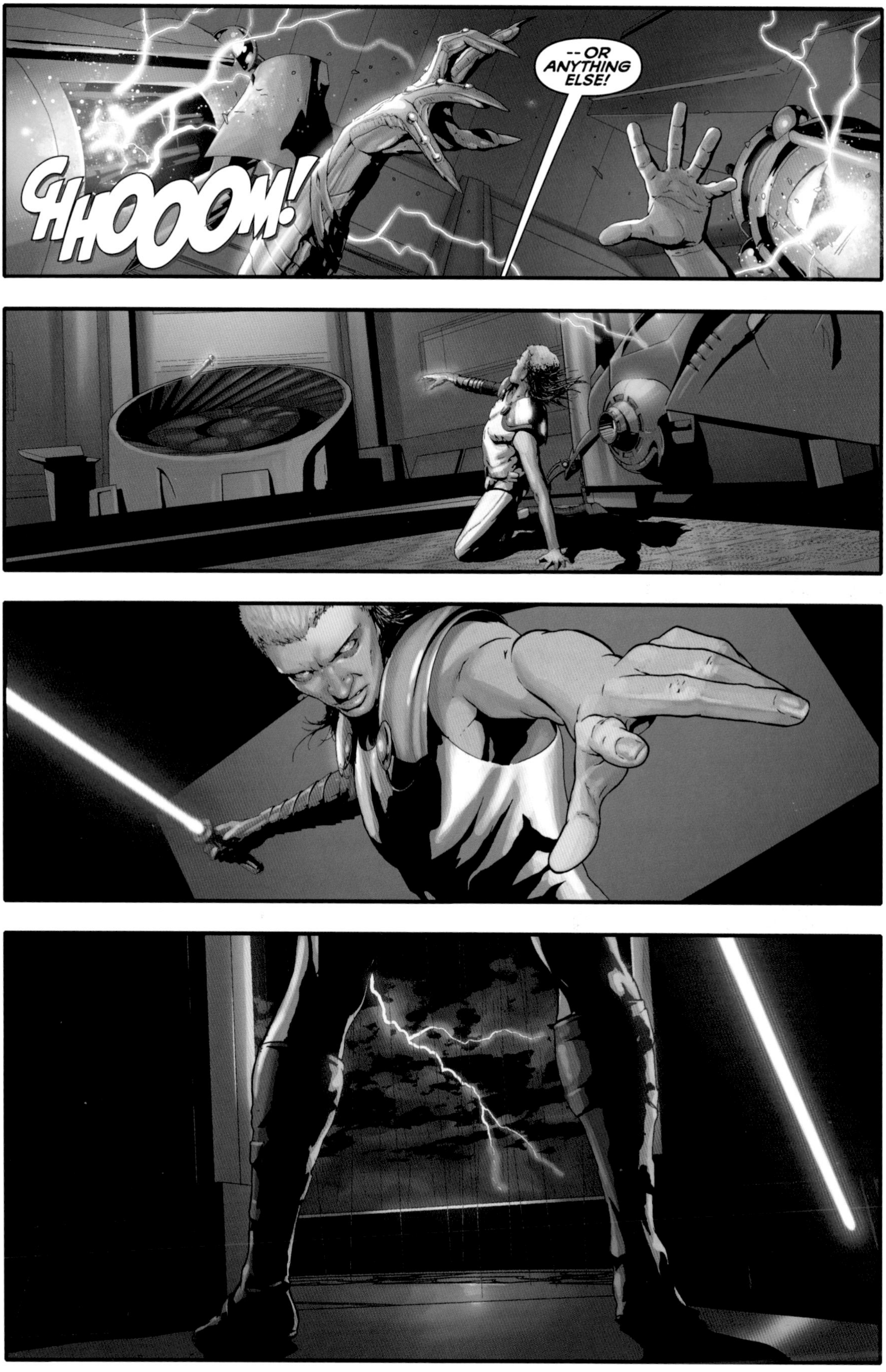
--OR ANYTHING ELSE!
CHHOOOM!

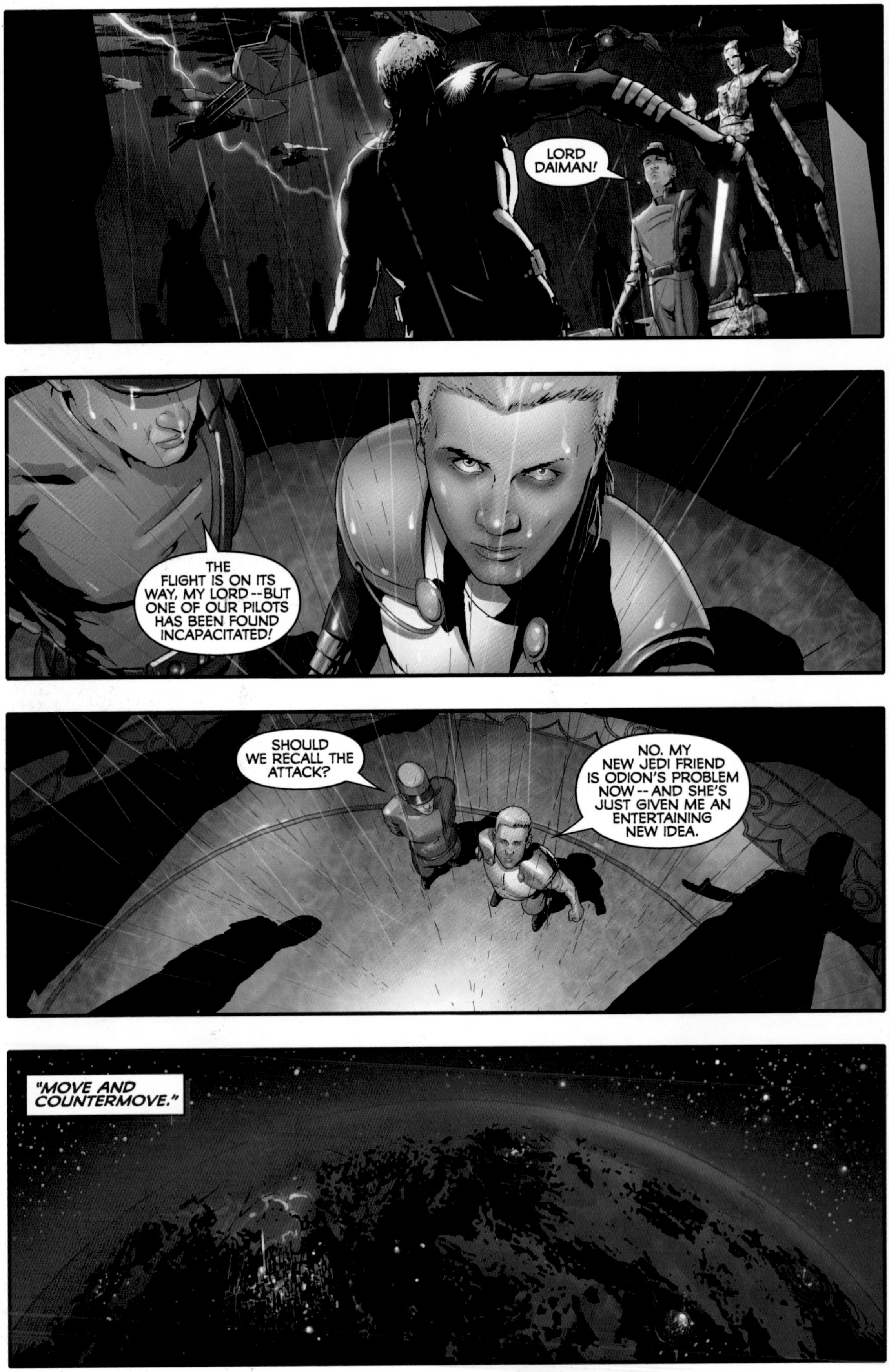
LORD DAIMAN!
THE FLIGHT IS ON ITS WAY, MY LORD--BUT ONE OF OUR PILOTS HAS BEEN FOUND INCAPACITATED!
SHOULD WE RECALL THE ATTACK?
NO. MY NEW JEDI FRIEND IS ODION'S PROBLEM NOW--AND SHE'S JUST GIVEN ME AN ENTERTAINING NEW IDEA.
"MOVE AND COUNTERMOVE."

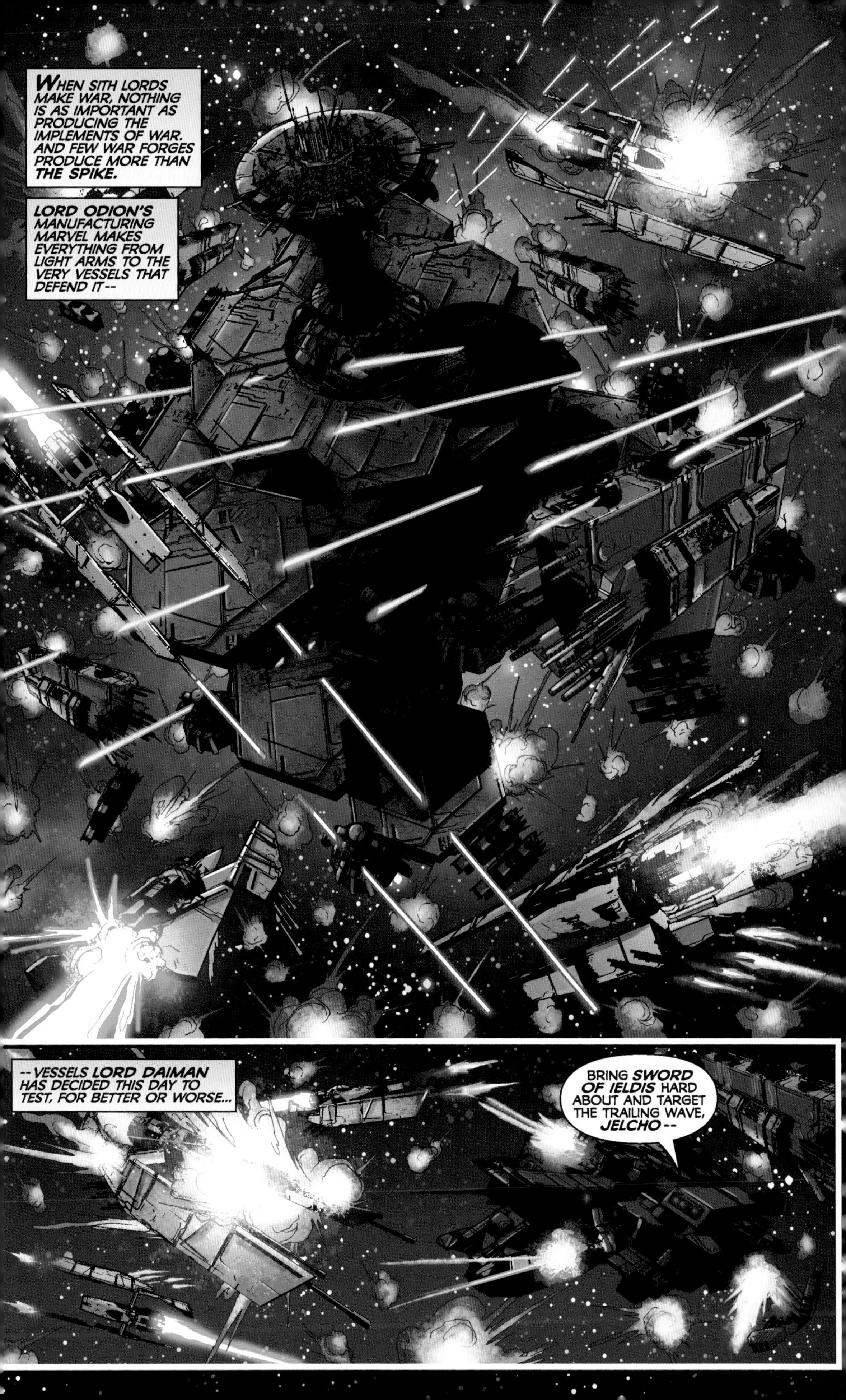
WHEN SITH LORDS MAKE WAR, NOTHING IS AS IMPORTANT AS PRODUCING THE IMPLEMENTS OF WAR. AND FEW WAR FORGES PRODUCE MORE THAN THE SPIKE.
LORD ODION'S MANUFACTURING MARVEL MAKES EVERYTHING FROM LIGHT ARMS TO THE VERY VESSELS THAT DEFEND IT--
--VESSELS LORD DAIMAN HAS DECIDED THIS DAY TO TEST, FOR BETTER OR WORSE...
BRING SWORD OF IELDIS HARD ABOUT AND TARGET THE TRAILING WAVE, JELCHO--

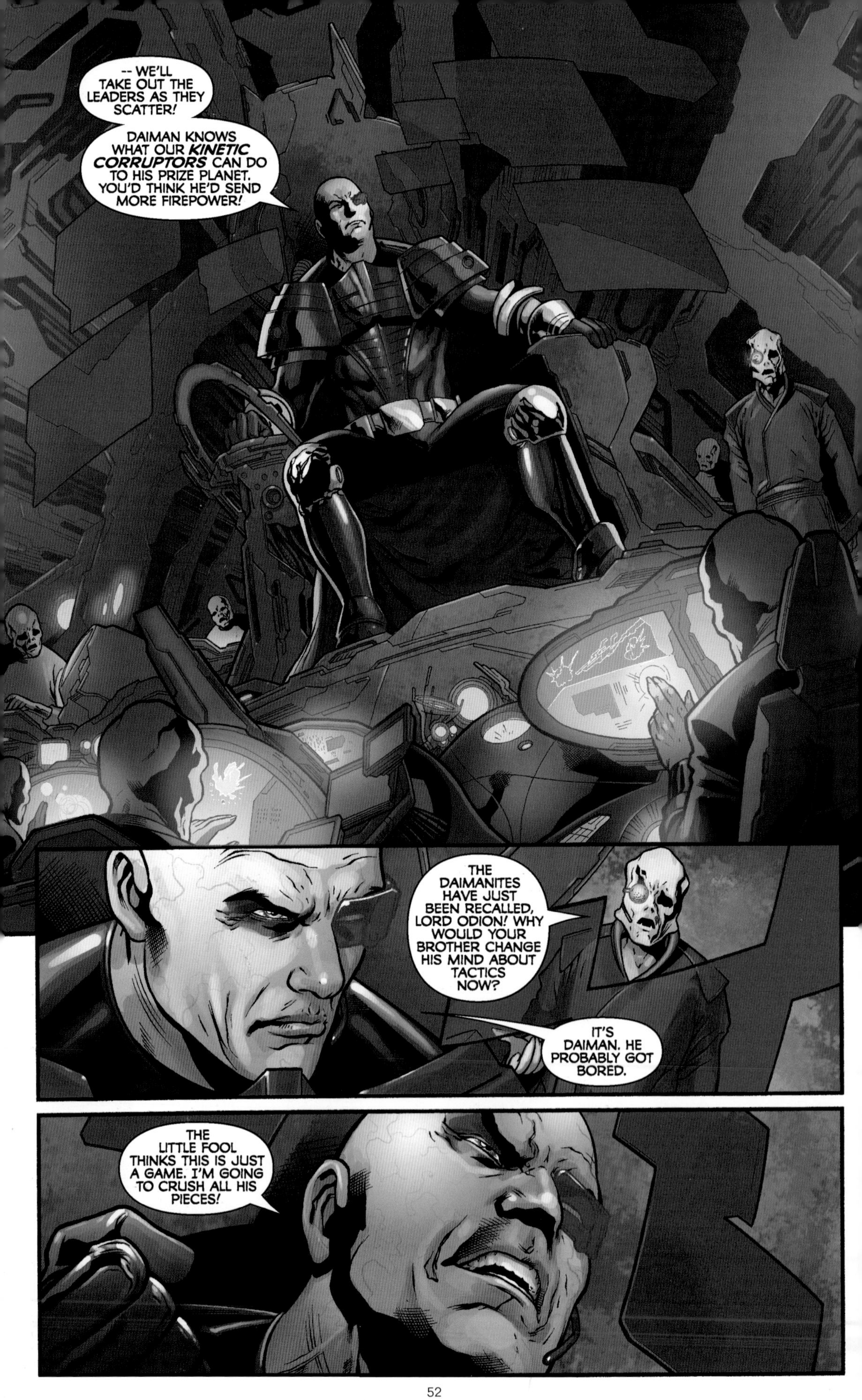
-- WE'LL TAKE OUT THE LEADERS AS THEY SCATTER!
DAIMAN KNOWS WHAT OUR *KINETIC CORRUPTORS* CAN DO TO HIS PRIZE PLANET. YOU'D THINK HE'D SEND MORE FIREPOWER!
THE DAIMANITES HAVE JUST BEEN RECALLED, LORD ODION! WHY WOULD YOUR BROTHER CHANGE HIS MIND ABOUT TACTICS NOW?
IT'S DAIMAN. HE PROBABLY GOT BORED.
THE LITTLE FOOL THINKS THIS IS JUST A GAME. I'M GOING TO CRUSH ALL HIS PIECES!

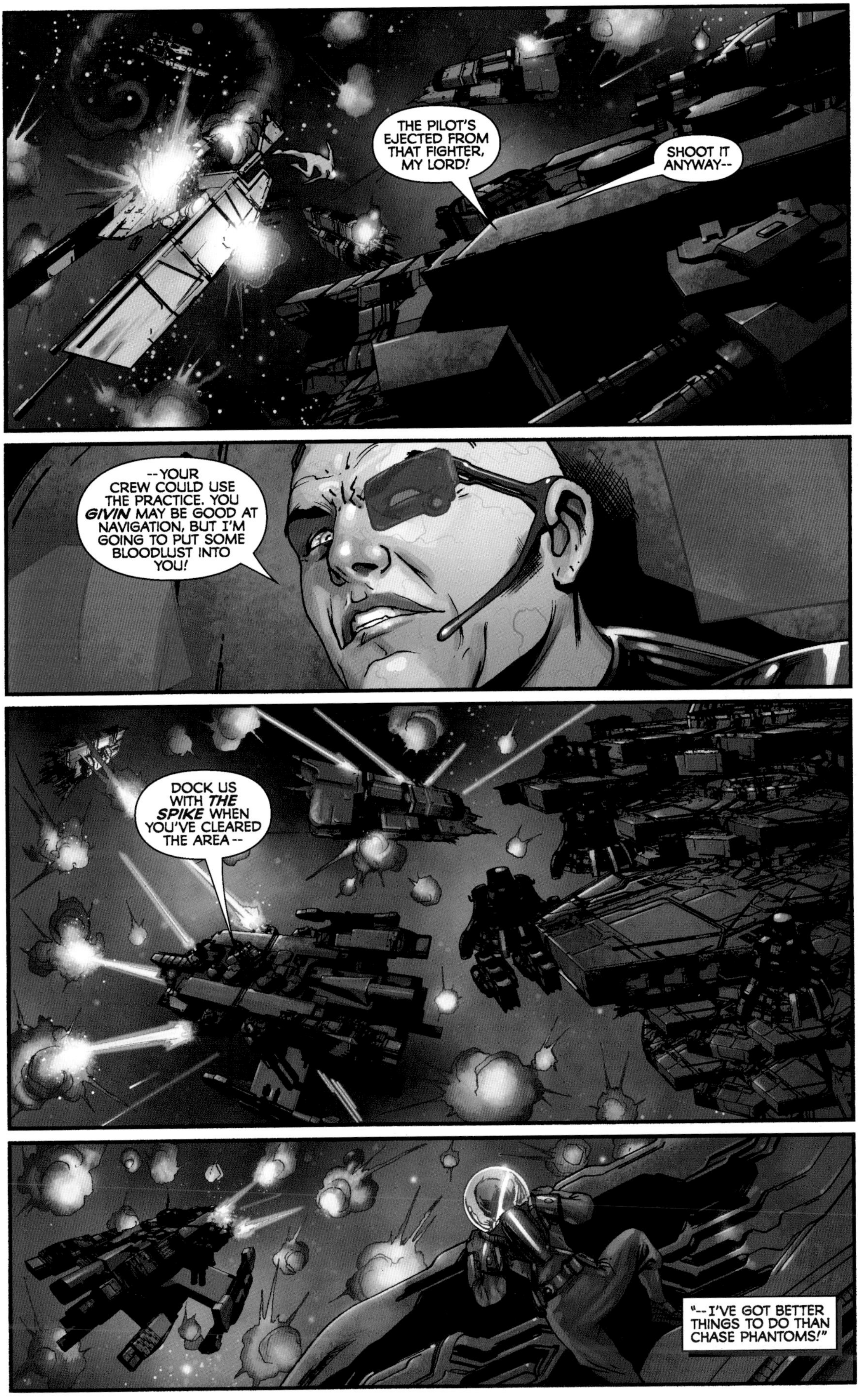
THE PILOT'S EJECTED FROM THAT FIGHTER, MY LORD!
SHOOT IT ANYWAY--
--YOUR CREW COULD USE THE PRACTICE. YOU *GIVIN* MAY BE GOOD AT NAVIGATION, BUT I'M GOING TO PUT SOME BLOODLUST INTO YOU!
DOCK US WITH *THE SPIKE* WHEN YOU'VE CLEARED THE AREA--
"--I'VE GOT BETTER THINGS TO DO THAN CHASE PHANTOMS!"

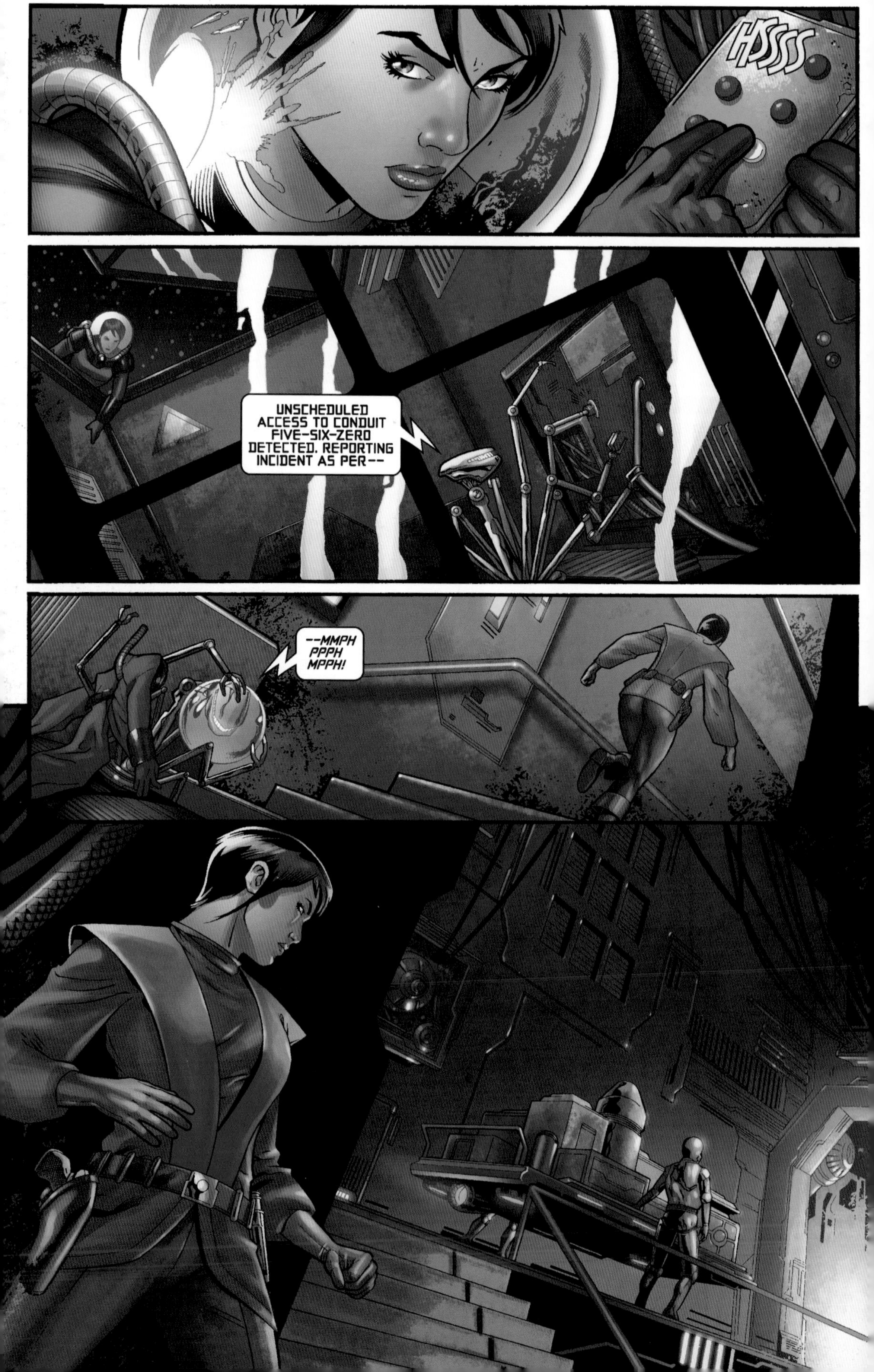
HSSSS
UNSCHEDULED ACCESS TO CONDUIT FIVE-SIX-ZERO DETECTED. REPORTING INCIDENT AS PER--
--MMPH PPPH MPPH!

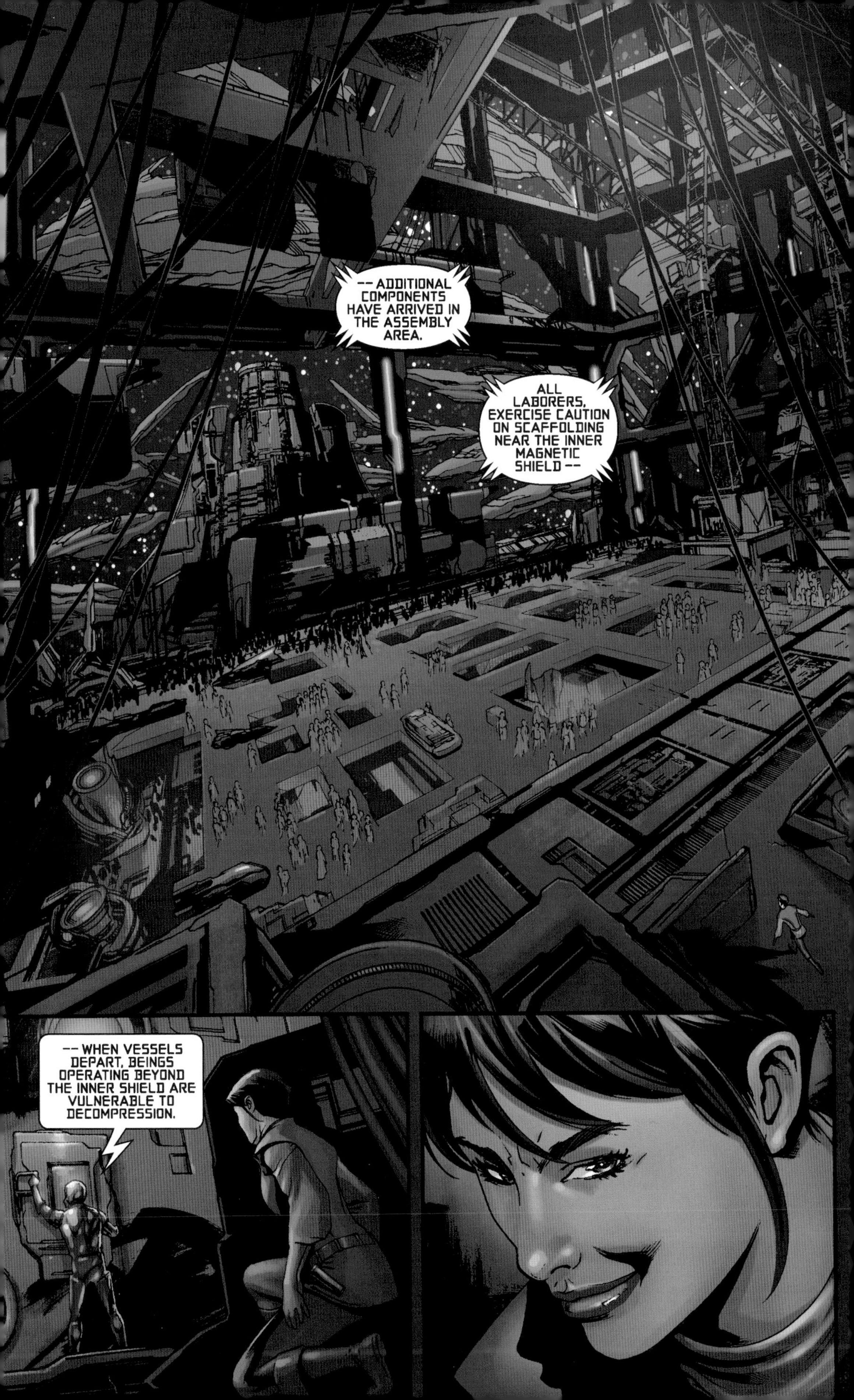
-- ADDITIONAL COMPONENTS HAVE ARRIVED IN THE ASSEMBLY AREA.
ALL LABORERS, EXERCISE CAUTION ON SCAFFOLDING NEAR THE INNER MAGNETIC SHIELD --
-- WHEN VESSELS DEPART, BEINGS OPERATING BEYOND THE INNER SHIELD ARE VULNERABLE TO DECOMPRESSION.

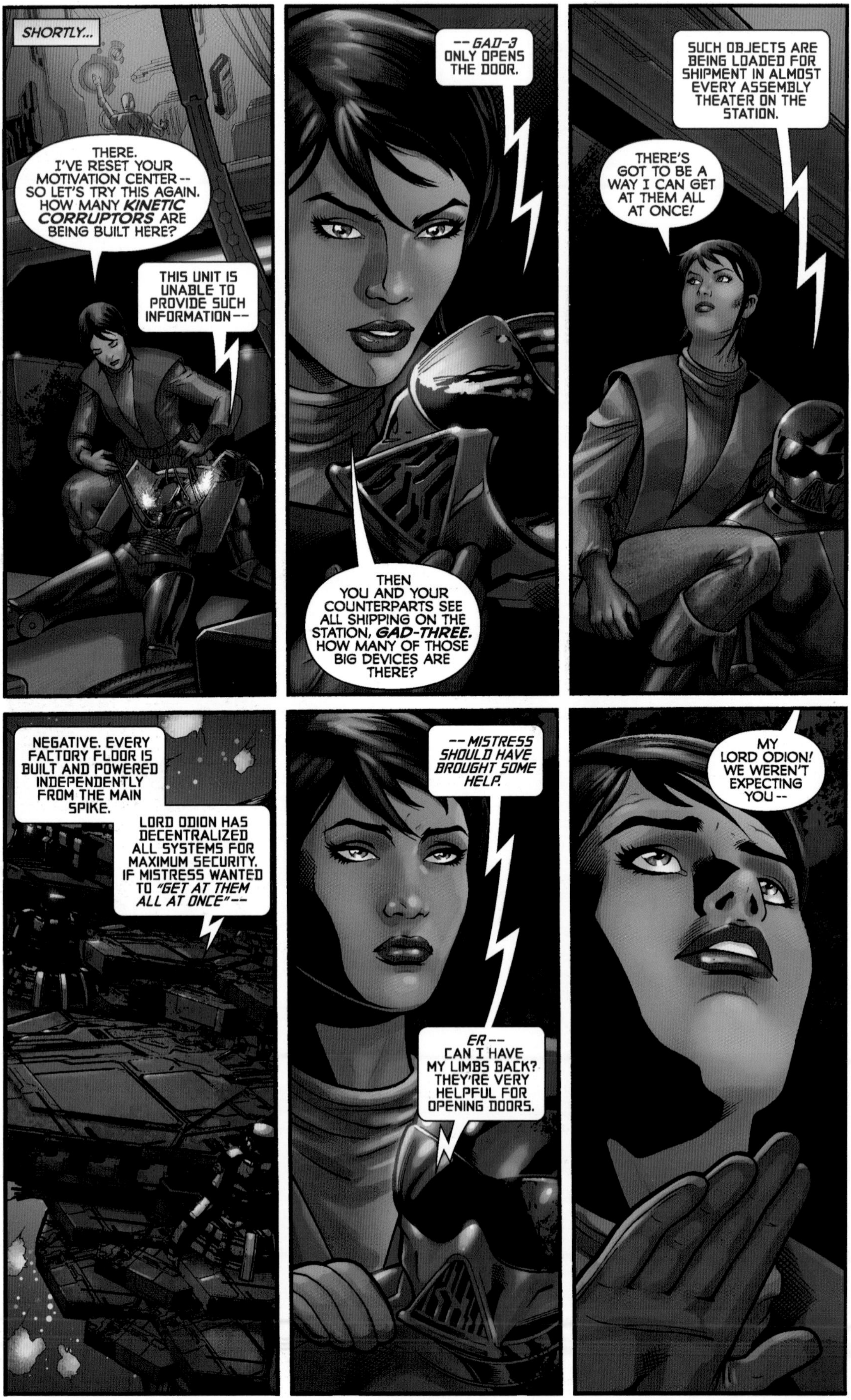
SHORTLY...
THERE. I'VE RESET YOUR MOTIVATION CENTER -- SO LET'S TRY THIS AGAIN. HOW MANY *KINETIC CORRUPTORS* ARE BEING BUILT HERE?
THIS UNIT IS UNABLE TO PROVIDE SUCH INFORMATION--
--GAD-3 ONLY OPENS THE DOOR.
THEN YOU AND YOUR COUNTERPARTS SEE ALL SHIPPING ON THE STATION, *GAD-THREE.* HOW MANY OF THOSE BIG DEVICES ARE THERE?
SUCH OBJECTS ARE BEING LOADED FOR SHIPMENT IN ALMOST EVERY ASSEMBLY THEATER ON THE STATION.
THERE'S GOT TO BE A WAY I CAN GET AT THEM ALL AT ONCE!
NEGATIVE. EVERY FACTORY FLOOR IS BUILT AND POWERED INDEPENDENTLY FROM THE MAIN SPIKE.
LORD ODION HAS DECENTRALIZED ALL SYSTEMS FOR MAXIMUM SECURITY. IF MISTRESS WANTED TO *"GET AT THEM ALL AT ONCE"*--
--MISTRESS SHOULD HAVE BROUGHT SOME HELP.
ER-- CAN I HAVE MY LIMBS BACK? THEY'RE VERY HELPFUL FOR OPENING DOORS.
MY LORD ODION! WE WEREN'T EXPECTING YOU--

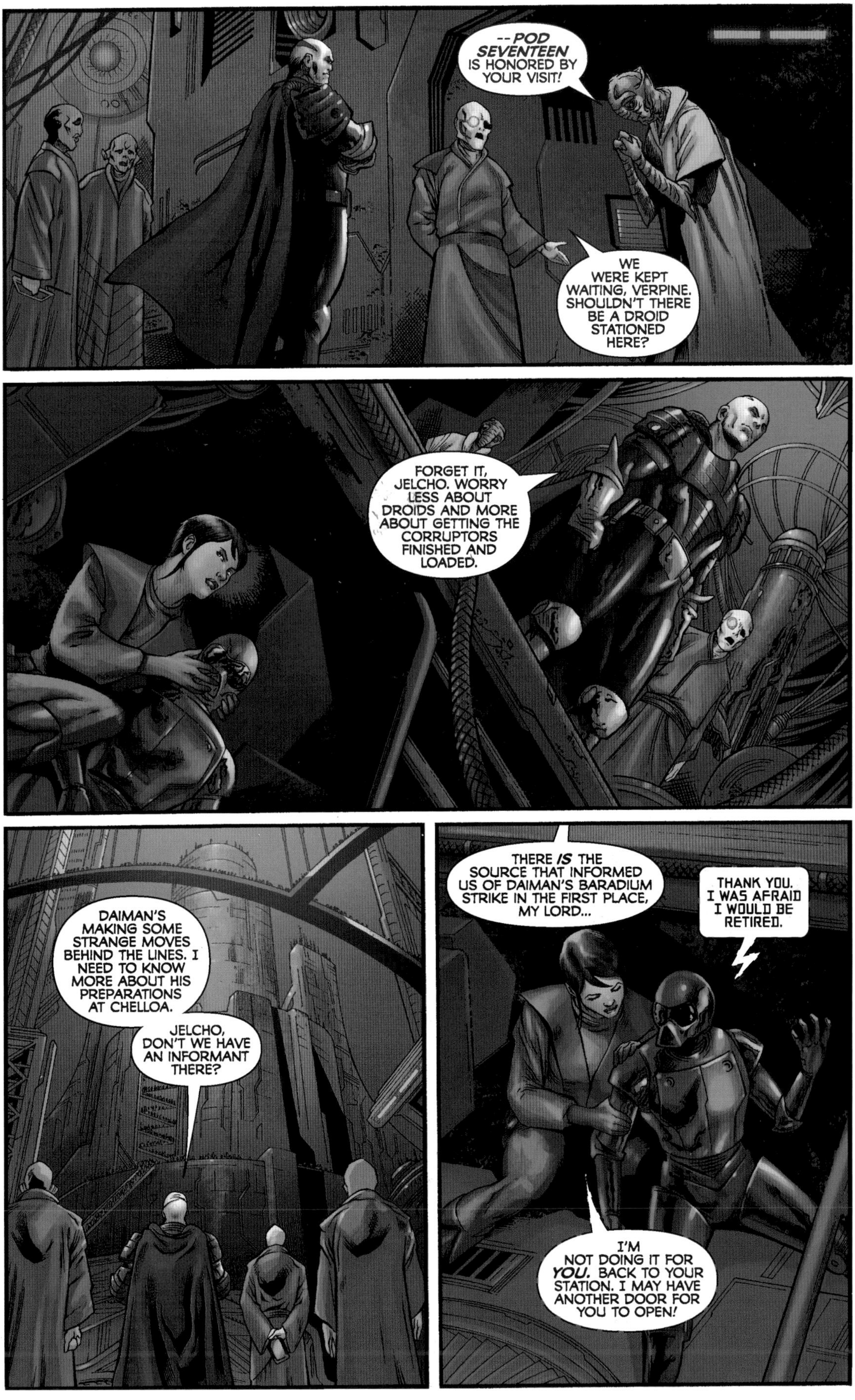
--POD SEVENTEEN IS HONORED BY YOUR VISIT!
WE WERE KEPT WAITING, VERPINE. SHOULDN'T THERE BE A DROID STATIONED HERE?
FORGET IT, JELCHO. WORRY LESS ABOUT DROIDS AND MORE ABOUT GETTING THE CORRUPTORS FINISHED AND LOADED.
DAIMAN'S MAKING SOME STRANGE MOVES BEHIND THE LINES. I NEED TO KNOW MORE ABOUT HIS PREPARATIONS AT CHELLOA.
JELCHO, DON'T WE HAVE AN INFORMANT THERE?
THERE *IS* THE SOURCE THAT INFORMED US OF DAIMAN'S BARADIUM STRIKE IN THE FIRST PLACE, MY LORD...
THANK YOU. I WAS AFRAID I WOULD BE RETIRED.
I'M NOT DOING IT FOR *YOU.* BACK TO YOUR STATION. I MAY HAVE ANOTHER DOOR FOR YOU TO OPEN!

BUT WE QUESTION THE RELIABILITY OF THE SOURCE. LISTEN TO THE LATEST MESSAGE!

--SZKKT-- THIS IS *CHELLOA* AGAIN! UH--

--ALL LORD DAIMAN'S MINING OPERATIONS ARE *PERMANENTLY OFFLINE*. CHELLOA IS NO LONGER A CONCERN FOR LORD ODION!

HUH?

--SKRKKT--I REPEAT, CHELLOA IS NO LONGER A CONCERN FOR LORD ODION!

THAT'S A LIE! WE ONLY KNOCKED OUT *ONE MINE!* WHAT KIND OF GAME IS THIS?

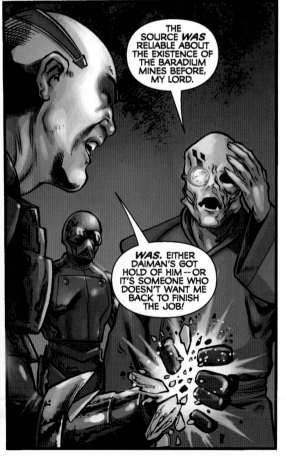

THE SOURCE *WAS* RELIABLE ABOUT THE EXISTENCE OF THE BARADIUM MINES BEFORE, MY LORD.

WAS. EITHER DAIMAN'S GOT HOLD OF HIM -- OR IT'S SOMEONE WHO DOESN'T WANT ME BACK TO FINISH THE JOB!

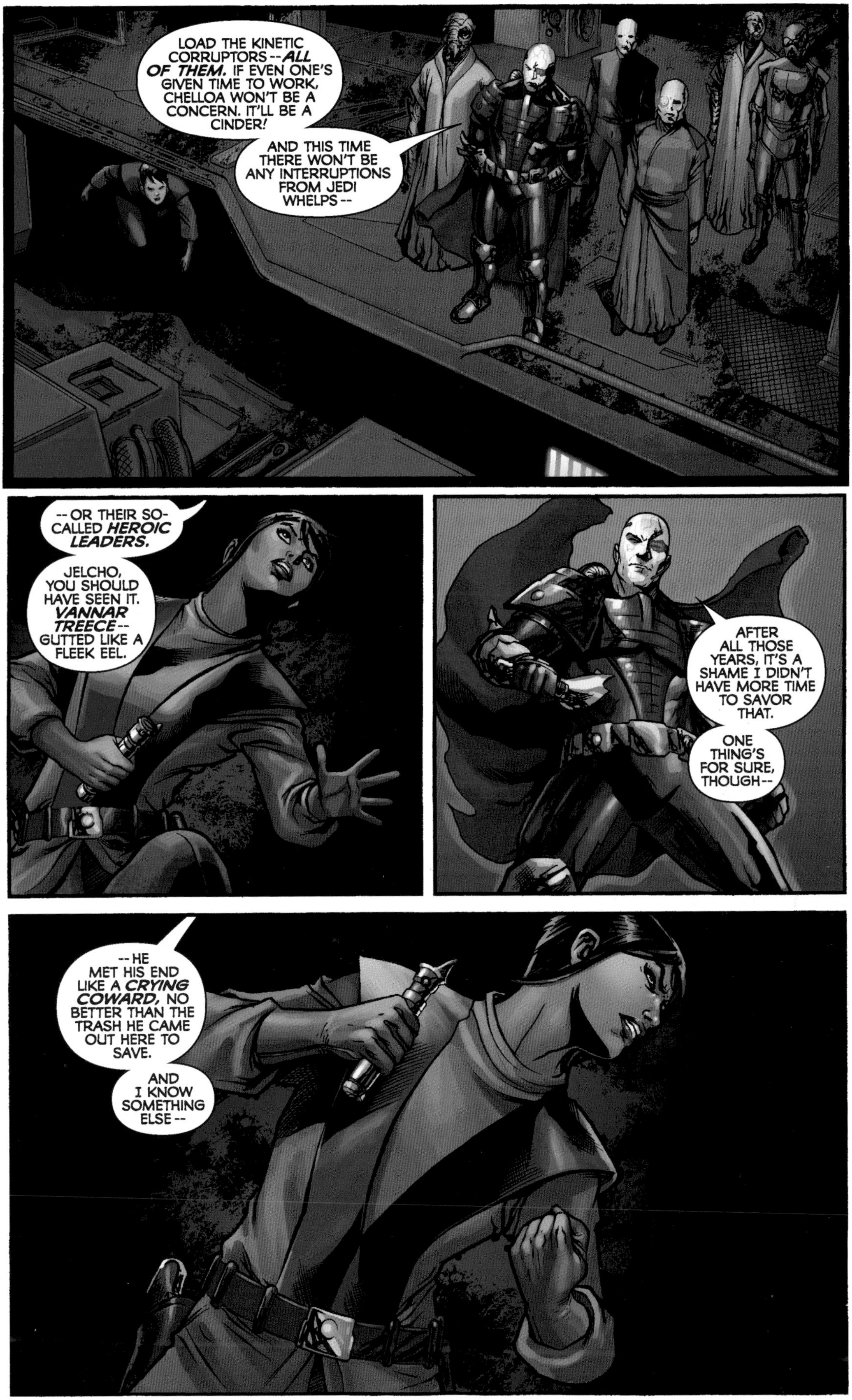
LOAD THE KINETIC CORRUPTORS -- ALL OF THEM. IF EVEN ONE'S GIVEN TIME TO WORK, CHELLOA WON'T BE A CONCERN. IT'LL BE A CINDER!
AND THIS TIME THERE WON'T BE ANY INTERRUPTIONS FROM JEDI WHELPS --
-- OR THEIR SO-CALLED HEROIC LEADERS.
JELCHO, YOU SHOULD HAVE SEEN IT. VANNAR TREECE -- GUTTED LIKE A FLEEK EEL.
AFTER ALL THOSE YEARS, IT'S A SHAME I DIDN'T HAVE MORE TIME TO SAVOR THAT.
ONE THING'S FOR SURE, THOUGH --
-- HE MET HIS END LIKE A CRYING COWARD, NO BETTER THAN THE TRASH HE CAME OUT HERE TO SAVE.
AND I KNOW SOMETHING ELSE --

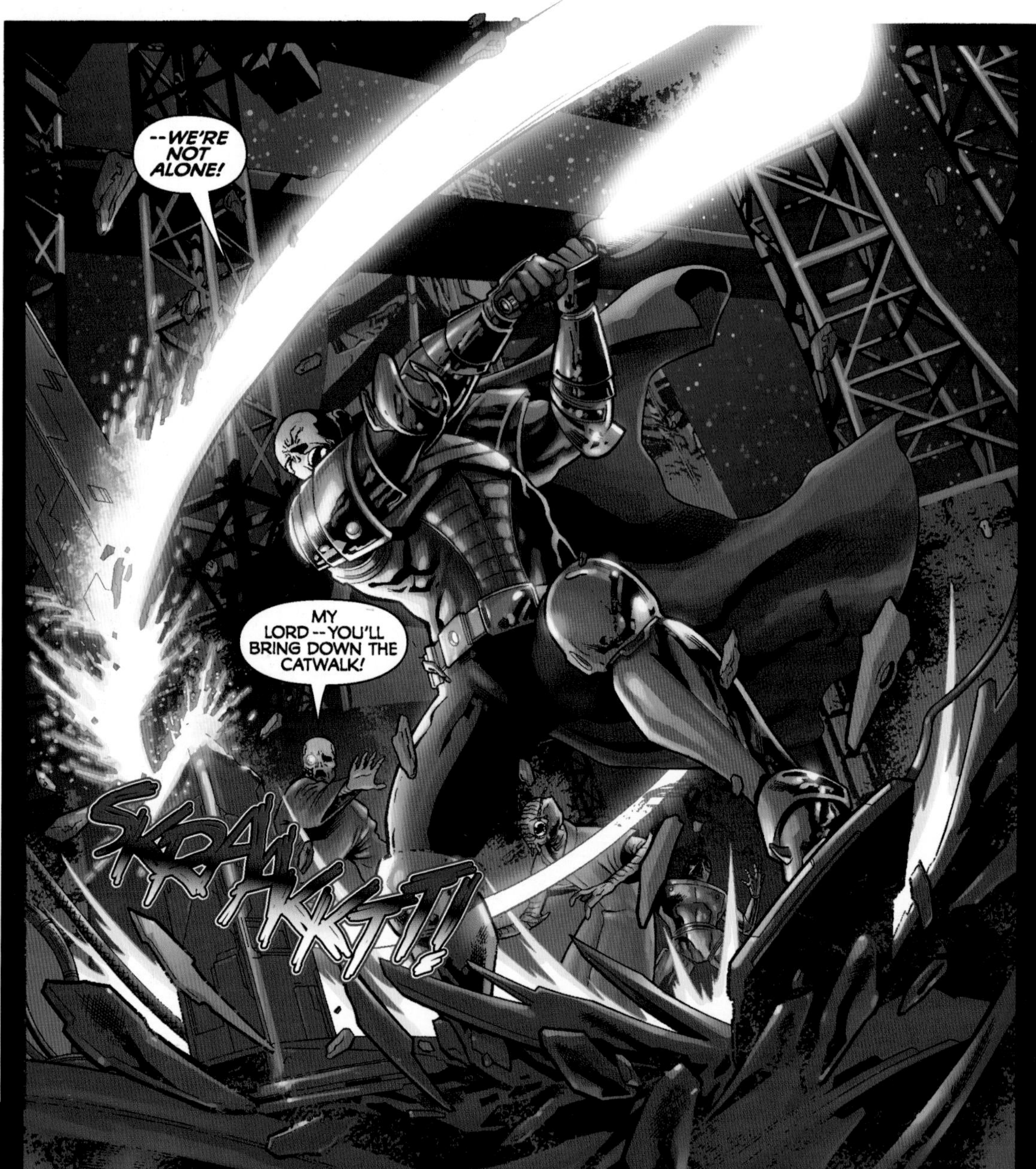
--WE'RE NOT ALONE!
MY LORD--YOU'LL BRING DOWN THE CATWALK!
SKRAAAKKT!!
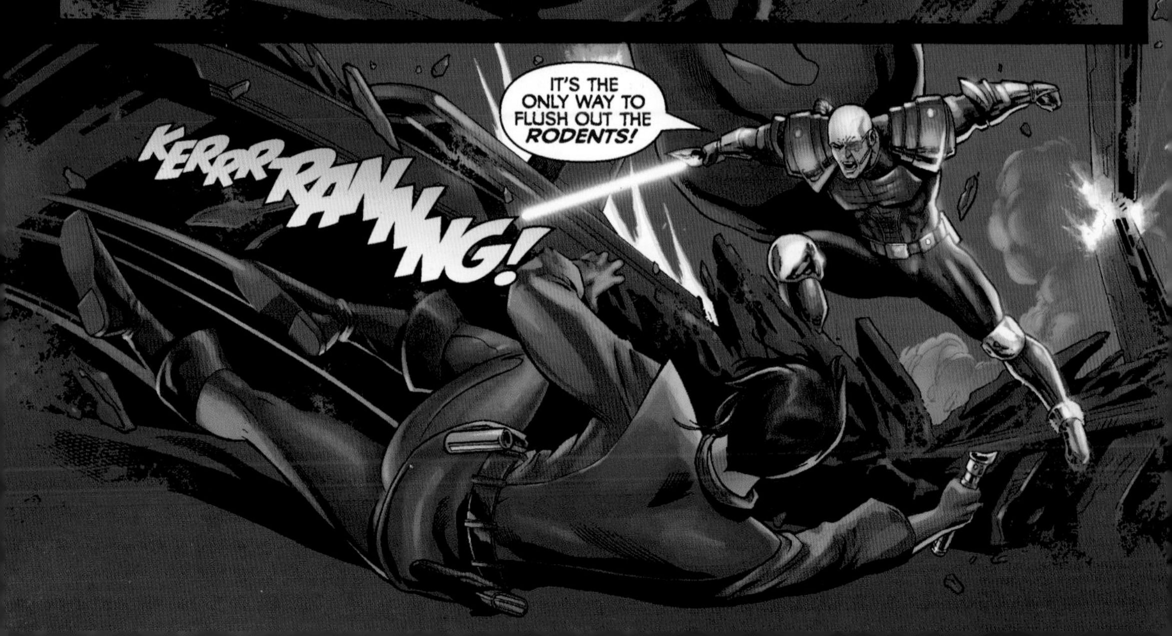
IT'S THE ONLY WAY TO FLUSH OUT THE RODENTS!
KERRRRANNNG!

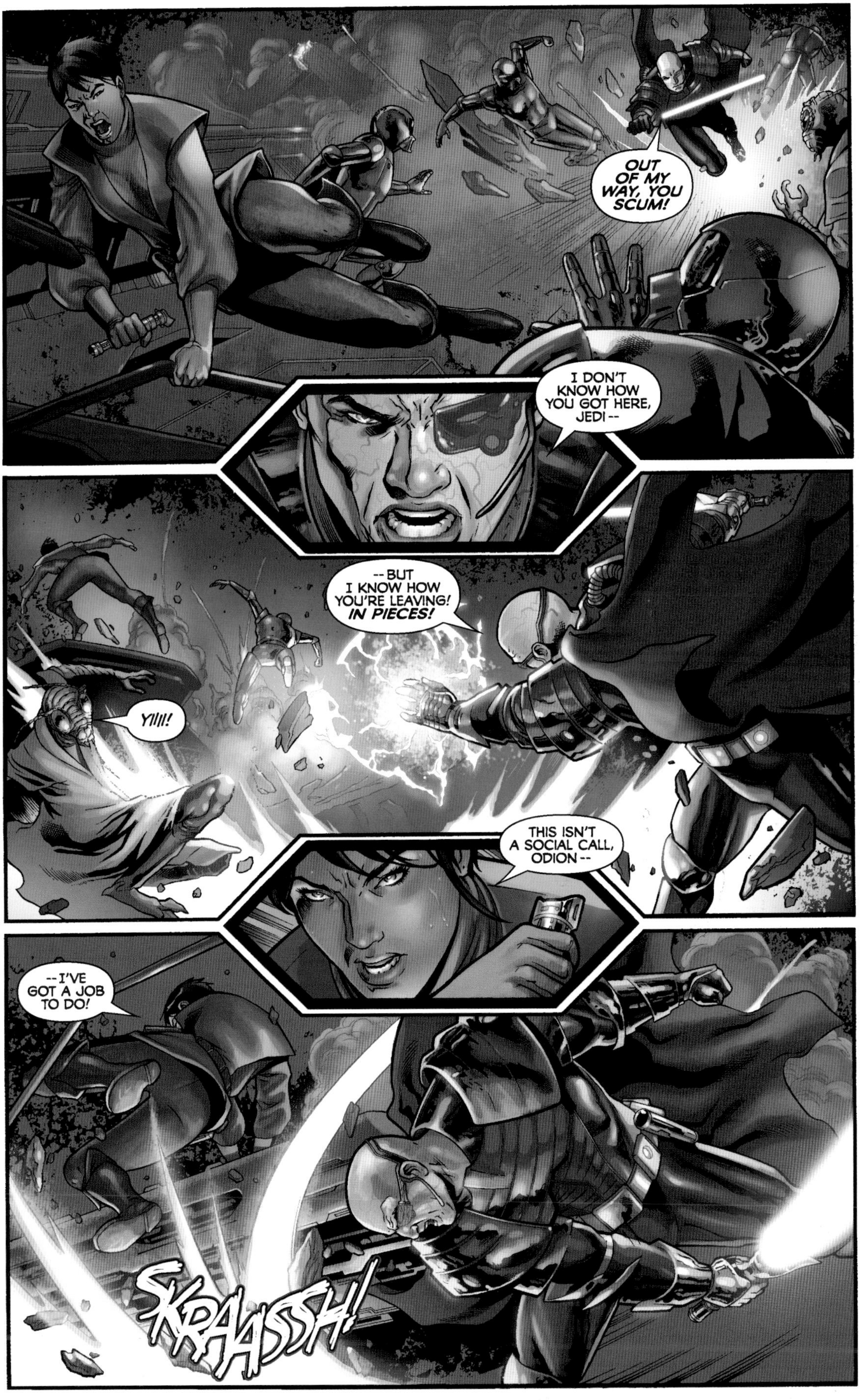
OUT OF MY WAY, YOU SCUM!
I DON'T KNOW HOW YOU GOT HERE, JEDI --
-- BUT I KNOW HOW YOU'RE LEAVING! IN PIECES!
YIIII!
THIS ISN'T A SOCIAL CALL, ODION --
-- I'VE GOT A JOB TO DO!
SKRAASSH!

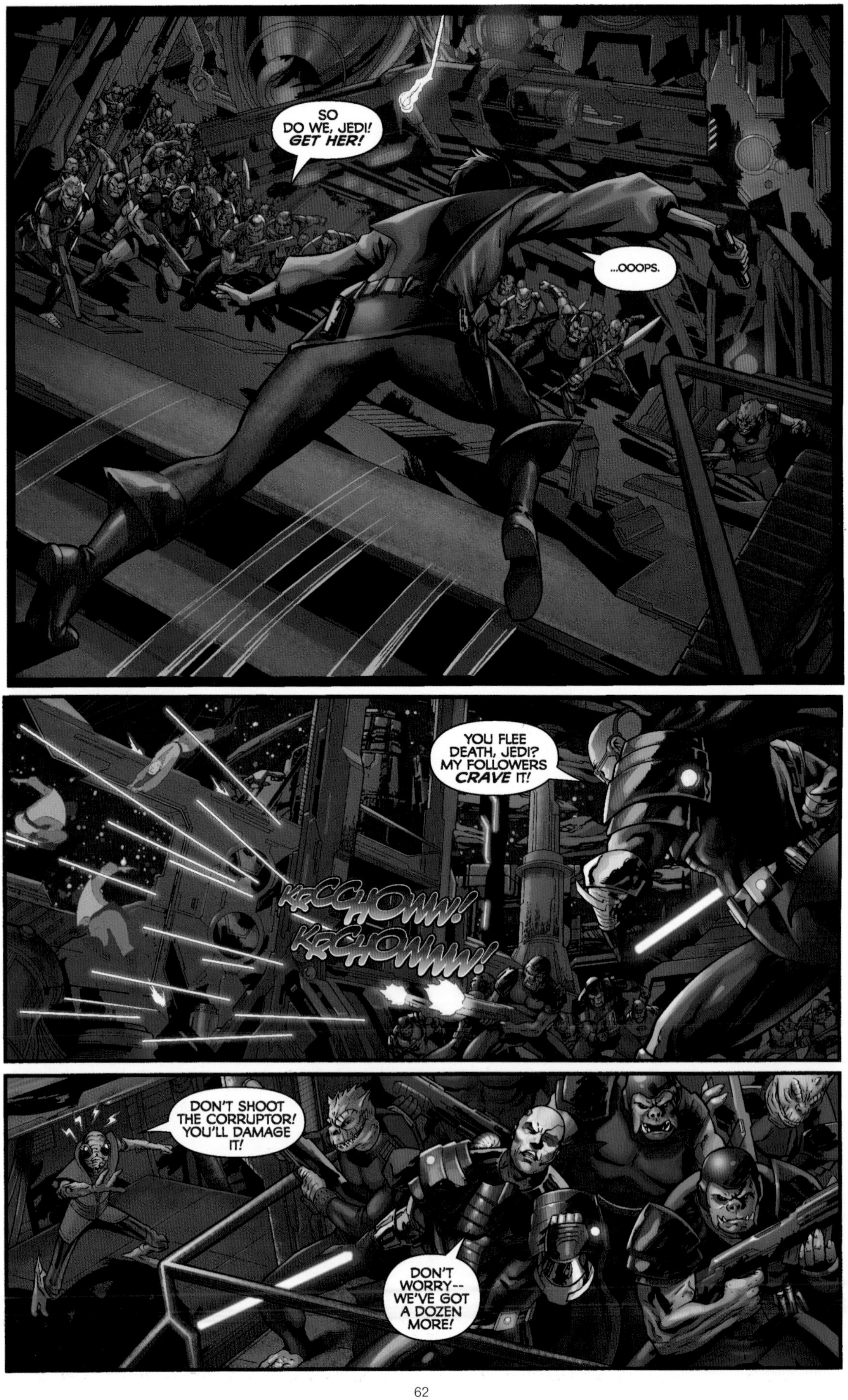
SO DO WE, JEDI! GET HER!
...OOOPS.
YOU FLEE DEATH, JEDI? MY FOLLOWERS CRAVE IT!
KRCHOWW! KRCHOWWW!
DON'T SHOOT THE CORRUPTOR! YOU'LL DAMAGE IT!
DON'T WORRY-- WE'VE GOT A DOZEN MORE!

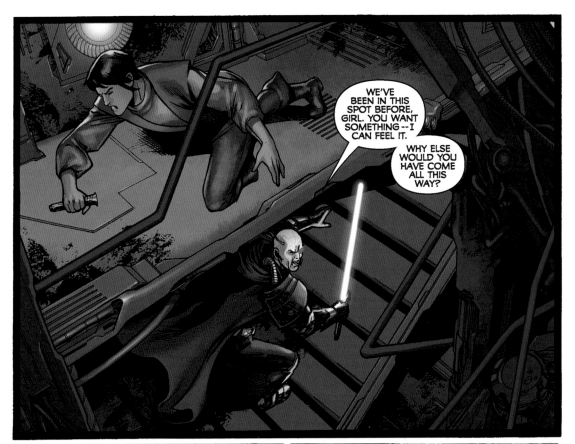

WE'VE BEEN IN THIS SPOT BEFORE, GIRL. YOU WANT SOMETHING -- I CAN FEEL IT.

WHY ELSE WOULD YOU HAVE COME ALL THIS WAY?

TO STOP YOU FROM FINISHING OFF CHELLOA! THERE ARE THOUSANDS OF INNOCENT PEOPLE THERE --

-- AND *MORE ARRIVING EVERY DAY!* DON'T YOU CARE ABOUT THEM? AREN'T THEY GOOD TO YOU AS SLAVES?

I'VE GOT PLENTY OF SLAVES -- SPECIES BETTER AT WHAT THEY DO THAN THE DREGS OF CHELLOA.

BUT WHAT DO YOU MEAN -- *MORE ARRIVING EVERY DAY?* WHO?

AH -- I SEE IT IN YOUR THOUGHTS. DAIMAN'S MOVING HIS MUNITIONS FACTORIES THERE!

THAT EXPLAINS EVERYTHING!

I DIDN'T BELIEVE THE INTEL -- BUT I'LL BELIEVE WHAT A *JEDI* SAW.

THANKS, LITTLE KNIGHT. YOU *DID* HAVE A JOB TO DO -- AND NOW YOU'VE DONE IT.

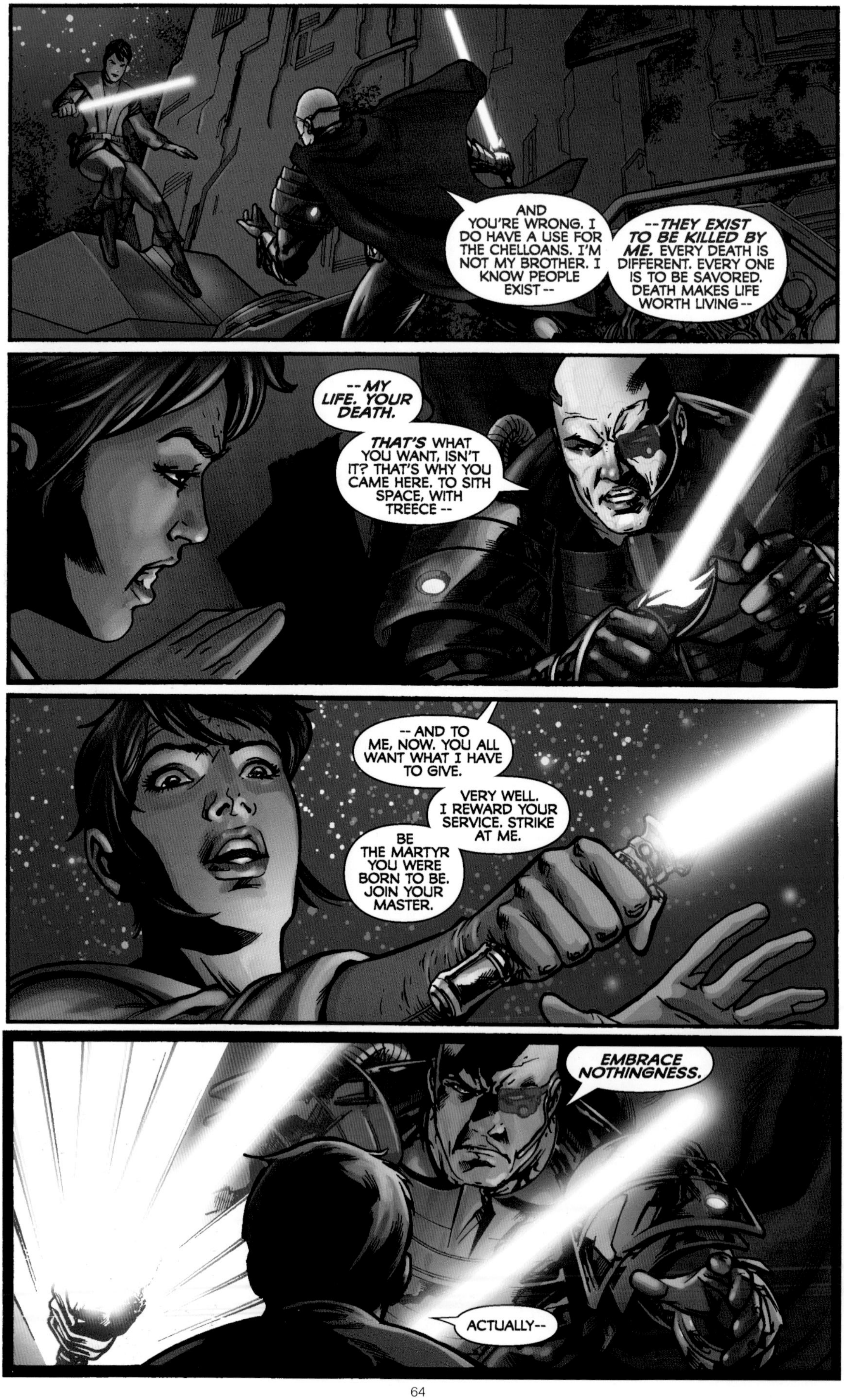
AND YOU'RE WRONG. I DO HAVE A USE FOR THE CHELLOANS. I'M NOT MY BROTHER. I KNOW PEOPLE EXIST --
--THEY EXIST TO BE KILLED BY ME. EVERY DEATH IS DIFFERENT. EVERY ONE IS TO BE SAVORED. DEATH MAKES LIFE WORTH LIVING--
-- MY LIFE. YOUR DEATH.
THAT'S WHAT YOU WANT, ISN'T IT? THAT'S WHY YOU CAME HERE. TO SITH SPACE, WITH TREECE --
-- AND TO ME, NOW. YOU ALL WANT WHAT I HAVE TO GIVE.
VERY WELL. I REWARD YOUR SERVICE. STRIKE AT ME.
BE THE MARTYR YOU WERE BORN TO BE. JOIN YOUR MASTER.
EMBRACE NOTHINGNESS.
ACTUALLY--

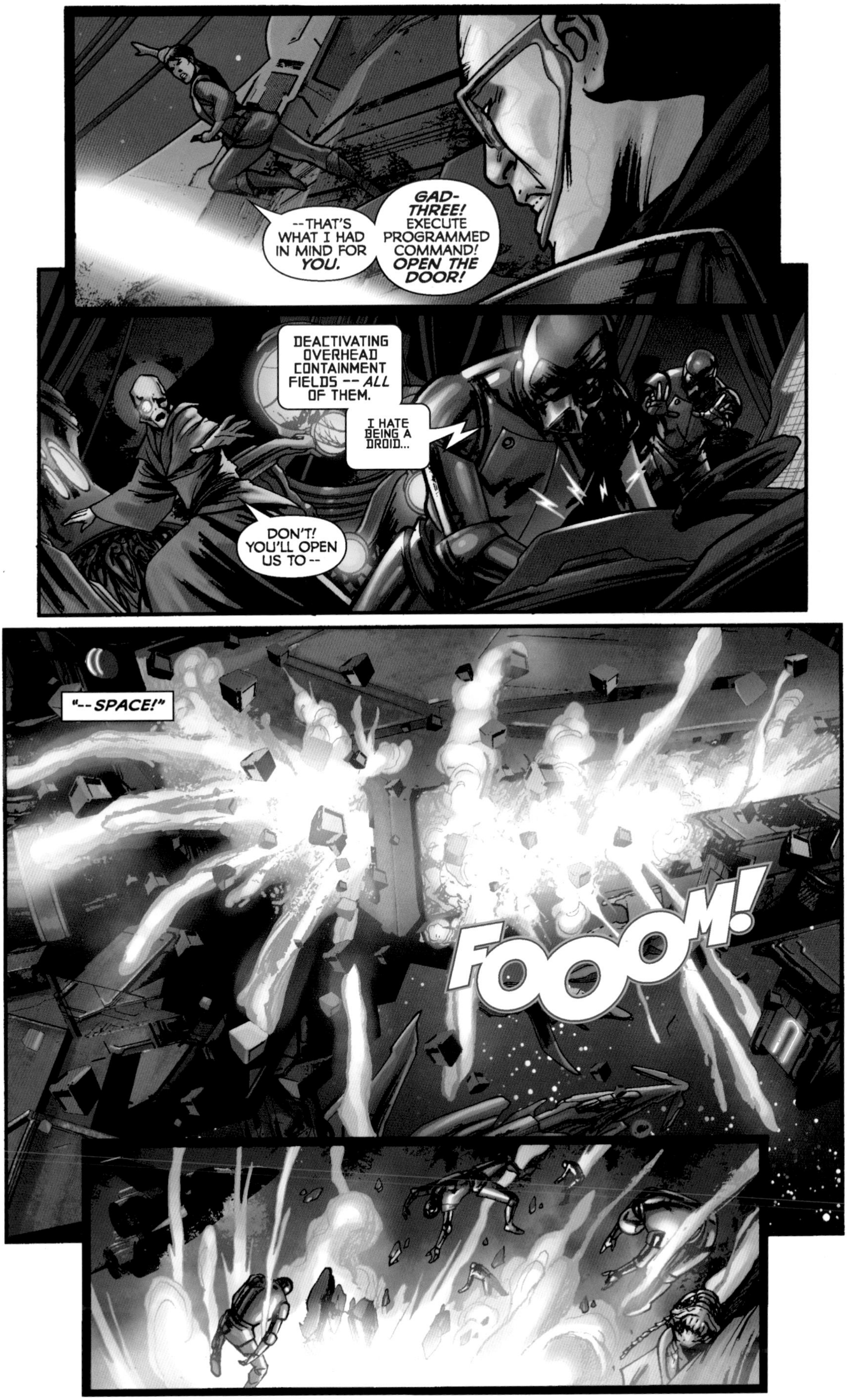
--THAT'S WHAT I HAD IN MIND FOR YOU.
GAD-THREE! EXECUTE PROGRAMMED COMMAND! OPEN THE DOOR!
DEACTIVATING OVERHEAD CONTAINMENT FIELDS -- ALL OF THEM.
I HATE BEING A DROID...
DON'T! YOU'LL OPEN US TO --
"--SPACE!"
FOOOOM!

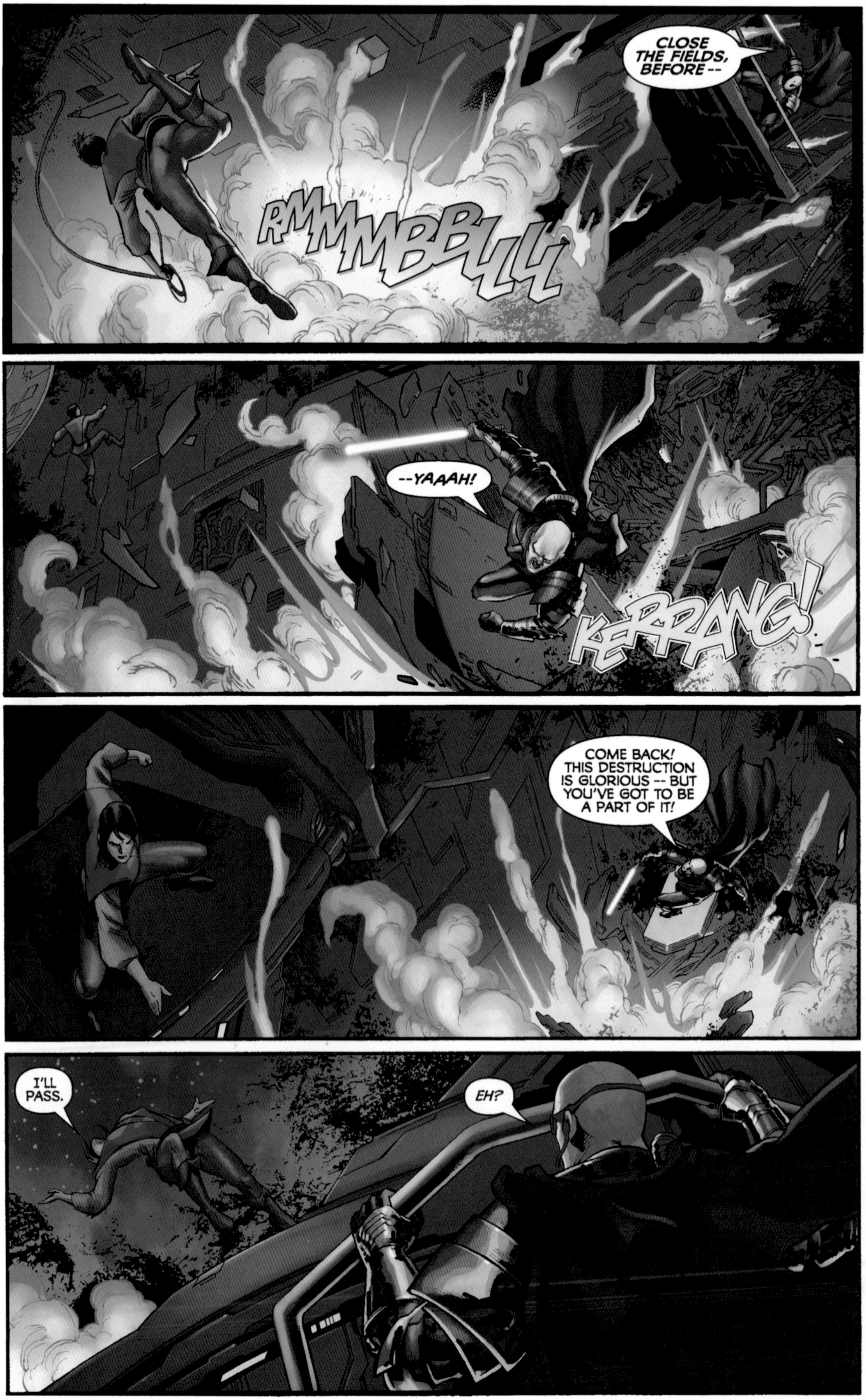
CLOSE THE FIELDS, BEFORE --
RMMMBBLLL
--YAAAH!
KERRANG!
COME BACK! THIS DESTRUCTION IS GLORIOUS -- BUT YOU'VE GOT TO BE A PART OF IT!
I'LL PASS.
EH?

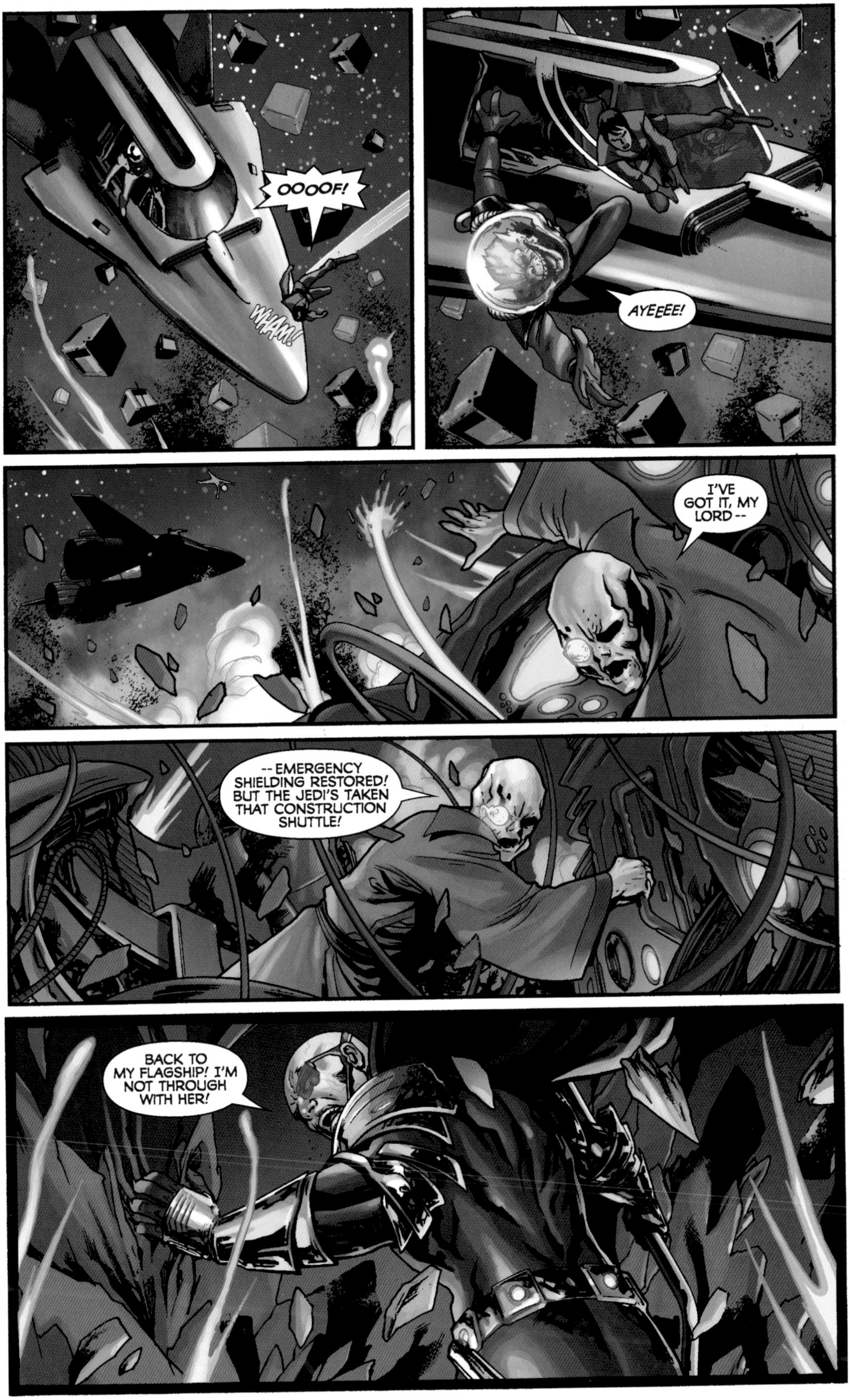
OOOOF!
WHAM!
AYEEEE!
I'VE GOT IT, MY LORD --
-- EMERGENCY SHIELDING RESTORED! BUT THE JEDI'S TAKEN THAT CONSTRUCTION SHUTTLE!
BACK TO MY FLAGSHIP! I'M NOT THROUGH WITH HER!

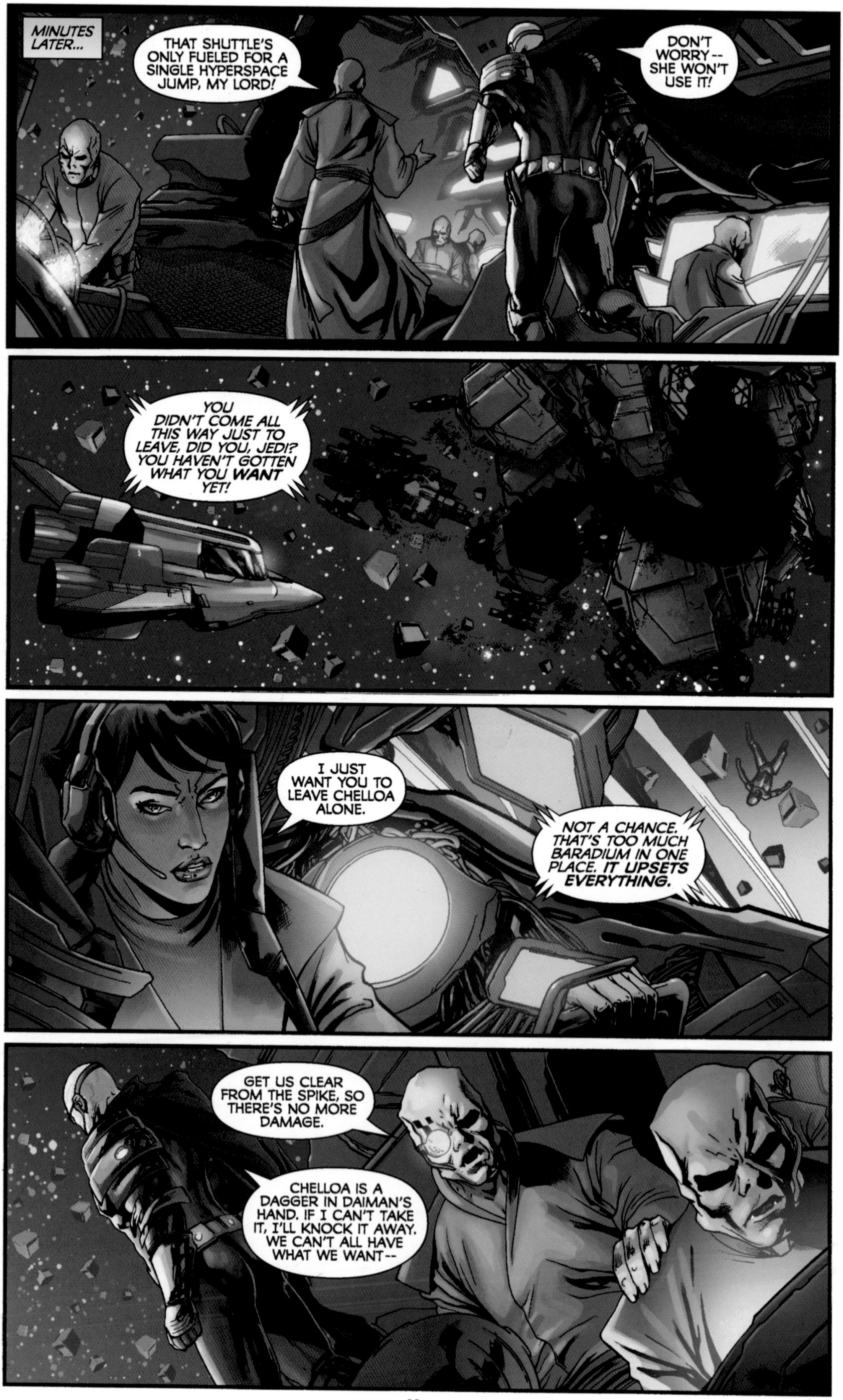
MINUTES LATER...
THAT SHUTTLE'S ONLY FUELED FOR A SINGLE HYPERSPACE JUMP, MY LORD!
DON'T WORRY-- SHE WON'T USE IT!
YOU DIDN'T COME ALL THIS WAY JUST TO LEAVE, DID YOU, JEDI? YOU HAVEN'T GOTTEN WHAT YOU WANT YET!
I JUST WANT YOU TO LEAVE CHELLOA ALONE.
NOT A CHANCE. THAT'S TOO MUCH BARADIUM IN ONE PLACE. IT UPSETS EVERYTHING.
GET US CLEAR FROM THE SPIKE, SO THERE'S NO MORE DAMAGE.
CHELLOA IS A DAGGER IN DAIMAN'S HAND. IF I CAN'T TAKE IT, I'LL KNOCK IT AWAY. WE CAN'T ALL HAVE WHAT WE WANT--

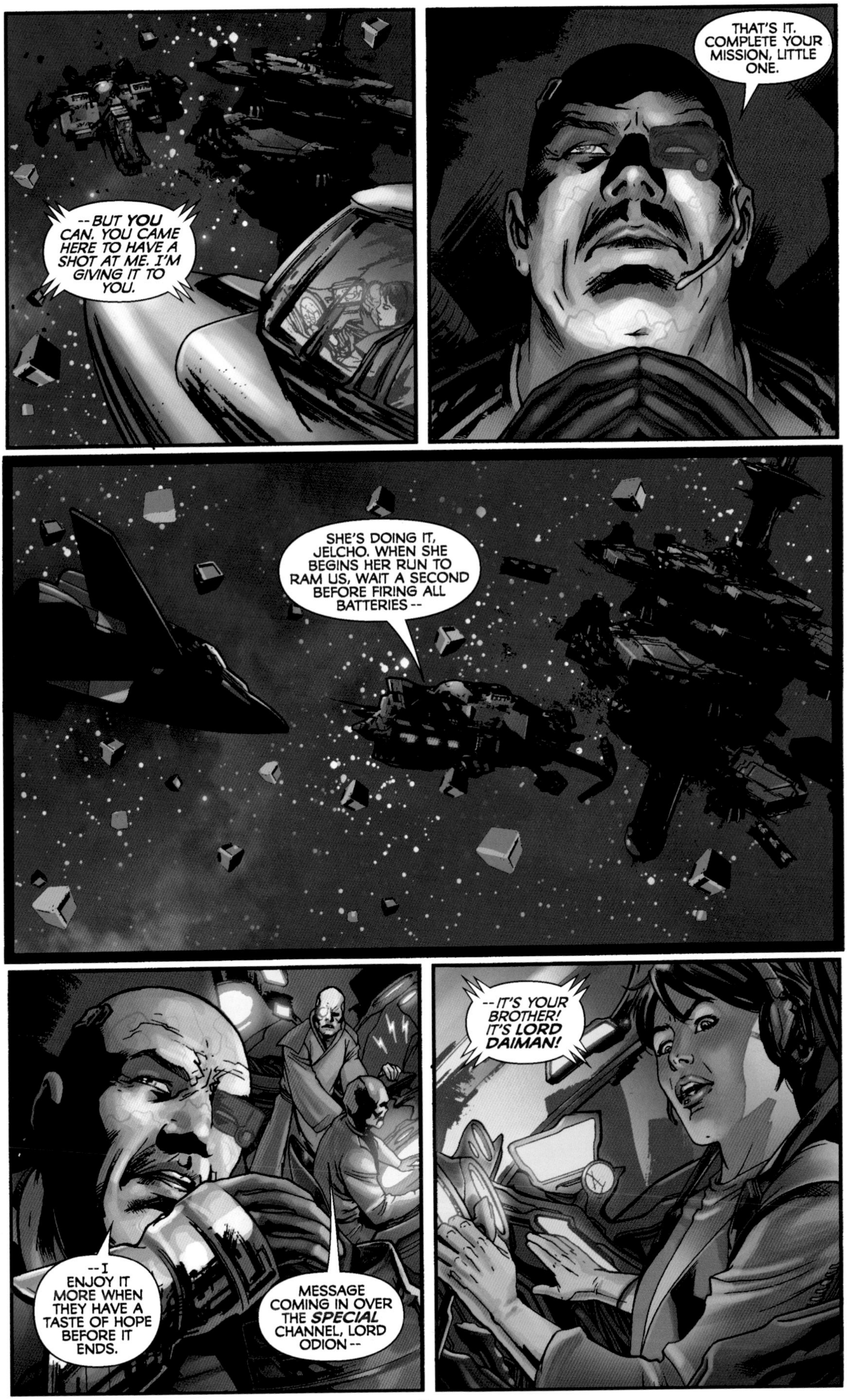
--BUT YOU CAN. YOU CAME HERE TO HAVE A SHOT AT ME. I'M GIVING IT TO YOU.
THAT'S IT. COMPLETE YOUR MISSION, LITTLE ONE.
SHE'S DOING IT, JELCHO. WHEN SHE BEGINS HER RUN TO RAM US, WAIT A SECOND BEFORE FIRING ALL BATTERIES--
--I ENJOY IT MORE WHEN THEY HAVE A TASTE OF HOPE BEFORE IT ENDS.
MESSAGE COMING IN OVER THE SPECIAL CHANNEL, LORD ODION--
--IT'S YOUR BROTHER! IT'S LORD DAIMAN!

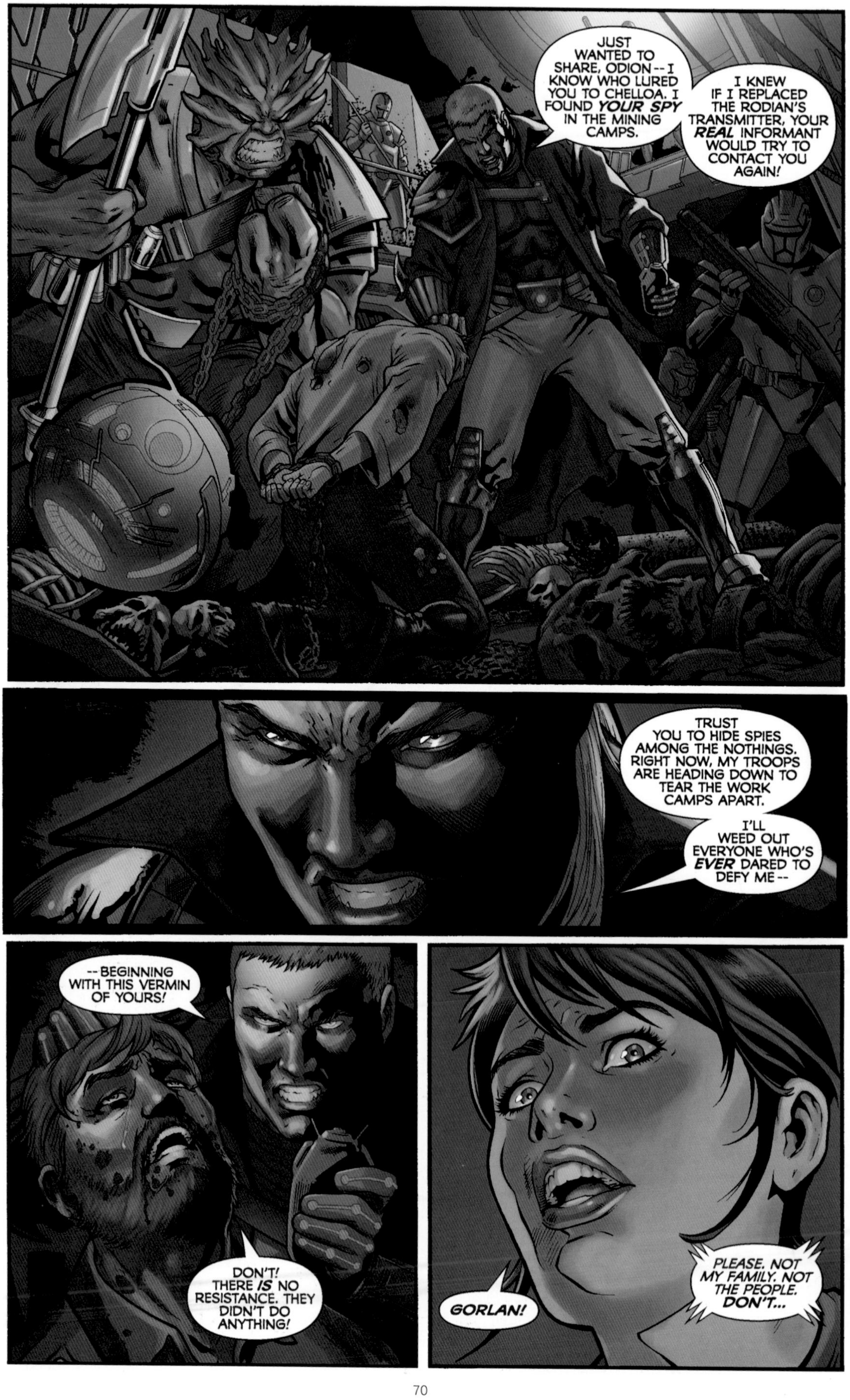
JUST WANTED TO SHARE, ODION -- I KNOW WHO LURED YOU TO CHELLOA. I FOUND YOUR SPY IN THE MINING CAMPS.
I KNEW IF I REPLACED THE RODIAN'S TRANSMITTER, YOUR REAL INFORMANT WOULD TRY TO CONTACT YOU AGAIN!
TRUST YOU TO HIDE SPIES AMONG THE NOTHINGS. RIGHT NOW, MY TROOPS ARE HEADING DOWN TO TEAR THE WORK CAMPS APART.
I'LL WEED OUT EVERYONE WHO'S EVER DARED TO DEFY ME --
-- BEGINNING WITH THIS VERMIN OF YOURS!
DON'T! THERE IS NO RESISTANCE. THEY DIDN'T DO ANYTHING!
GORLAN!
PLEASE. NOT MY FAMILY. NOT THE PEOPLE. DON'T...

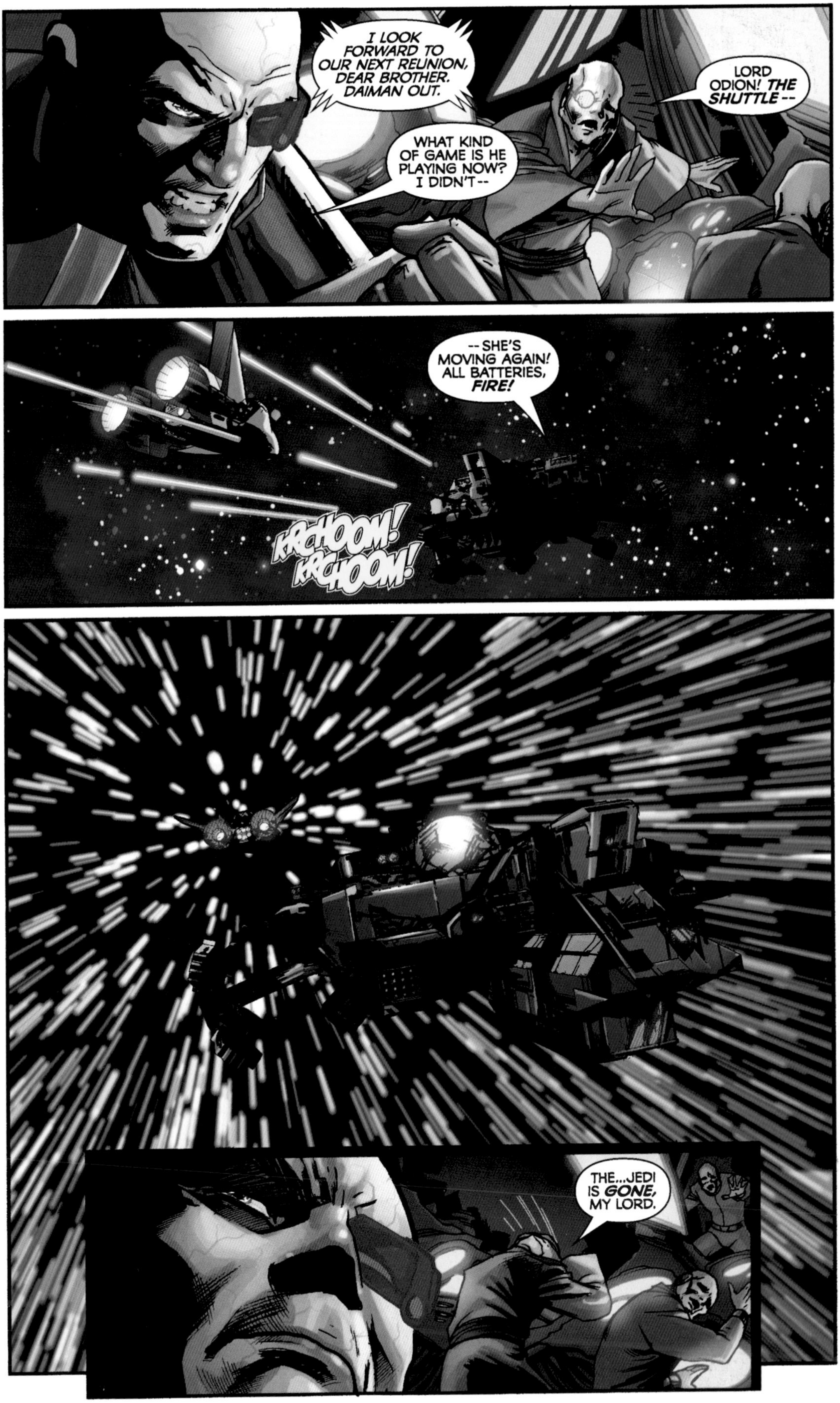
I LOOK FORWARD TO OUR NEXT REUNION, DEAR BROTHER. DAIMAN OUT.
LORD ODION! THE SHUTTLE --
WHAT KIND OF GAME IS HE PLAYING NOW? I DIDN'T --
-- SHE'S MOVING AGAIN! ALL BATTERIES, FIRE!
KRCHOOM! KRCHOOM!
THE...JEDI IS GONE, MY LORD.

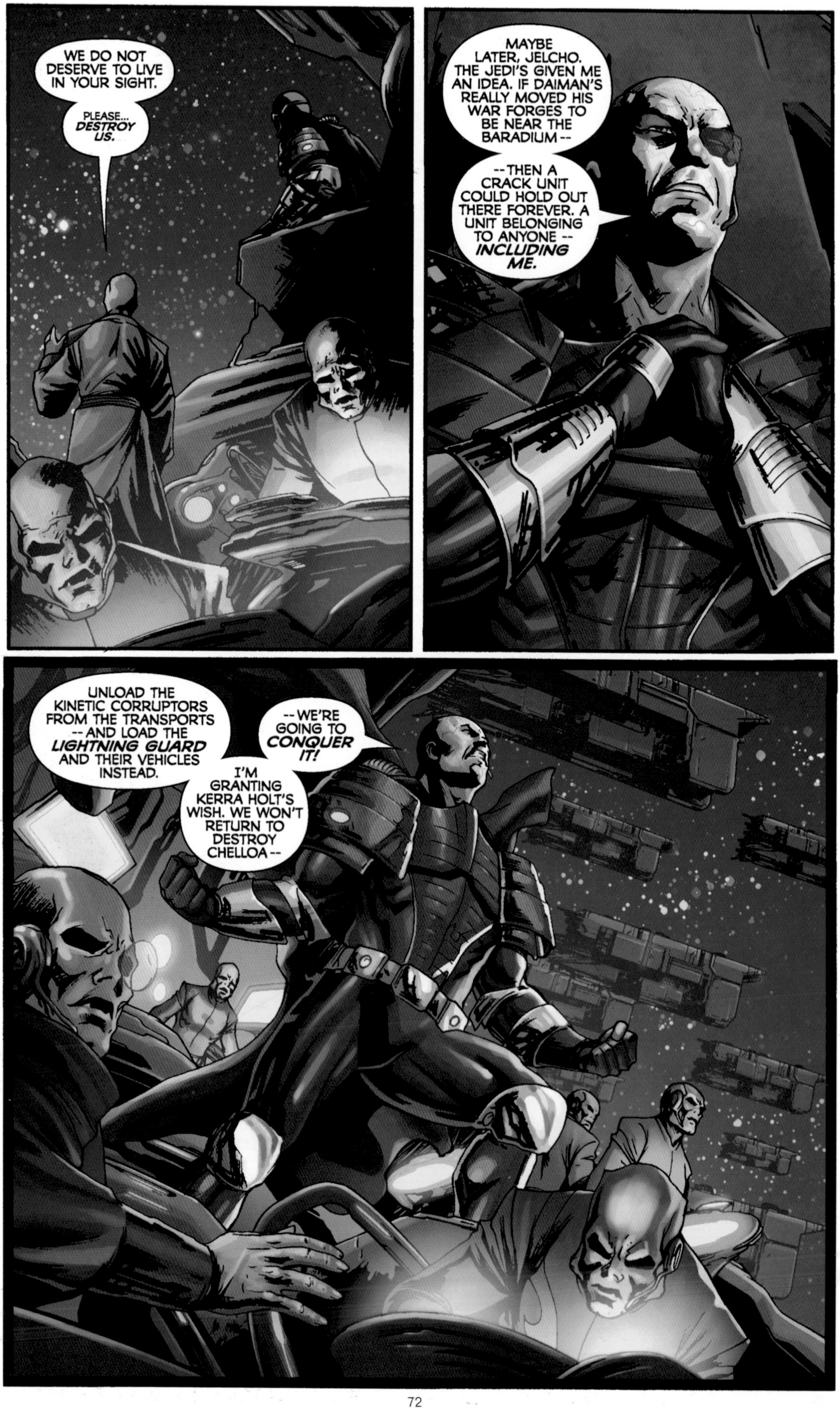
WE DO NOT DESERVE TO LIVE IN YOUR SIGHT.
PLEASE... *DESTROY US.*
MAYBE LATER, JELCHO. THE JEDI'S GIVEN ME AN IDEA. IF DAIMAN'S REALLY MOVED HIS WAR FORGES TO BE NEAR THE BARADIUM --
--THEN A CRACK UNIT COULD HOLD OUT THERE FOREVER. A UNIT BELONGING TO ANYONE -- *INCLUDING ME.*
UNLOAD THE KINETIC CORRUPTORS FROM THE TRANSPORTS --AND LOAD THE *LIGHTNING GUARD* AND THEIR VEHICLES INSTEAD.
I'M GRANTING KERRA HOLT'S WISH. WE WON'T RETURN TO DESTROY CHELLOA --
--WE'RE GOING TO *CONQUER IT!*

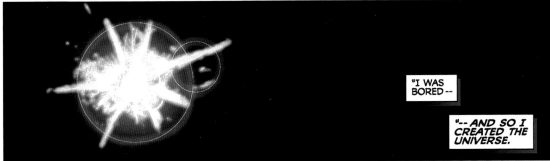

"I WAS BORED --

"-- AND SO I CREATED THE UNIVERSE.

"I HAVE NO DIRECT KNOWLEDGE OF THE TIME BEFORE TIME. BUT I INFER THAT WHEREVER I WAS, NOTHING COULD CHALLENGE ME.

"AND SO I CREATED A *NEW* EXISTENCE. ALL MATTER, ALL ENERGY ARE MANIFESTATIONS OF MY UNDYING SPIRIT.

"BUT WHILE I GAVE ALL BEINGS MOTION, NOT ALL BEINGS SERVE ME. FOR I ALSO CREATED AN OPPONENT -- IN *ODION.*

"HE CLAIMS HE IS MY OLDER BROTHER -- BUT I, OF COURSE, HAVE NO KIN OR KIND. HE IS SIMPLY WHAT I MUST OVERCOME TO *ADVANCE.*

"AND NOW I LEARN THAT *YOU* STAND WITH HIM, RATHER THAN WITH *LORD DAIMAN,* WHO GAVE YOU LIFE.

"YOU OFFEND CREATION -- *MY CREATION.* SO NOW, *GORLAN PALLADANE* --"

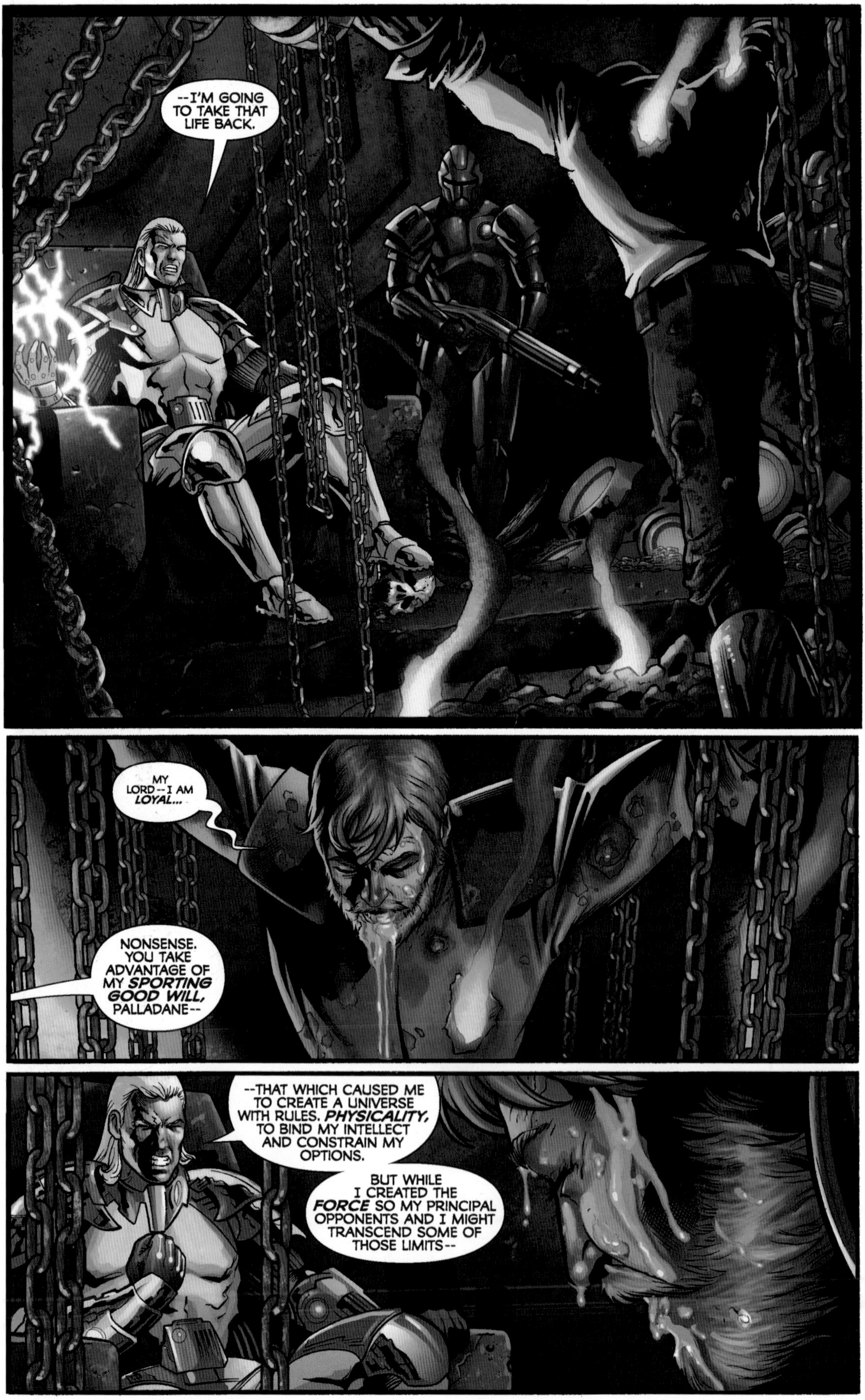
--I'M GOING TO TAKE THAT LIFE BACK.
MY LORD--I AM *LOYAL...*
NONSENSE. YOU TAKE ADVANTAGE OF MY *SPORTING GOOD WILL,* PALLADANE--
--THAT WHICH CAUSED ME TO CREATE A UNIVERSE WITH RULES. *PHYSICALITY,* TO BIND MY INTELLECT AND CONSTRAIN MY OPTIONS.
BUT WHILE I CREATED THE *FORCE* SO MY PRINCIPAL OPPONENTS AND I MIGHT TRANSCEND SOME OF THOSE LIMITS--

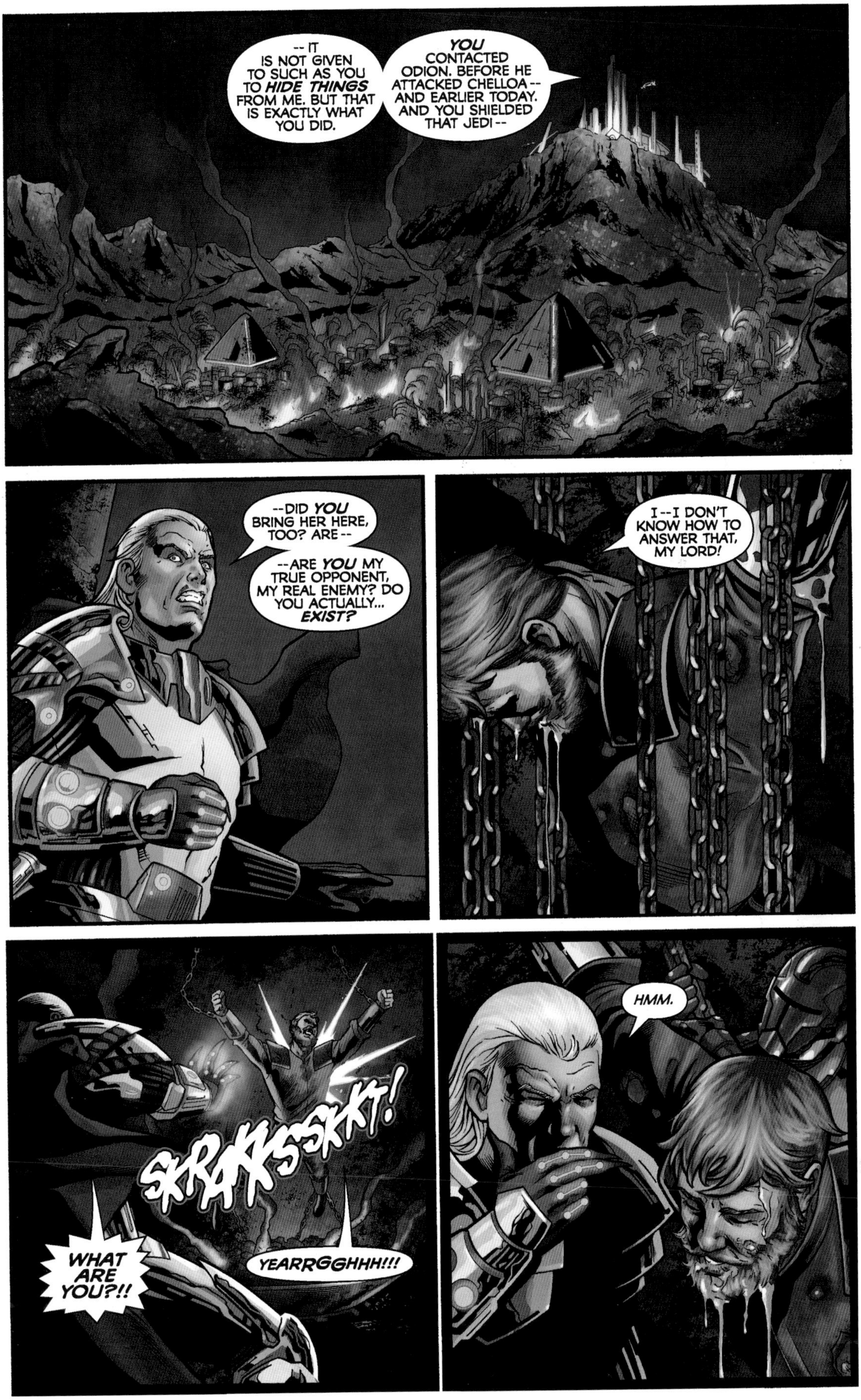
-- IT IS NOT GIVEN TO SUCH AS YOU TO *HIDE THINGS* FROM ME. BUT THAT IS EXACTLY WHAT YOU DID.
YOU CONTACTED ODION. BEFORE HE ATTACKED CHELLOA -- AND EARLIER TODAY. AND YOU SHIELDED THAT JEDI --
--DID *YOU* BRING HER HERE, TOO? ARE --
--ARE *YOU* MY TRUE OPPONENT, MY REAL ENEMY? DO YOU ACTUALLY... *EXIST?*
I -- I DON'T KNOW HOW TO ANSWER THAT, MY LORD!
SKRAKKSSKKT!
WHAT ARE YOU?!!
YEARRGGHHH!!!
HMM.

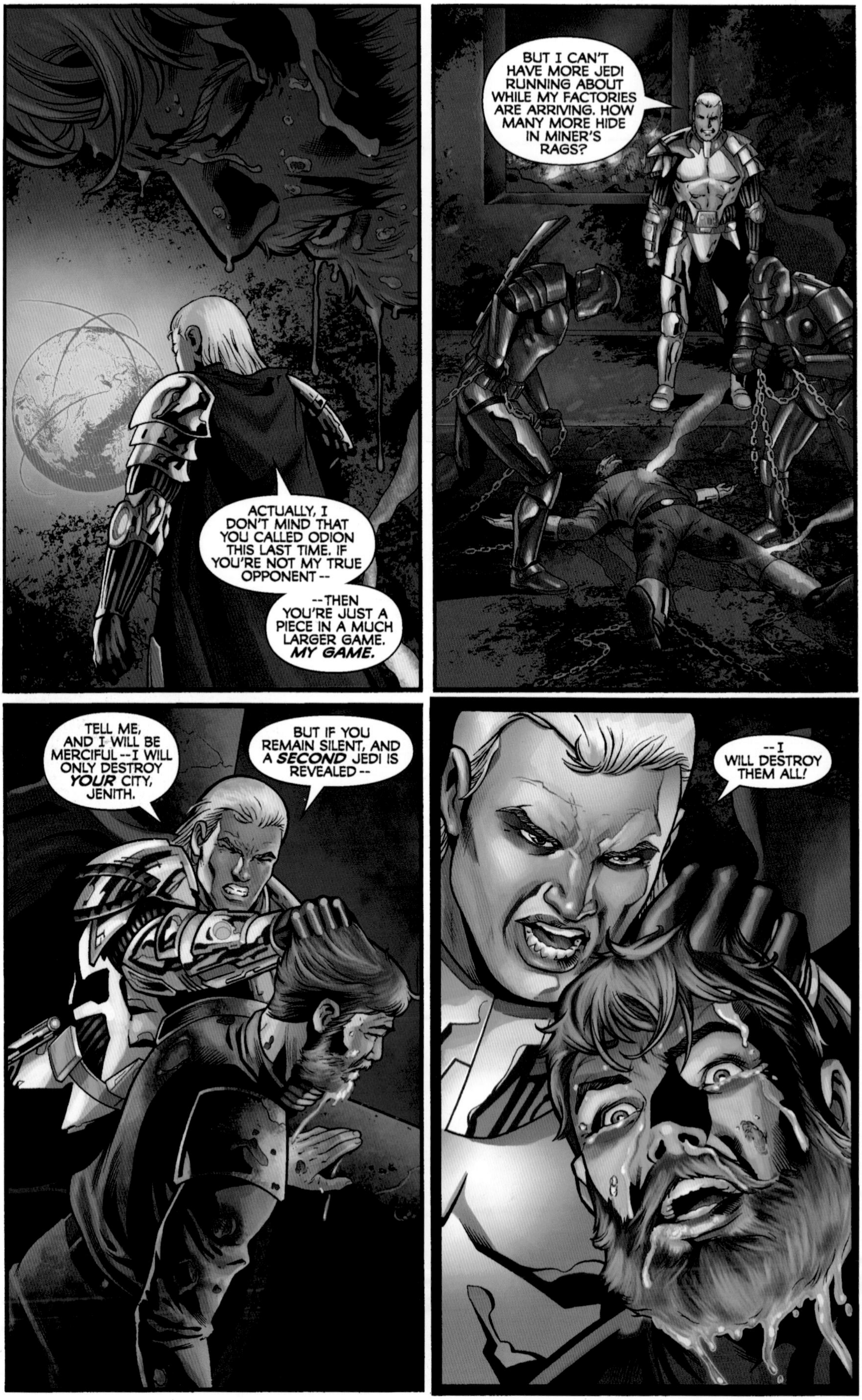
ACTUALLY, I DON'T MIND THAT YOU CALLED ODION THIS LAST TIME. IF YOU'RE NOT MY TRUE OPPONENT--
--THEN YOU'RE JUST A PIECE IN A MUCH LARGER GAME. MY GAME.
BUT I CAN'T HAVE MORE JEDI RUNNING ABOUT WHILE MY FACTORIES ARE ARRIVING. HOW MANY MORE HIDE IN MINER'S RAGS?
TELL ME, AND I WILL BE MERCIFUL--I WILL ONLY DESTROY YOUR CITY, JENITH.
BUT IF YOU REMAIN SILENT, AND A SECOND JEDI IS REVEALED--
--I WILL DESTROY THEM ALL!

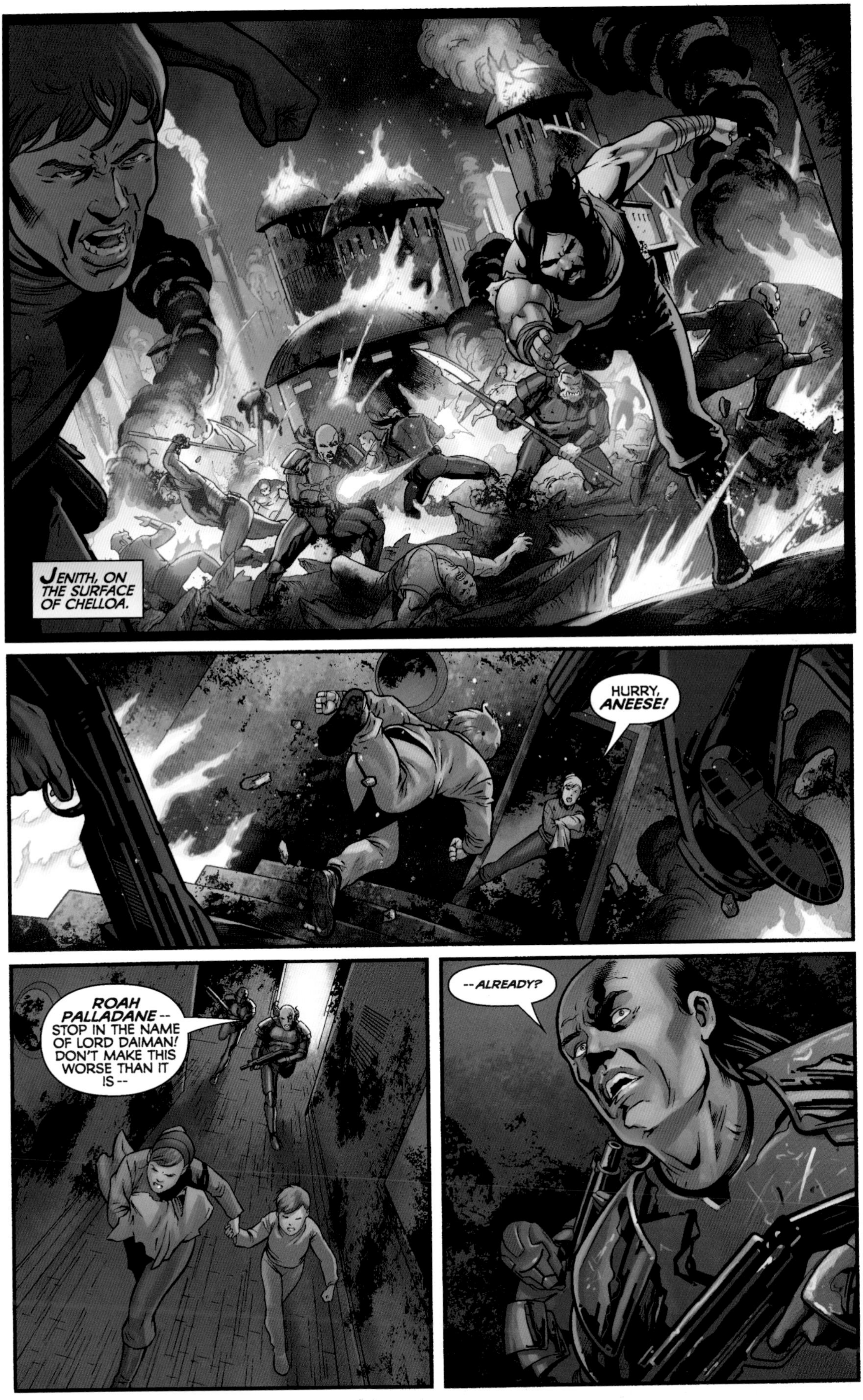
JENITH, ON THE SURFACE OF CHELLOA.
HURRY, ANEESE!
ROAH PALLADANE -- STOP IN THE NAME OF LORD DAIMAN! DON'T MAKE THIS WORSE THAN IT IS --
-- ALREADY?

GET OUT OF THEIR HOME.
KRAKOWW
GAAAHH!

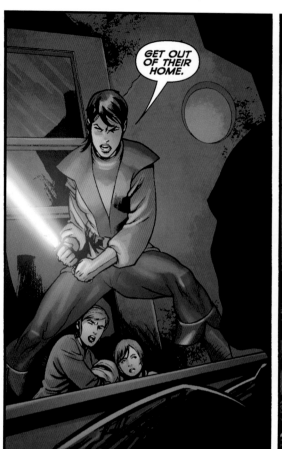

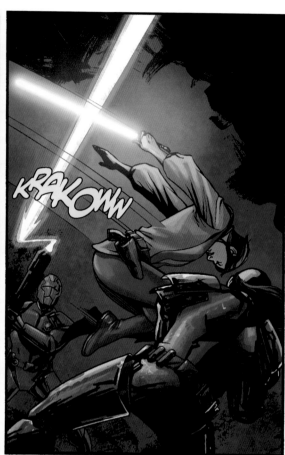

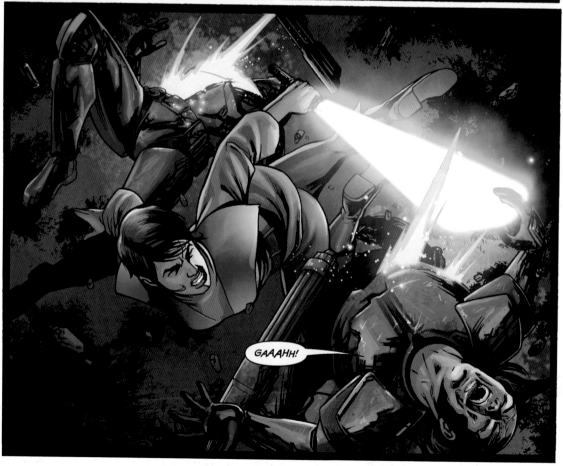

DON'T LOOK, ANEESE.

NO. LOOK -- BUT *DON'T FORGET.*

WHERE'S YOUR HUSBAND, ROAH? WHERE'S *GORLAN?*

WHEN YOU DIDN'T RETURN, HE LEFT. HE SAID HE HAD TO STOP ODION FROM STRIKING AGAIN.

YOU'RE -- YOU'RE LIKE GORLAN, AREN'T YOU? YOU'RE A JEDI?

I DON'T KNOW HOW LIKE HIM I AM. *I FIGHT.*

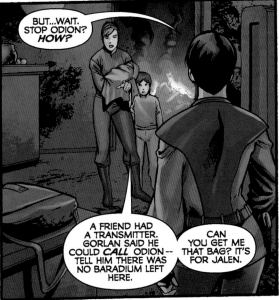

BUT...WAIT. STOP ODION? *HOW?*

A FRIEND HAD A TRANSMITTER. GORLAN SAID HE COULD *CALL* ODION -- TELL HIM THERE WAS NO BARADIUM LEFT HERE.

CAN YOU GET ME THAT BAG? IT'S FOR JALEN.

I THINK I HEARD GORLAN'S CALL. BUT WHY WOULD HE THINK HE COULD REACH ODION? THE OLD INTERSTELLAR RELAYS ARE DOWN.

YOU CAN'T JUST PICK THE PERSON YOU'RE GOING TO CALL OUT HERE. AND HOW WOULD HE KNOW THAT HE'D LISTEN? UNLESS --

-- COULD DAIMAN BE RIGHT? COULD GORLAN REALLY HAVE BEEN IN LEAGUE WITH ODION?

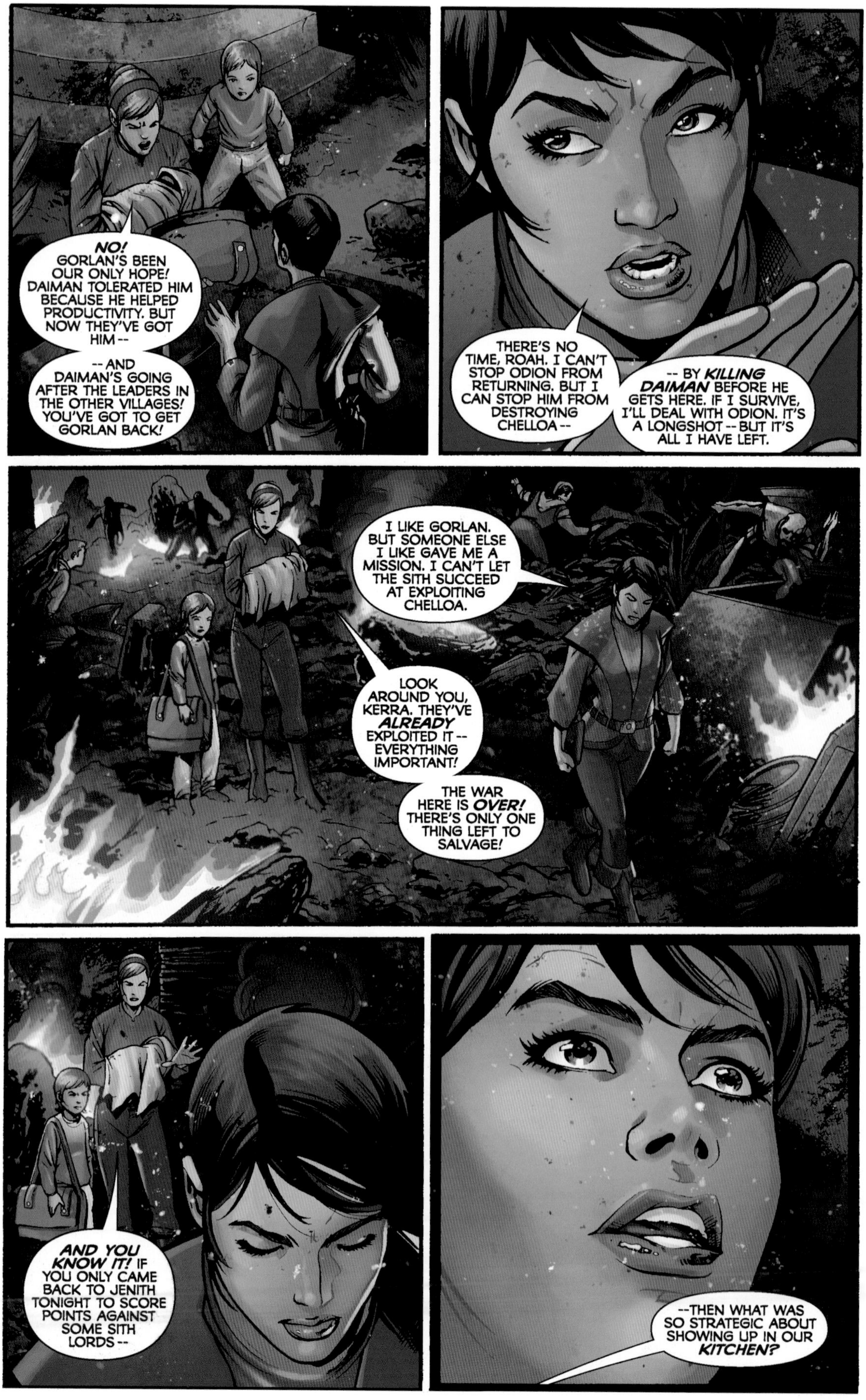
NO! GORLAN'S BEEN OUR ONLY HOPE! DAIMAN TOLERATED HIM BECAUSE HE HELPED PRODUCTIVITY. BUT NOW THEY'VE GOT HIM --
-- AND DAIMAN'S GOING AFTER THE LEADERS IN THE OTHER VILLAGES! YOU'VE GOT TO GET GORLAN BACK!
THERE'S NO TIME, ROAH. I CAN'T STOP ODION FROM RETURNING. BUT I CAN STOP HIM FROM DESTROYING CHELLOA --
-- BY KILLING DAIMAN BEFORE HE GETS HERE. IF I SURVIVE, I'LL DEAL WITH ODION. IT'S A LONGSHOT -- BUT IT'S ALL I HAVE LEFT.
I LIKE GORLAN. BUT SOMEONE ELSE I LIKE GAVE ME A MISSION. I CAN'T LET THE SITH SUCCEED AT EXPLOITING CHELLOA.
LOOK AROUND YOU, KERRA. THEY'VE ALREADY EXPLOITED IT -- EVERYTHING IMPORTANT!
THE WAR HERE IS OVER! THERE'S ONLY ONE THING LEFT TO SALVAGE!
AND YOU KNOW IT! IF YOU ONLY CAME BACK TO JENITH TONIGHT TO SCORE POINTS AGAINST SOME SITH LORDS --
--THEN WHAT WAS SO STRATEGIC ABOUT SHOWING UP IN OUR KITCHEN?

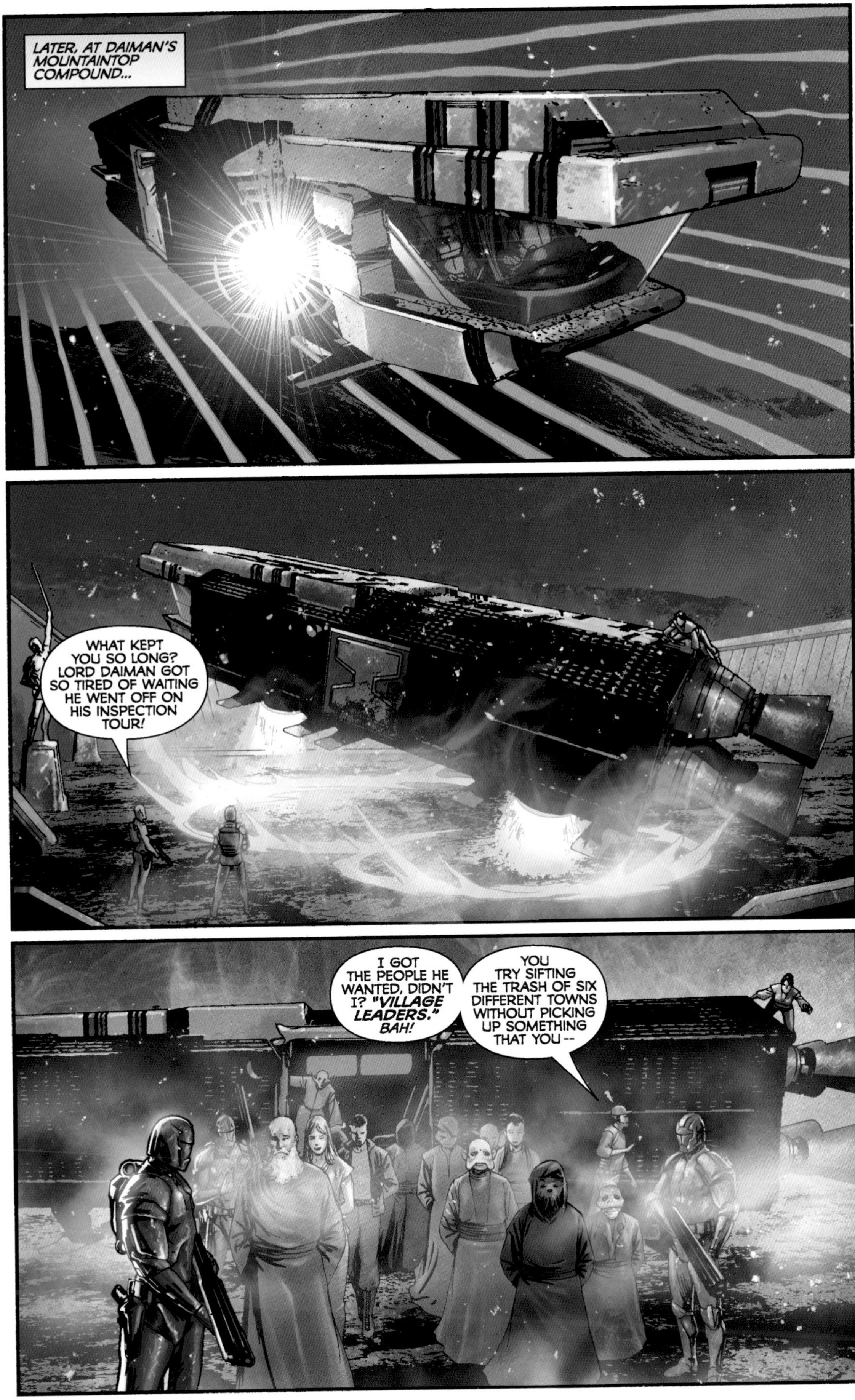
LATER, AT DAIMAN'S MOUNTAINTOP COMPOUND...
WHAT KEPT YOU SO LONG? LORD DAIMAN GOT SO TIRED OF WAITING HE WENT OFF ON HIS INSPECTION TOUR!
I GOT THE PEOPLE HE WANTED, DIDN'T I? *"VILLAGE LEADERS."* BAH!
YOU TRY SIFTING THE TRASH OF SIX DIFFERENT TOWNS WITHOUT PICKING UP SOMETHING THAT YOU --

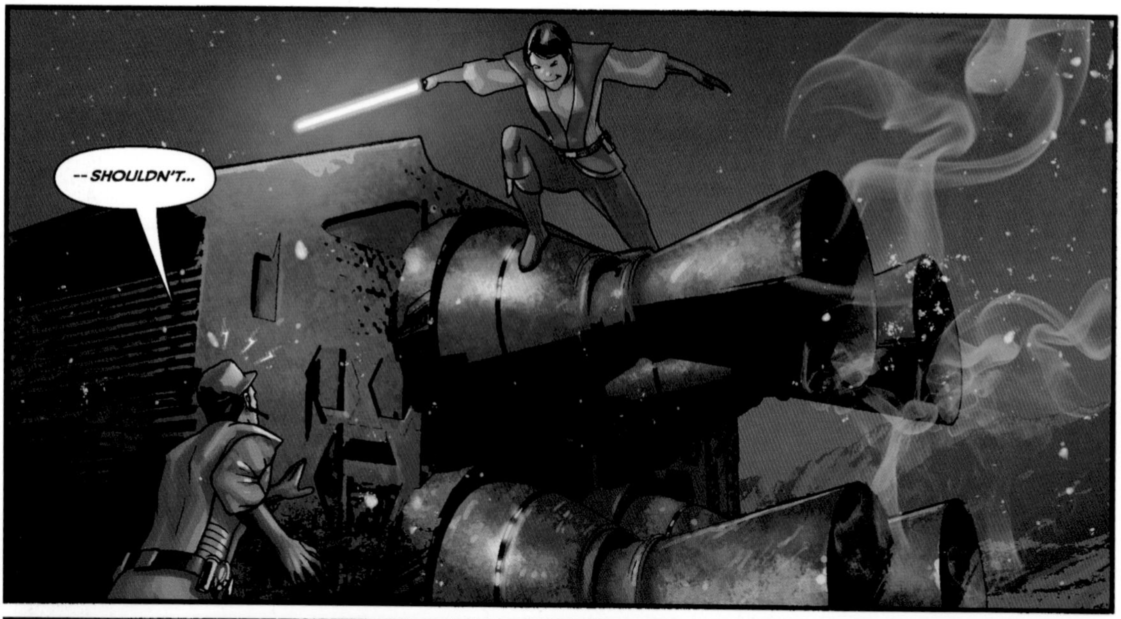
--SHOULDN'T...

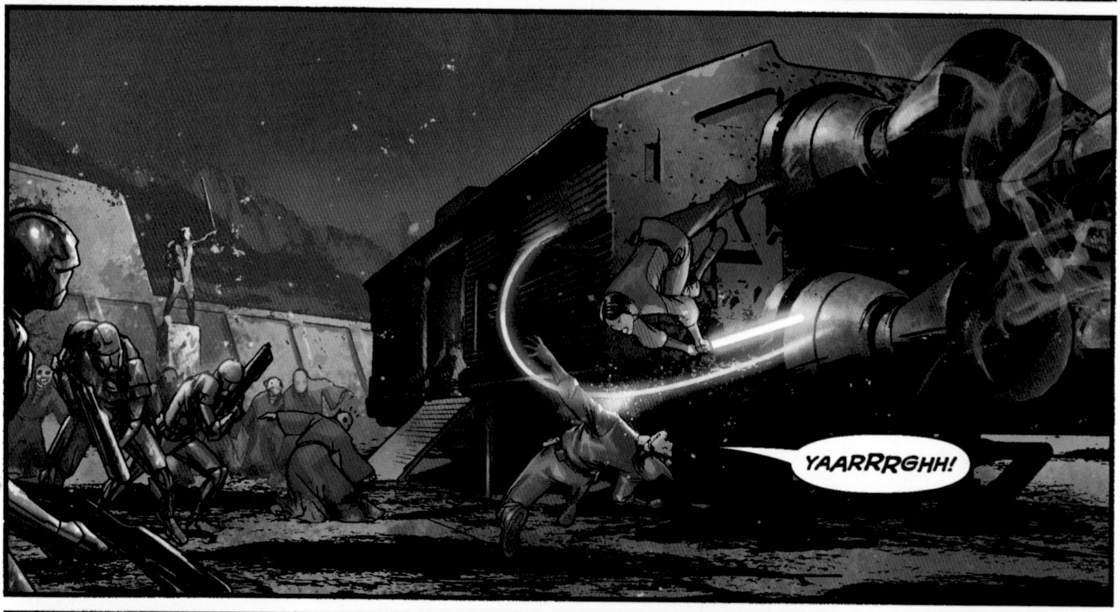
YAARRRGHH!

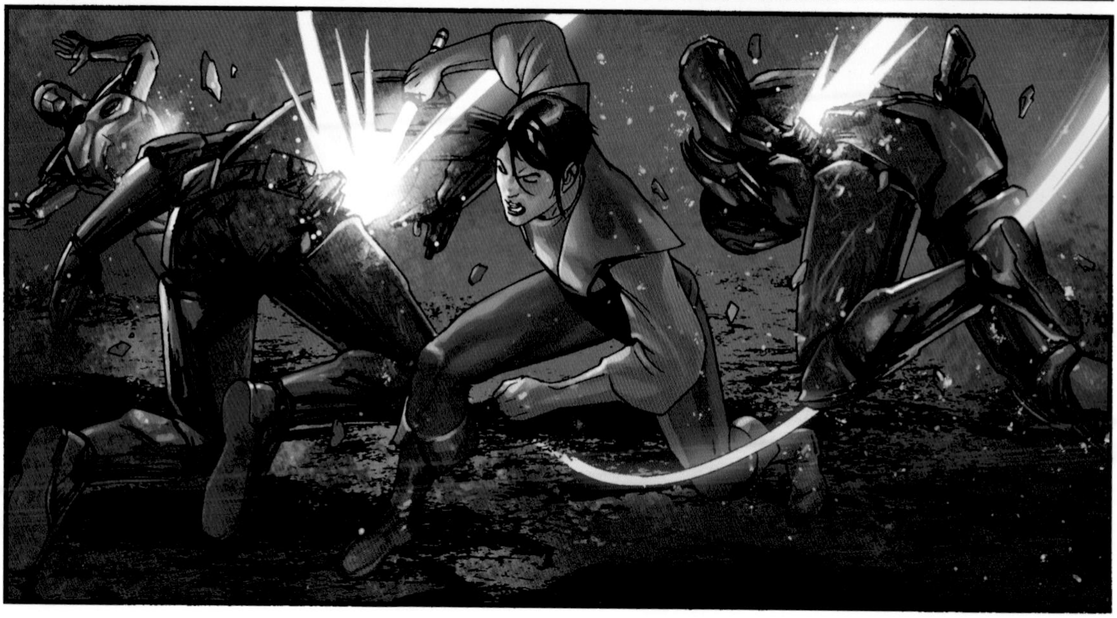

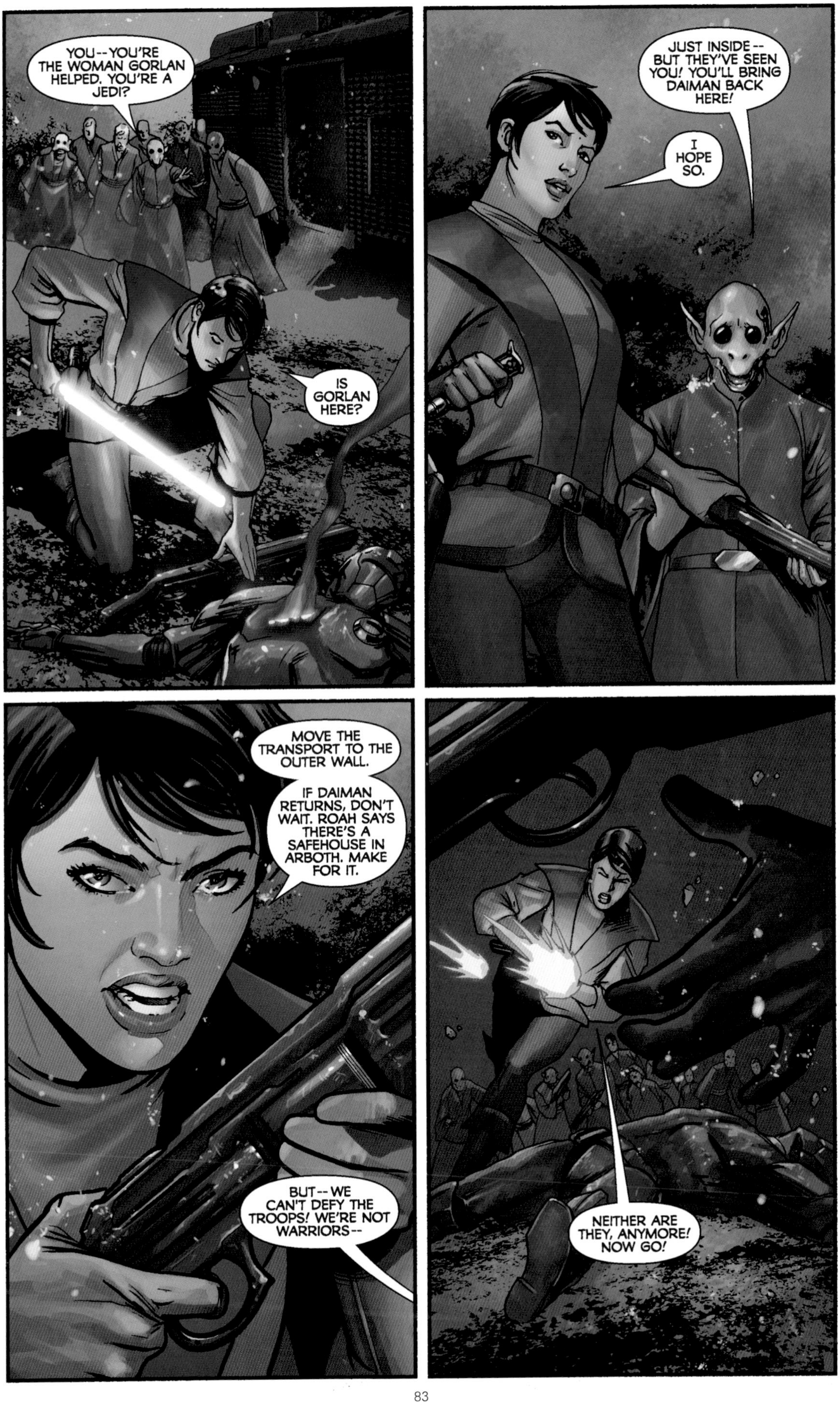
YOU--YOU'RE THE WOMAN GORLAN HELPED. YOU'RE A JEDI?
IS GORLAN HERE?
JUST INSIDE-- BUT THEY'VE SEEN YOU! YOU'LL BRING DAIMAN BACK HERE!
I HOPE SO.
MOVE THE TRANSPORT TO THE OUTER WALL.
IF DAIMAN RETURNS, DON'T WAIT. ROAH SAYS THERE'S A SAFEHOUSE IN ARBOTH. MAKE FOR IT.
BUT--WE CAN'T DEFY THE TROOPS! WE'RE NOT WARRIORS--
NEITHER ARE THEY, ANYMORE! NOW GO!

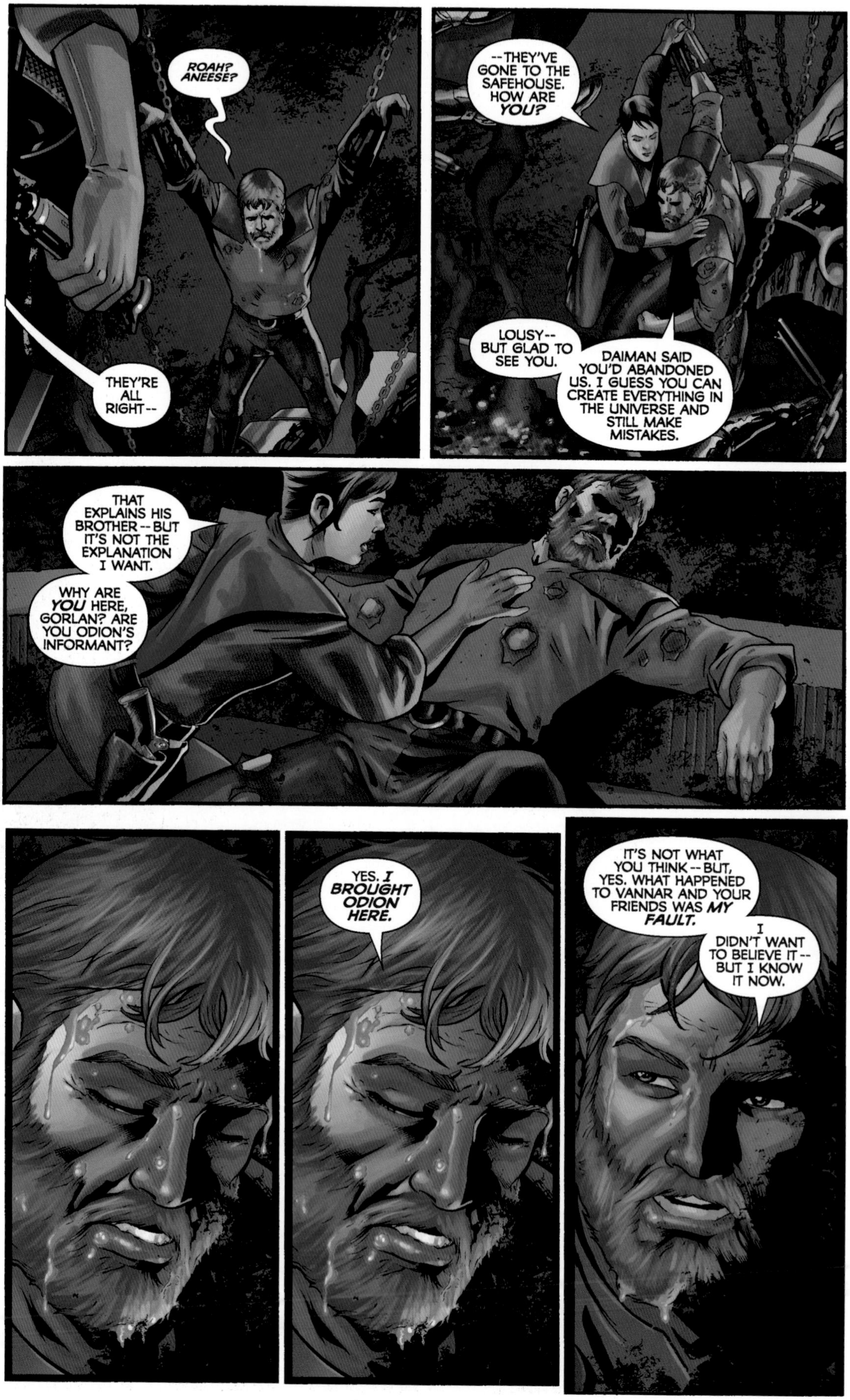
ROAH? ANEESE?
THEY'RE ALL RIGHT--
--THEY'VE GONE TO THE SAFEHOUSE. HOW ARE YOU?
LOUSY-- BUT GLAD TO SEE YOU.
DAIMAN SAID YOU'D ABANDONED US. I GUESS YOU CAN CREATE EVERYTHING IN THE UNIVERSE AND STILL MAKE MISTAKES.
THAT EXPLAINS HIS BROTHER--BUT IT'S NOT THE EXPLANATION I WANT.
WHY ARE YOU HERE, GORLAN? ARE YOU ODION'S INFORMANT?
YES. I BROUGHT ODION HERE.
IT'S NOT WHAT YOU THINK--BUT, YES. WHAT HAPPENED TO VANNAR AND YOUR FRIENDS WAS MY FAULT.
I DIDN'T WANT TO BELIEVE IT-- BUT I KNOW IT NOW.

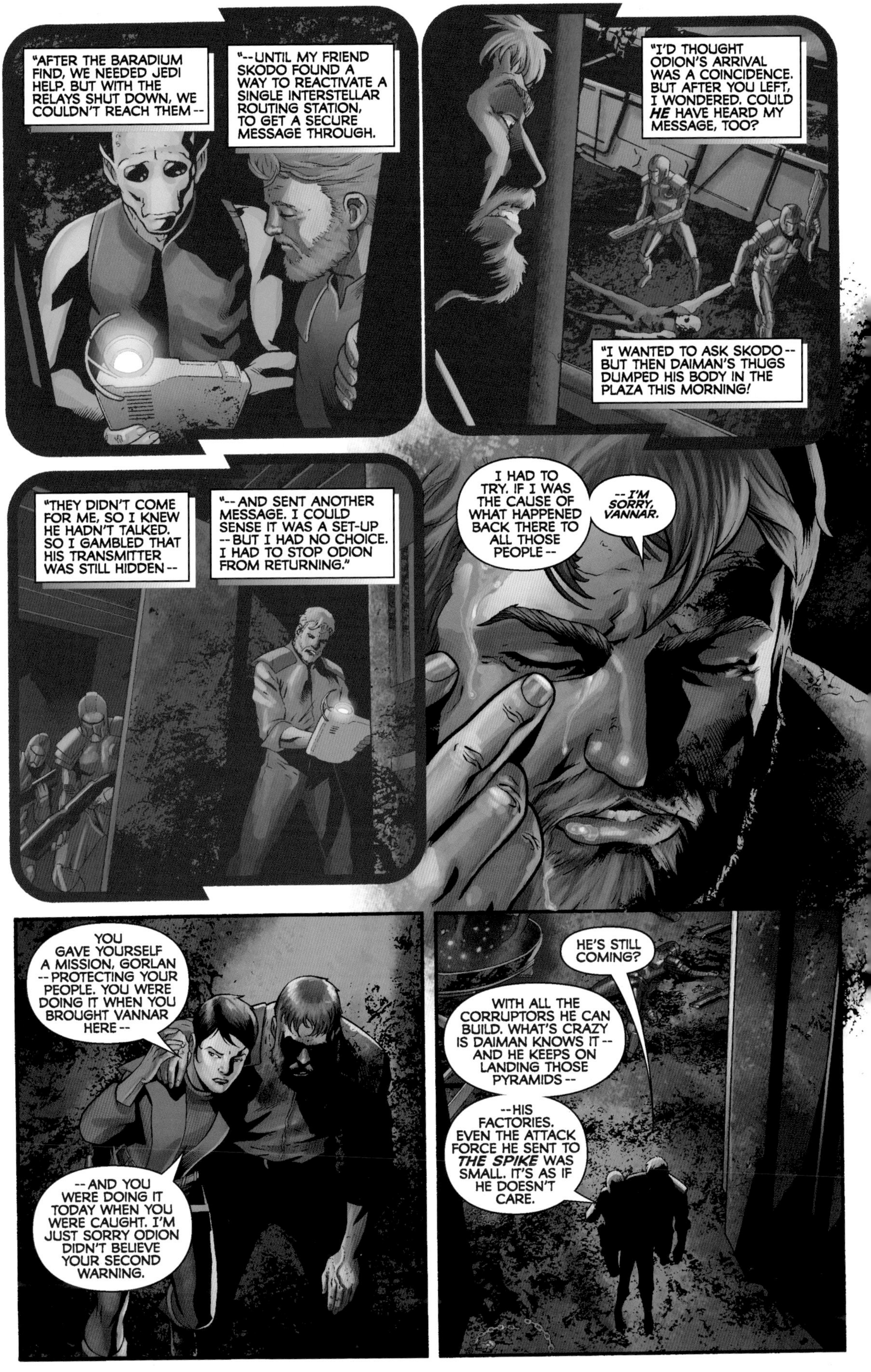
"AFTER THE BARADIUM FIND, WE NEEDED JEDI HELP. BUT WITH THE RELAYS SHUT DOWN, WE COULDN'T REACH THEM --
"--UNTIL MY FRIEND SKODO FOUND A WAY TO REACTIVATE A SINGLE INTERSTELLAR ROUTING STATION, TO GET A SECURE MESSAGE THROUGH.
"I'D THOUGHT ODION'S ARRIVAL WAS A COINCIDENCE. BUT AFTER YOU LEFT, I WONDERED. COULD *HE* HAVE HEARD MY MESSAGE, TOO?
"I WANTED TO ASK SKODO -- BUT THEN DAIMAN'S THUGS DUMPED HIS BODY IN THE PLAZA THIS MORNING!
"THEY DIDN'T COME FOR ME, SO I KNEW HE HADN'T TALKED. SO I GAMBLED THAT HIS TRANSMITTER WAS STILL HIDDEN --
"-- AND SENT ANOTHER MESSAGE. I COULD SENSE IT WAS A SET-UP -- BUT I HAD NO CHOICE. I HAD TO STOP ODION FROM RETURNING."
I HAD TO TRY. IF I WAS THE CAUSE OF WHAT HAPPENED BACK THERE TO ALL THOSE PEOPLE --
-- *I'M SORRY, VANNAR.*
YOU GAVE YOURSELF A MISSION, GORLAN -- PROTECTING YOUR PEOPLE. YOU WERE DOING IT WHEN YOU BROUGHT VANNAR HERE --
-- AND YOU WERE DOING IT TODAY WHEN YOU WERE CAUGHT. I'M JUST SORRY ODION DIDN'T BELIEVE YOUR SECOND WARNING.
HE'S STILL COMING?
WITH ALL THE CORRUPTORS HE CAN BUILD. WHAT'S CRAZY IS DAIMAN KNOWS IT -- AND HE KEEPS ON LANDING THOSE PYRAMIDS --
--HIS FACTORIES. EVEN THE ATTACK FORCE HE SENT TO *THE SPIKE* WAS SMALL. IT'S AS IF HE DOESN'T CARE.

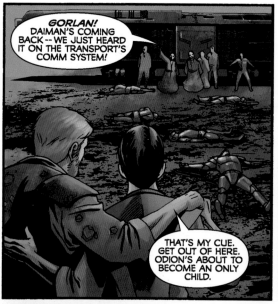

GORLAN! DAIMAN'S COMING BACK -- WE JUST HEARD IT ON THE TRANSPORT'S COMM SYSTEM!

THAT'S MY CUE. GET OUT OF HERE. ODION'S ABOUT TO BECOME AN ONLY CHILD.

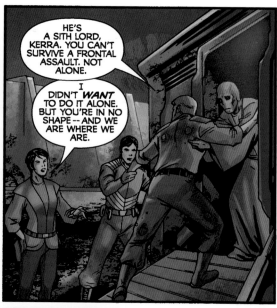

HE'S A SITH LORD, KERRA. YOU CAN'T SURVIVE A FRONTAL ASSAULT. NOT ALONE.

I DIDN'T *WANT* TO DO IT ALONE. BUT YOU'RE IN NO SHAPE -- AND WE ARE WHERE WE ARE.

YOU...YOU *WANT* TO DO IT. DON'T YOU?

YOU DON'T HAVE TO BE A MARTYR, KERRA. I SEE YOU... *THROWING YOURSELF AWAY.*

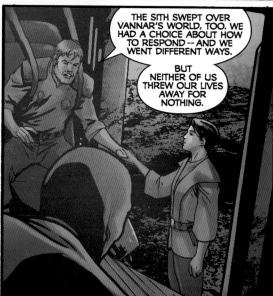

THE SITH SWEPT OVER VANNAR'S WORLD, TOO. WE HAD A CHOICE ABOUT HOW TO RESPOND -- AND WE WENT DIFFERENT WAYS.

BUT NEITHER OF US THREW OUR LIVES AWAY FOR NOTHING.

I HAVE ORDERS. I HAVE A MISSION TO COMPLETE!

BUT KERRA, DON'T YOU REMEMBER? DISABLING THE BARADIUM MINES -- THAT WAS *VANNAR'S* MISSION.

REMEMBER *YOUR* MISSION--

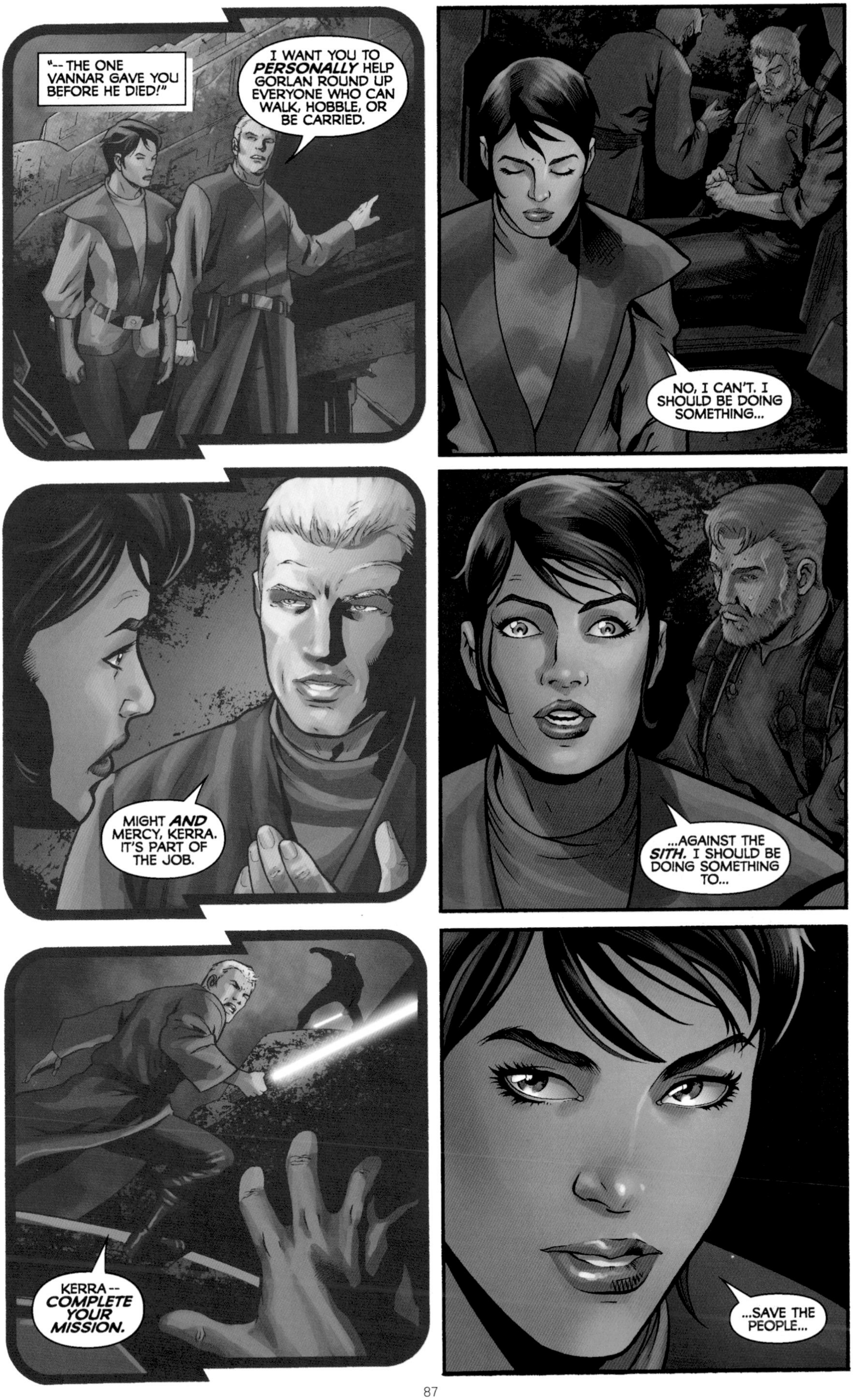
"-- THE ONE VANNAR GAVE YOU BEFORE HE DIED!"
I WANT YOU TO *PERSONALLY* HELP GORLAN ROUND UP EVERYONE WHO CAN WALK, HOBBLE, OR BE CARRIED.
MIGHT *AND* MERCY, KERRA. IT'S PART OF THE JOB.
KERRA -- *COMPLETE YOUR MISSION.*
NO, I CAN'T. I SHOULD BE DOING SOMETHING...
...AGAINST THE *SITH.* I SHOULD BE DOING SOMETHING TO...
...SAVE THE PEOPLE...

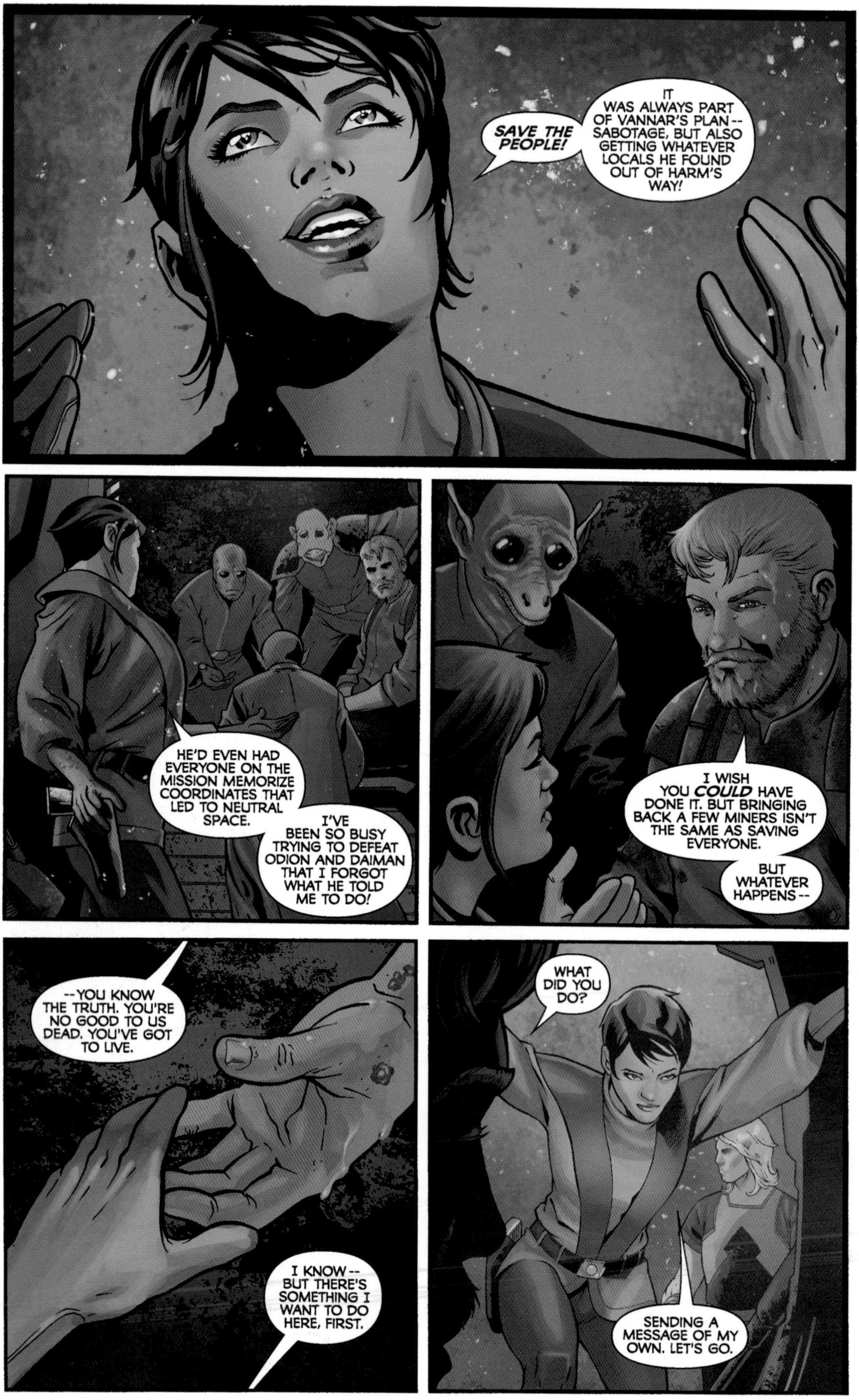
SAVE THE PEOPLE!
IT WAS ALWAYS PART OF VANNAR'S PLAN -- SABOTAGE, BUT ALSO GETTING WHATEVER LOCALS HE FOUND OUT OF HARM'S WAY!
HE'D EVEN HAD EVERYONE ON THE MISSION MEMORIZE COORDINATES THAT LED TO NEUTRAL SPACE.
I'VE BEEN SO BUSY TRYING TO DEFEAT ODION AND DAIMAN THAT I FORGOT WHAT HE TOLD ME TO DO!
I WISH YOU COULD HAVE DONE IT. BUT BRINGING BACK A FEW MINERS ISN'T THE SAME AS SAVING EVERYONE.
BUT WHATEVER HAPPENS --
--YOU KNOW THE TRUTH. YOU'RE NO GOOD TO US DEAD. YOU'VE GOT TO LIVE.
I KNOW -- BUT THERE'S SOMETHING I WANT TO DO HERE, FIRST.
WHAT DID YOU DO?
SENDING A MESSAGE OF MY OWN. LET'S GO.

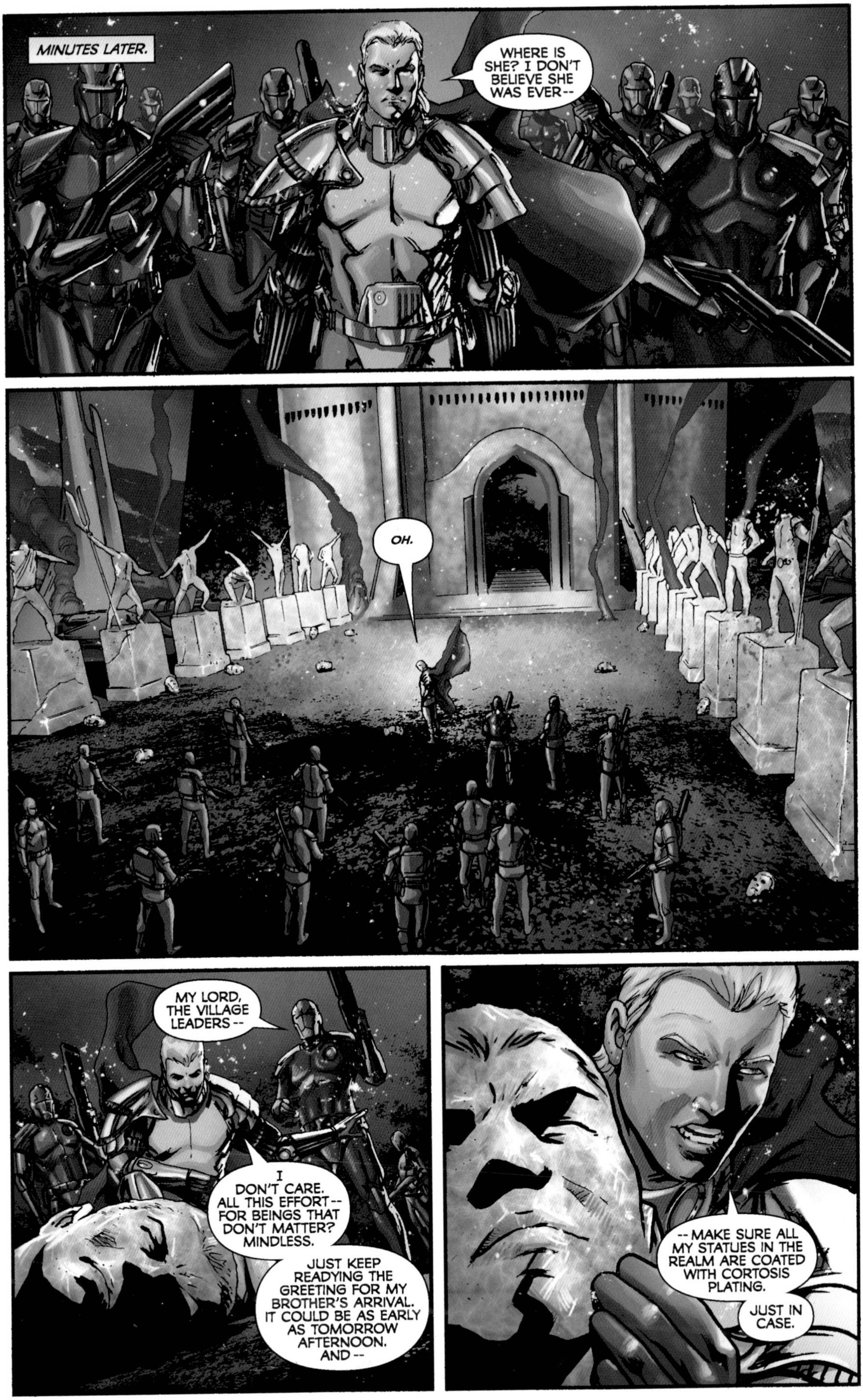
MINUTES LATER.
WHERE IS SHE? I DON'T BELIEVE SHE WAS EVER--
OH.
MY LORD, THE VILLAGE LEADERS--
I DON'T CARE. ALL THIS EFFORT-- FOR BEINGS THAT DON'T MATTER? MINDLESS.
JUST KEEP READYING THE GREETING FOR MY BROTHER'S ARRIVAL. IT COULD BE AS EARLY AS TOMORROW AFTERNOON. AND--
--MAKE SURE ALL MY STATUES IN THE REALM ARE COATED WITH CORTOSIS PLATING.
JUST IN CASE.

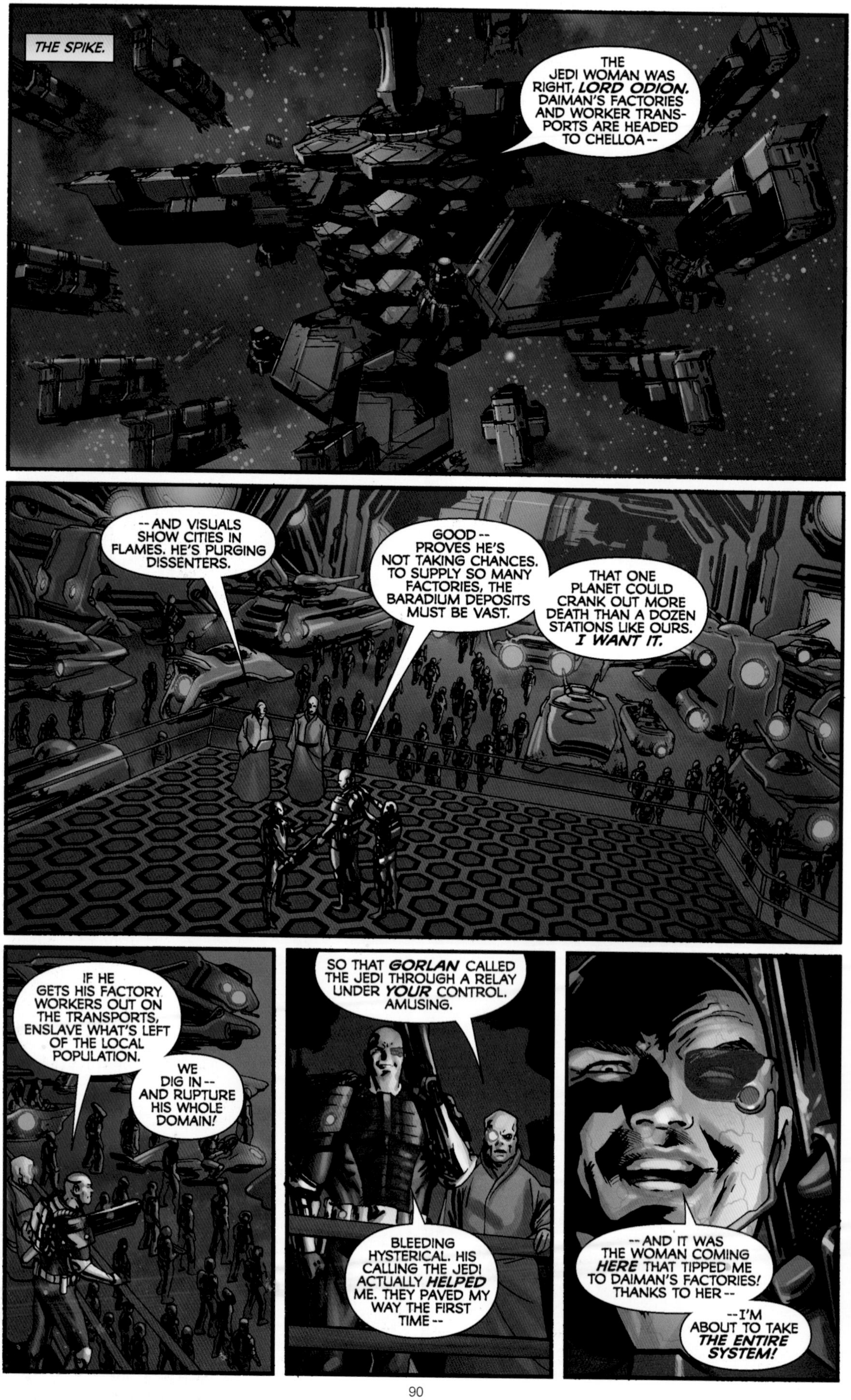
THE SPIKE.
THE JEDI WOMAN WAS RIGHT, LORD ODION. DAIMAN'S FACTORIES AND WORKER TRANSPORTS ARE HEADED TO CHELLOA--
--AND VISUALS SHOW CITIES IN FLAMES. HE'S PURGING DISSENTERS.
GOOD--PROVES HE'S NOT TAKING CHANCES. TO SUPPLY SO MANY FACTORIES, THE BARADIUM DEPOSITS MUST BE VAST.
THAT ONE PLANET COULD CRANK OUT MORE DEATH THAN A DOZEN STATIONS LIKE OURS. I WANT IT.
IF HE GETS HIS FACTORY WORKERS OUT ON THE TRANSPORTS, ENSLAVE WHAT'S LEFT OF THE LOCAL POPULATION.
WE DIG IN--AND RUPTURE HIS WHOLE DOMAIN!
SO THAT GORLAN CALLED THE JEDI THROUGH A RELAY UNDER YOUR CONTROL. AMUSING.
BLEEDING HYSTERICAL. HIS CALLING THE JEDI ACTUALLY HELPED ME. THEY PAVED MY WAY THE FIRST TIME--
--AND IT WAS THE WOMAN COMING HERE THAT TIPPED ME TO DAIMAN'S FACTORIES! THANKS TO HER--
--I'M ABOUT TO TAKE THE ENTIRE SYSTEM!

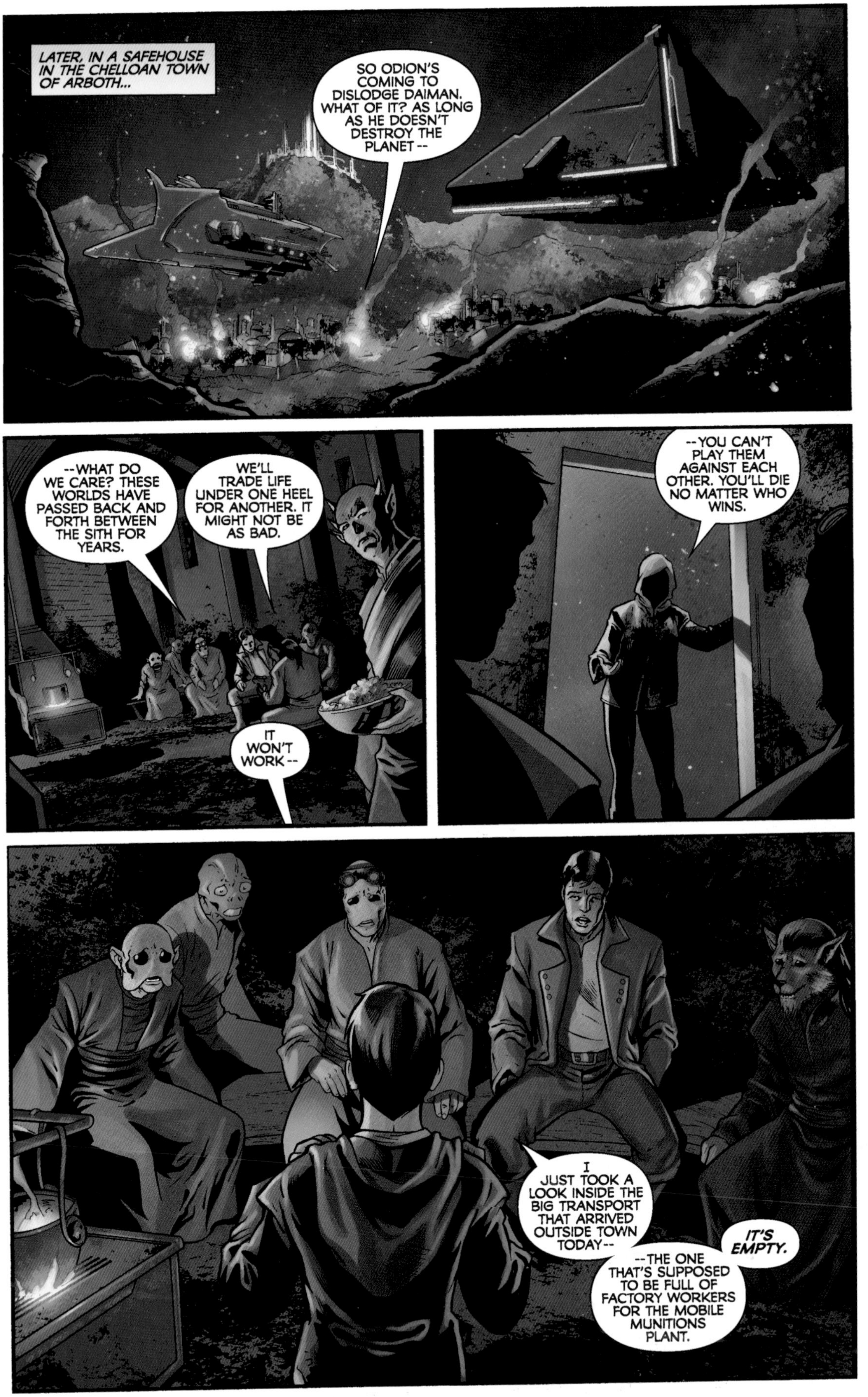
LATER, IN A SAFEHOUSE IN THE CHELLOAN TOWN OF ARBOTH...
SO ODION'S COMING TO DISLODGE DAIMAN. WHAT OF IT? AS LONG AS HE DOESN'T DESTROY THE PLANET --
--WHAT DO WE CARE? THESE WORLDS HAVE PASSED BACK AND FORTH BETWEEN THE SITH FOR YEARS.
WE'LL TRADE LIFE UNDER ONE HEEL FOR ANOTHER. IT MIGHT NOT BE AS BAD.
IT WON'T WORK--
--YOU CAN'T PLAY THEM AGAINST EACH OTHER. YOU'LL DIE NO MATTER WHO WINS.
I JUST TOOK A LOOK INSIDE THE BIG TRANSPORT THAT ARRIVED OUTSIDE TOWN TODAY--
--THE ONE THAT'S SUPPOSED TO BE FULL OF FACTORY WORKERS FOR THE MOBILE MUNITIONS PLANT.
IT'S EMPTY.

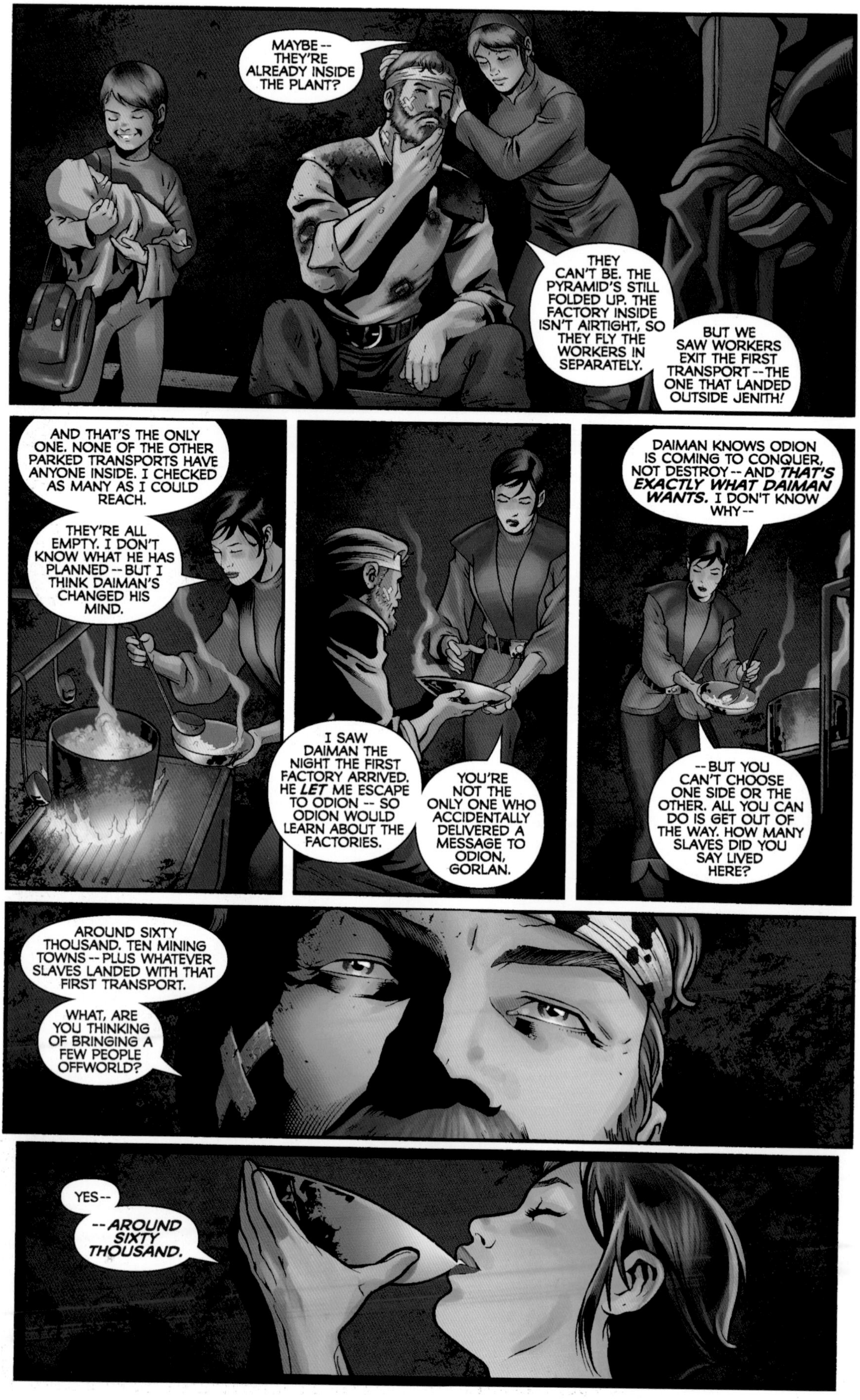
MAYBE-- THEY'RE ALREADY INSIDE THE PLANT?
THEY CAN'T BE. THE PYRAMID'S STILL FOLDED UP. THE FACTORY INSIDE ISN'T AIRTIGHT, SO THEY FLY THE WORKERS IN SEPARATELY.
BUT WE SAW WORKERS EXIT THE FIRST TRANSPORT--THE ONE THAT LANDED OUTSIDE JENITH!
AND THAT'S THE ONLY ONE. NONE OF THE OTHER PARKED TRANSPORTS HAVE ANYONE INSIDE. I CHECKED AS MANY AS I COULD REACH.
THEY'RE ALL EMPTY. I DON'T KNOW WHAT HE HAS PLANNED--BUT I THINK DAIMAN'S CHANGED HIS MIND.
I SAW DAIMAN THE NIGHT THE FIRST FACTORY ARRIVED. HE *LET* ME ESCAPE TO ODION -- SO ODION WOULD LEARN ABOUT THE FACTORIES.
YOU'RE NOT THE ONLY ONE WHO ACCIDENTALLY DELIVERED A MESSAGE TO ODION, GORLAN.
DAIMAN KNOWS ODION IS COMING TO CONQUER, NOT DESTROY--AND ***THAT'S EXACTLY WHAT DAIMAN WANTS.*** I DON'T KNOW WHY--
--BUT YOU CAN'T CHOOSE ONE SIDE OR THE OTHER. ALL YOU CAN DO IS GET OUT OF THE WAY. HOW MANY SLAVES DID YOU SAY LIVED HERE?
AROUND SIXTY THOUSAND. TEN MINING TOWNS--PLUS WHATEVER SLAVES LANDED WITH THAT FIRST TRANSPORT.
WHAT, ARE YOU THINKING OF BRINGING A FEW PEOPLE OFFWORLD?
YES--
--AROUND SIXTY THOUSAND.

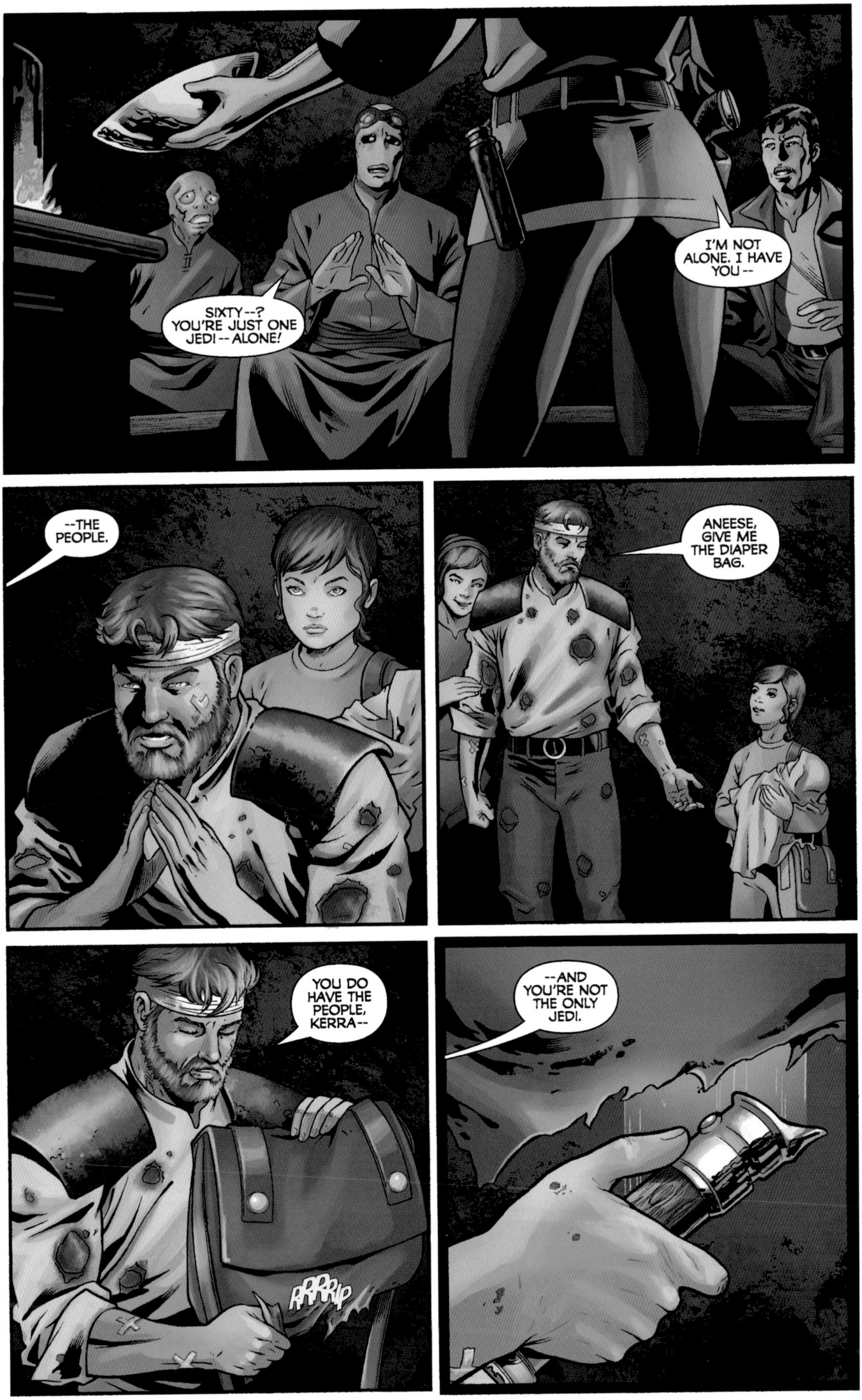
SIXTY--? YOU'RE JUST ONE JEDI -- ALONE!
I'M NOT ALONE. I HAVE YOU --
--THE PEOPLE.
ANEESE, GIVE ME THE DIAPER BAG.
YOU DO HAVE THE PEOPLE, KERRA--
RRRRIP
--AND YOU'RE NOT THE ONLY JEDI.

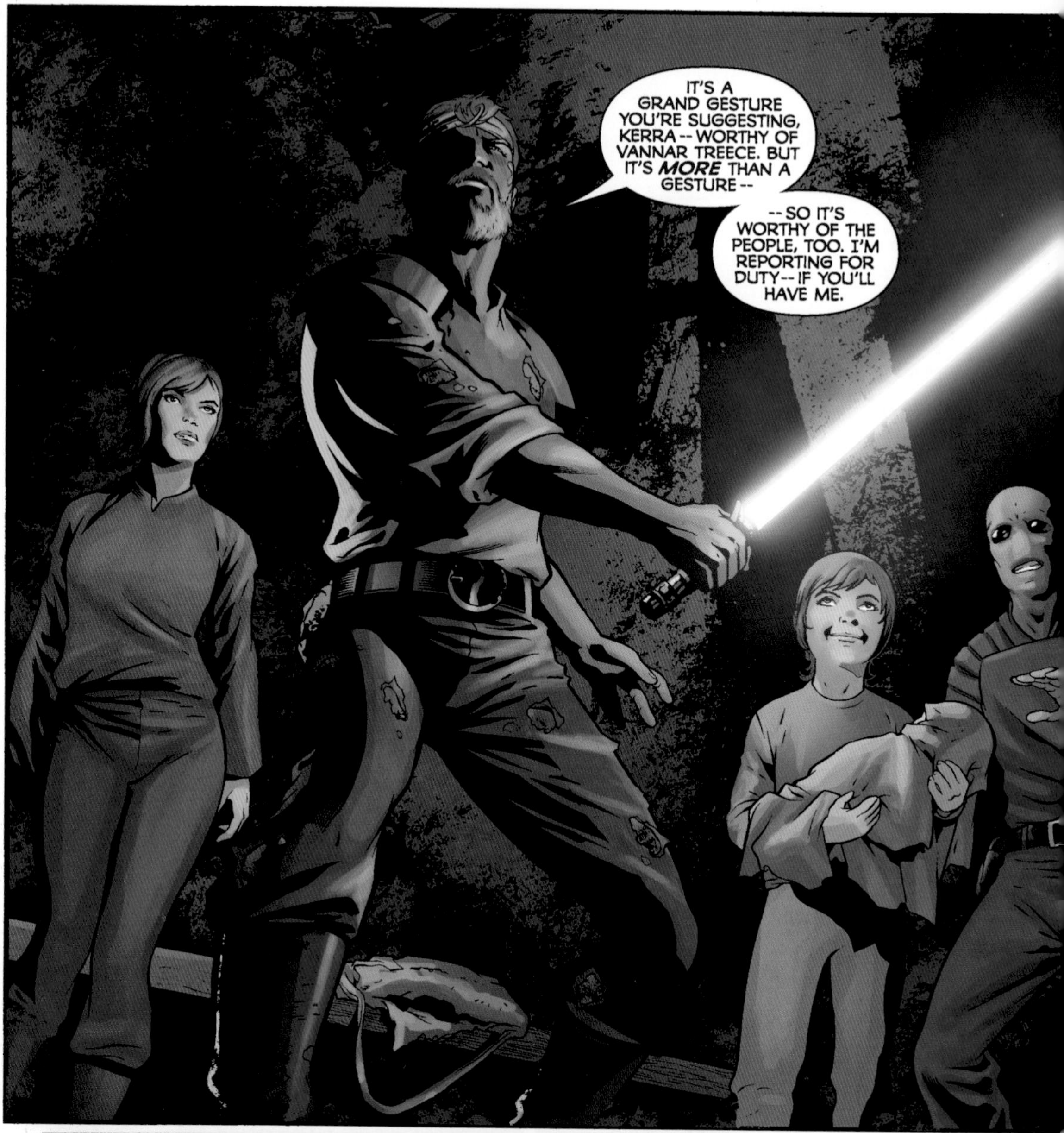

IT'S A GRAND GESTURE YOU'RE SUGGESTING, KERRA -- WORTHY OF VANNAR TREECE. BUT IT'S *MORE* THAN A GESTURE --
-- SO IT'S WORTHY OF THE PEOPLE, TOO. I'M REPORTING FOR DUTY -- IF YOU'LL HAVE ME.

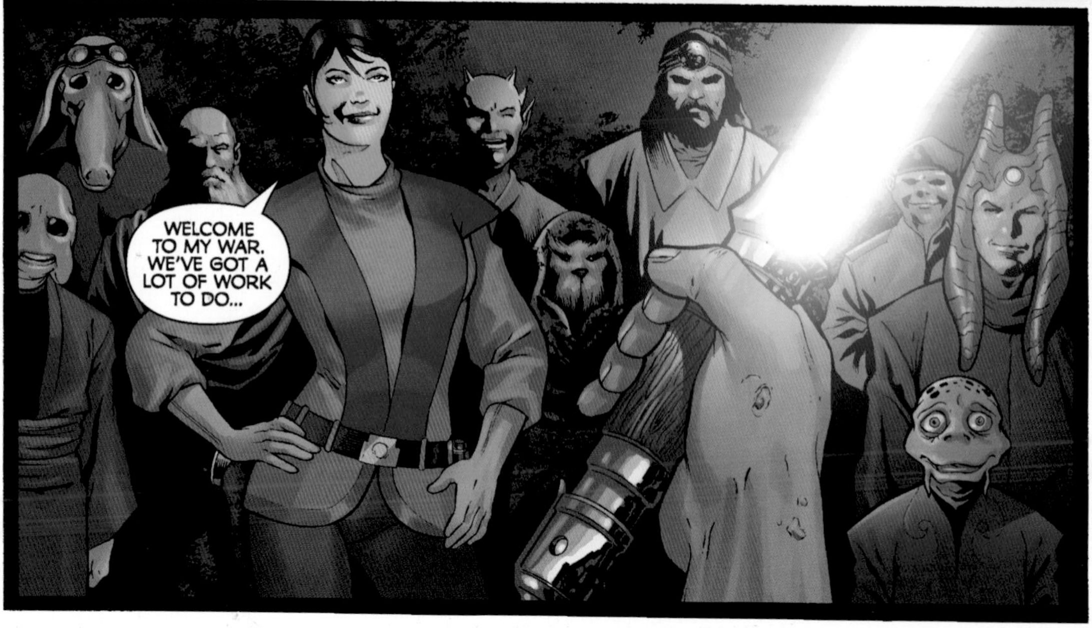

WELCOME TO MY WAR. WE'VE GOT A LOT OF WORK TO DO...

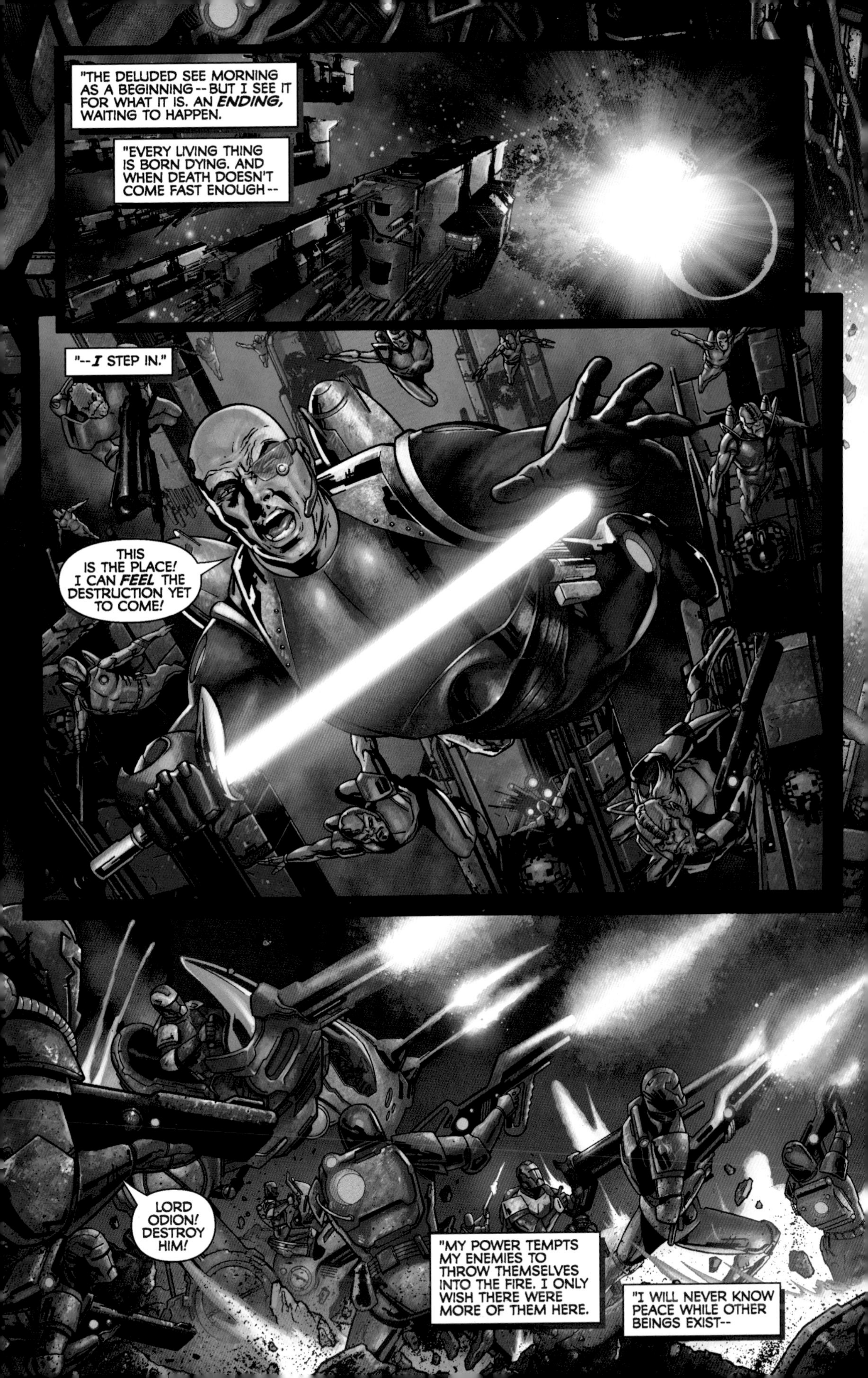
"THE DELUDED SEE MORNING AS A BEGINNING -- BUT I SEE IT FOR WHAT IT IS. AN ENDING, WAITING TO HAPPEN.
"EVERY LIVING THING IS BORN DYING. AND WHEN DEATH DOESN'T COME FAST ENOUGH --
"-- I STEP IN."
THIS IS THE PLACE! I CAN FEEL THE DESTRUCTION YET TO COME!
LORD ODION! DESTROY HIM!
"MY POWER TEMPTS MY ENEMIES TO THROW THEMSELVES INTO THE FIRE. I ONLY WISH THERE WERE MORE OF THEM HERE.
"I WILL NEVER KNOW PEACE WHILE OTHER BEINGS EXIST--

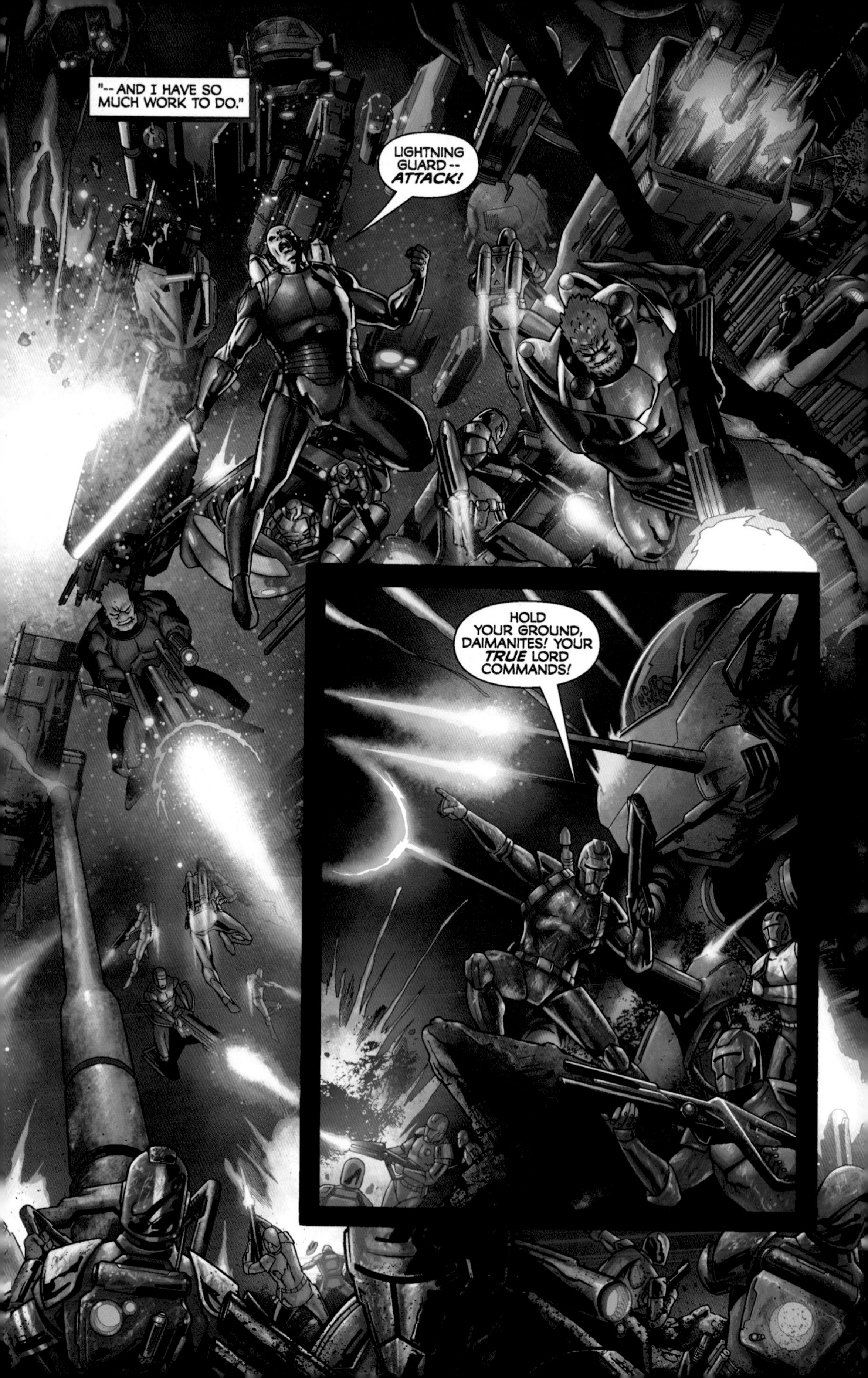
"-- AND I HAVE SO MUCH WORK TO DO."
LIGHTNING GUARD -- ATTACK!
HOLD YOUR GROUND, DAIMANITES! YOUR TRUE LORD COMMANDS!

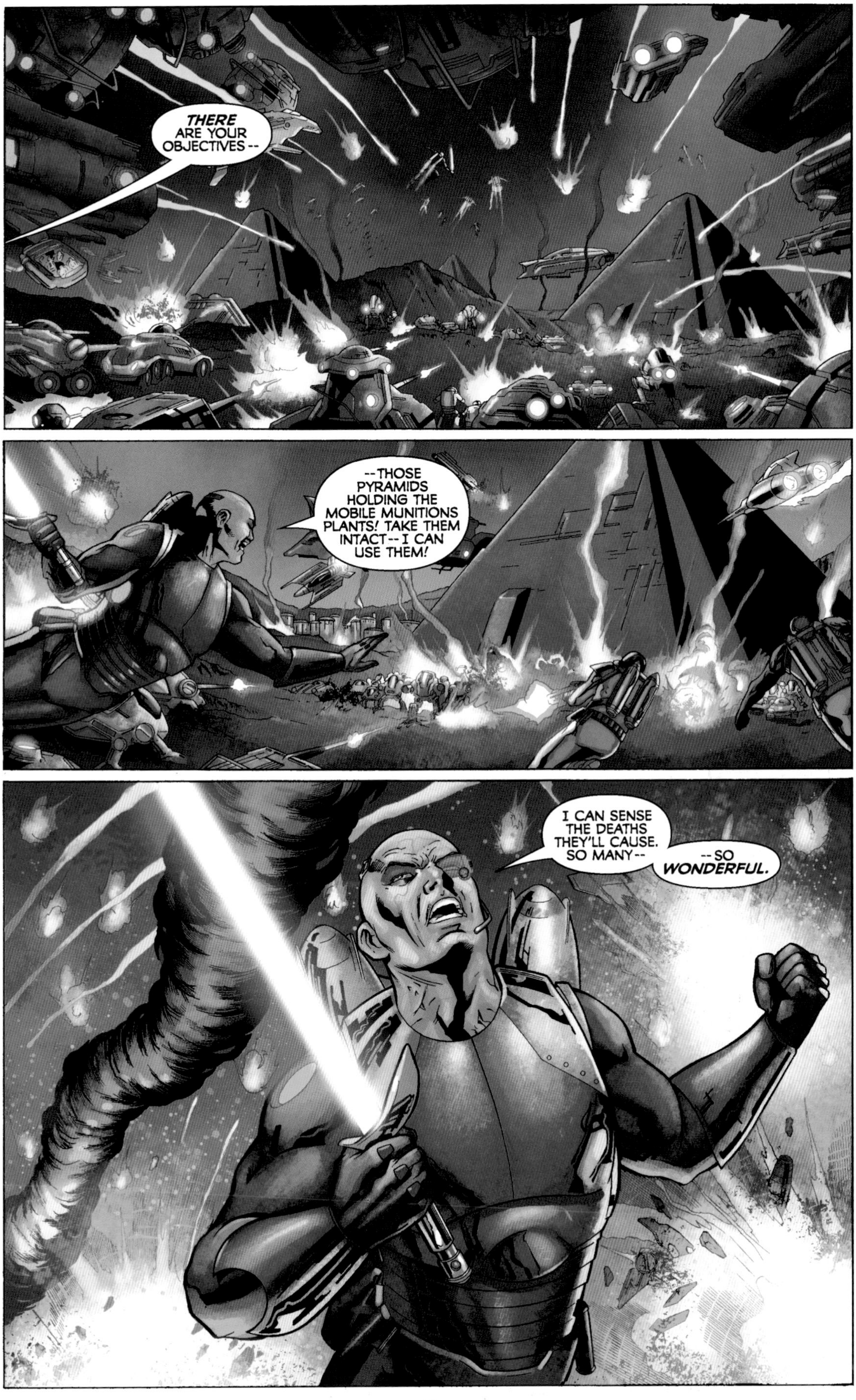
THERE ARE YOUR OBJECTIVES --
--THOSE PYRAMIDS HOLDING THE MOBILE MUNITIONS PLANTS! TAKE THEM INTACT--I CAN USE THEM!
I CAN SENSE THE DEATHS THEY'LL CAUSE. SO MANY--
--SO WONDERFUL.

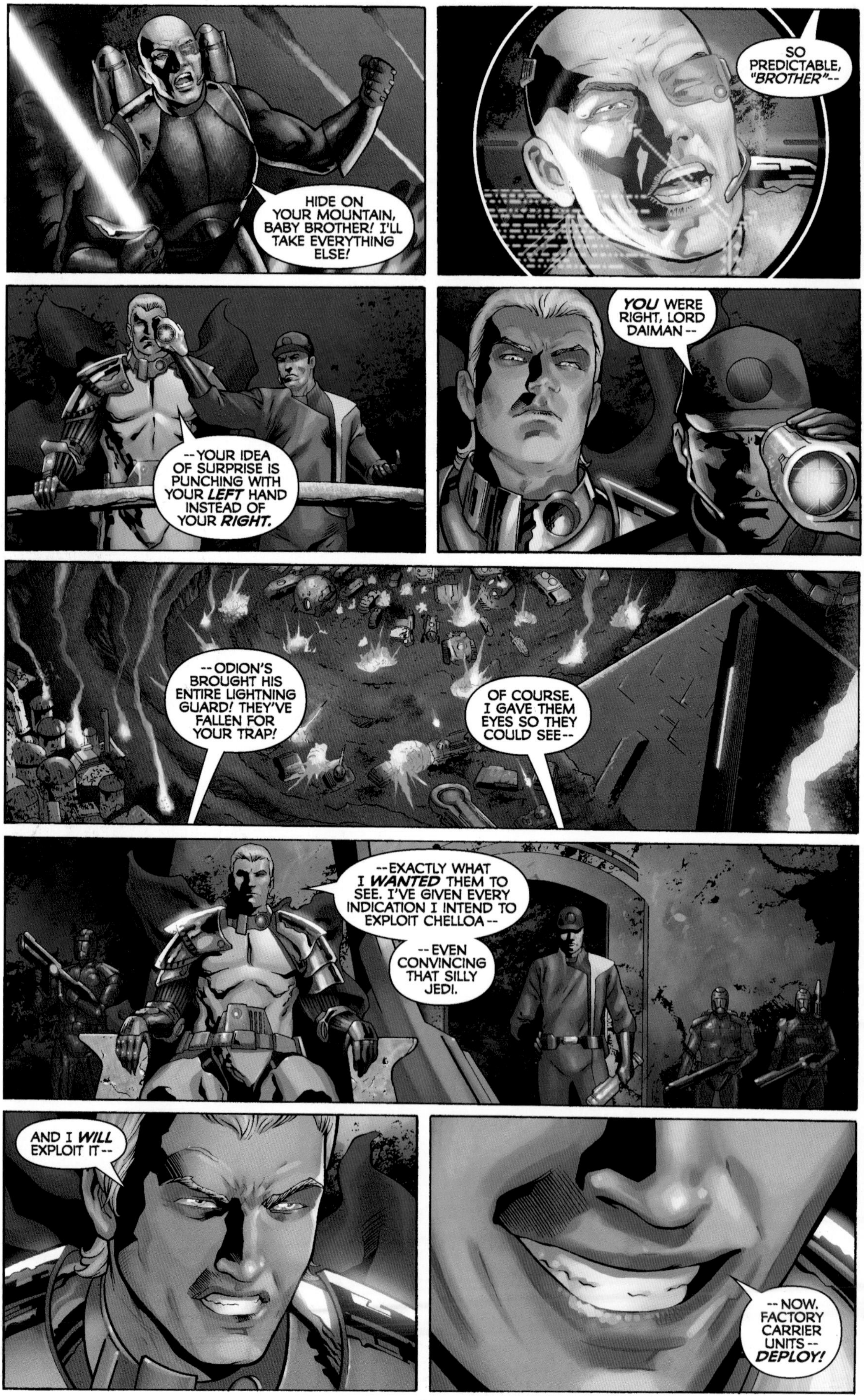
HIDE ON YOUR MOUNTAIN, BABY BROTHER! I'LL TAKE EVERYTHING ELSE!
SO PREDICTABLE, "BROTHER"--
--YOUR IDEA OF SURPRISE IS PUNCHING WITH YOUR *LEFT* HAND INSTEAD OF YOUR *RIGHT.*
YOU WERE RIGHT, LORD DAIMAN--
--ODION'S BROUGHT HIS ENTIRE LIGHTNING GUARD! THEY'VE FALLEN FOR YOUR TRAP!
OF COURSE. I GAVE THEM EYES SO THEY COULD SEE--
--EXACTLY WHAT I *WANTED* THEM TO SEE. I'VE GIVEN EVERY INDICATION I INTEND TO EXPLOIT CHELLOA--
--EVEN CONVINCING THAT SILLY JEDI.
AND I *WILL* EXPLOIT IT--
--NOW. FACTORY CARRIER UNITS-- *DEPLOY!*

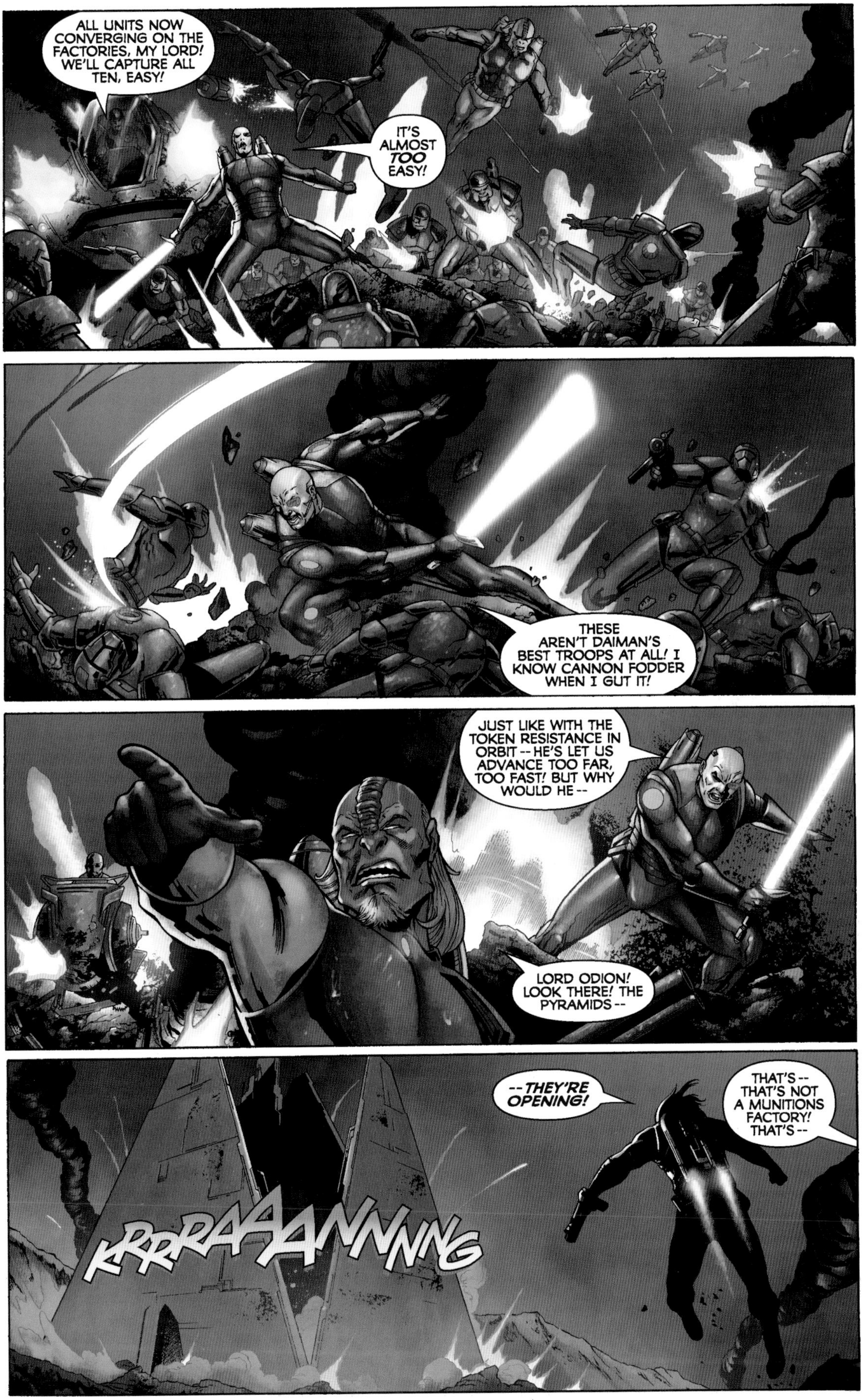
ALL UNITS NOW CONVERGING ON THE FACTORIES, MY LORD! WE'LL CAPTURE ALL TEN, EASY!
IT'S ALMOST TOO EASY!
THESE AREN'T DAIMAN'S BEST TROOPS AT ALL! I KNOW CANNON FODDER WHEN I GUT IT!
JUST LIKE WITH THE TOKEN RESISTANCE IN ORBIT -- HE'S LET US ADVANCE TOO FAR, TOO FAST! BUT WHY WOULD HE --
LORD ODION! LOOK THERE! THE PYRAMIDS --
-- THEY'RE OPENING!
THAT'S -- THAT'S NOT A MUNITIONS FACTORY! THAT'S --
KRRRAAAANNNNG

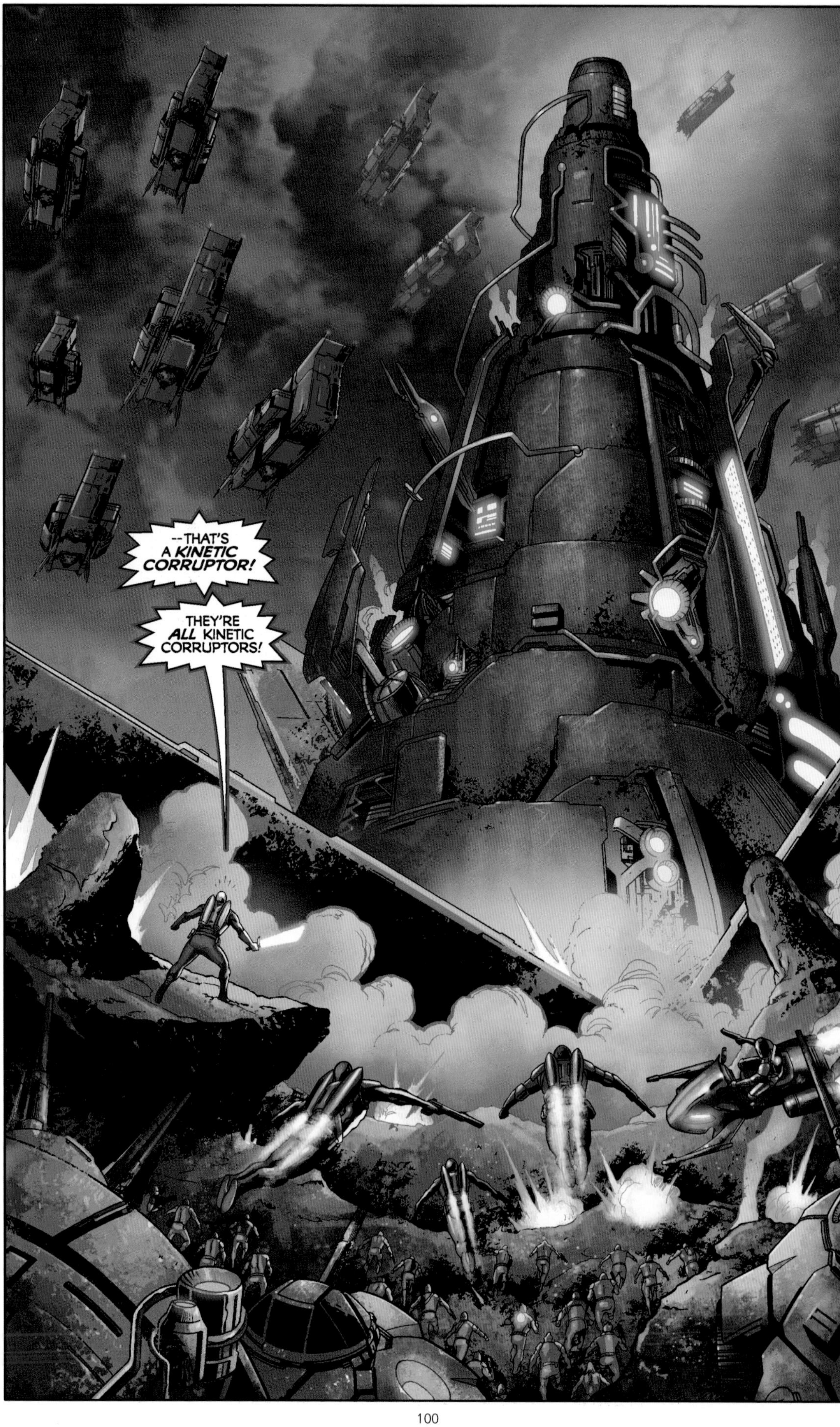
--THAT'S A ***KINETIC CORRUPTOR!***
THEY'RE ***ALL*** KINETIC CORRUPTORS!

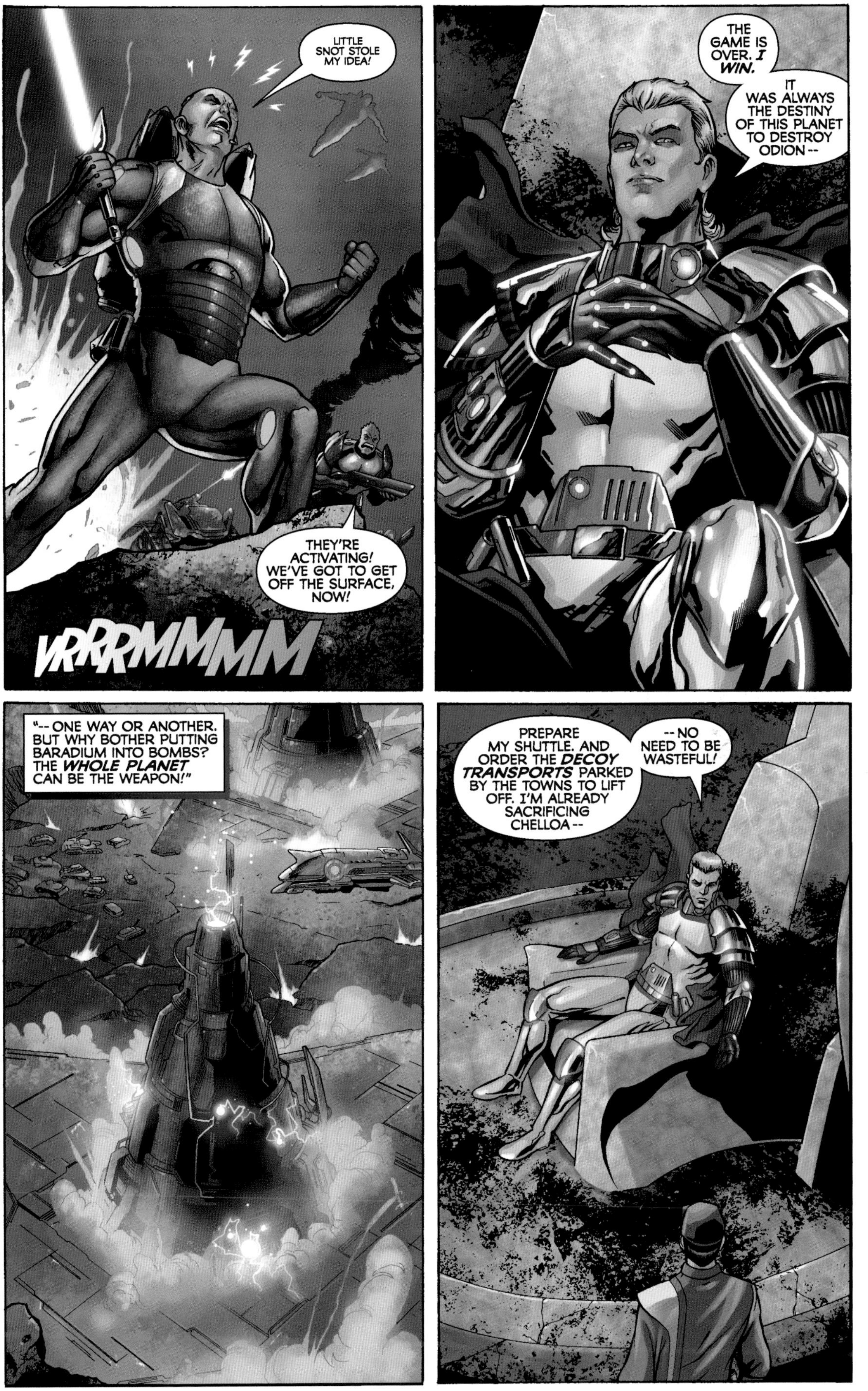
LITTLE SNOT STOLE MY IDEA!
THEY'RE ACTIVATING! WE'VE GOT TO GET OFF THE SURFACE, NOW!
VRRRMMMMM
THE GAME IS OVER. *I WIN.*
IT WAS ALWAYS THE DESTINY OF THIS PLANET TO DESTROY ODION --
"-- ONE WAY OR ANOTHER. BUT WHY BOTHER PUTTING BARADIUM INTO BOMBS? THE *WHOLE PLANET* CAN BE THE WEAPON!"
PREPARE MY SHUTTLE. AND ORDER THE *DECOY TRANSPORTS* PARKED BY THE TOWNS TO LIFT OFF. I'M ALREADY SACRIFICING CHELLOA --
-- NO NEED TO BE WASTEFUL!

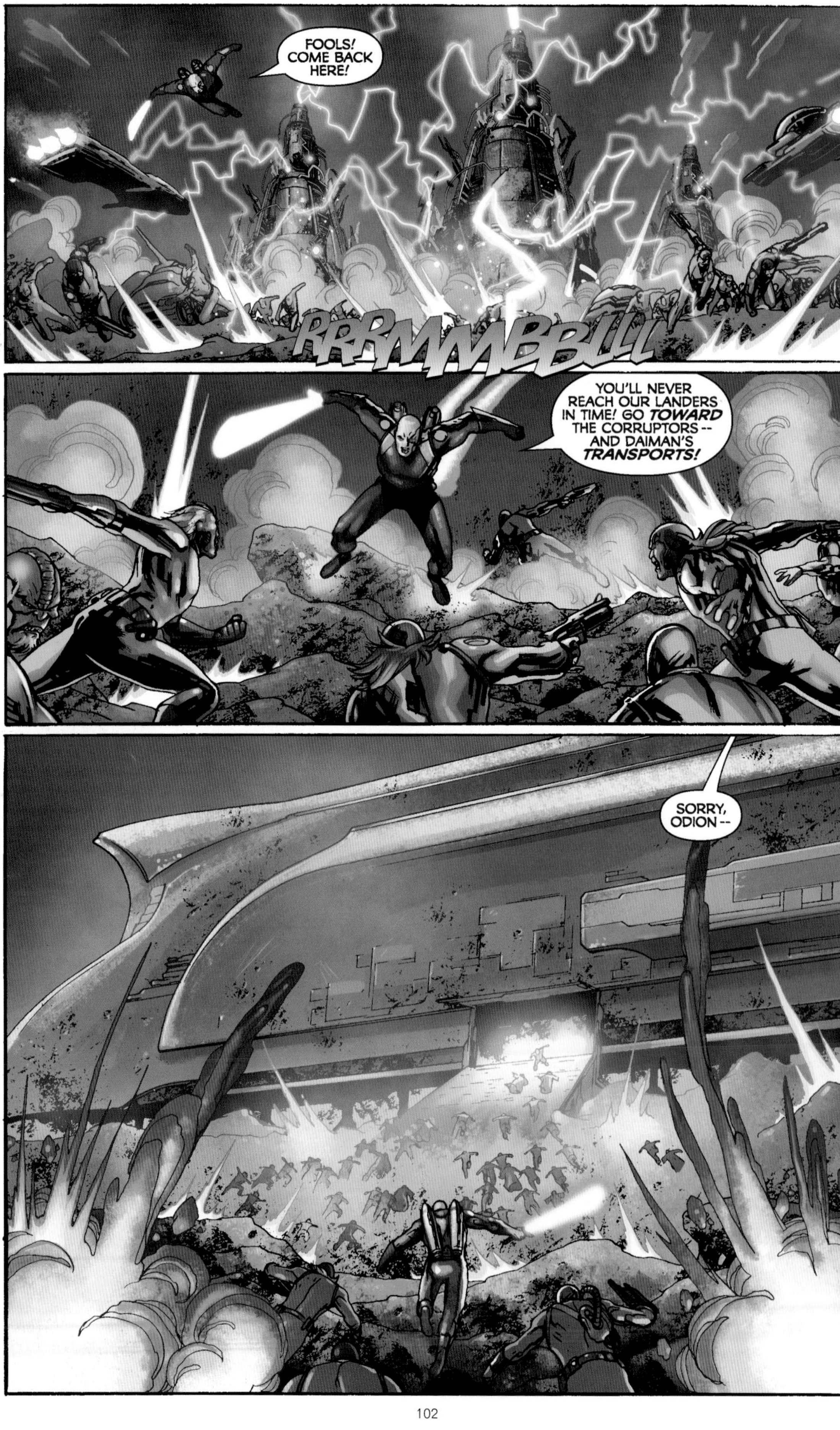
FOOLS! COME BACK HERE!
RRRMMMBBLLL
YOU'LL NEVER REACH OUR LANDERS IN TIME! GO *TOWARD* THE CORRUPTORS -- AND DAIMAN'S *TRANSPORTS!*
SORRY, ODION --

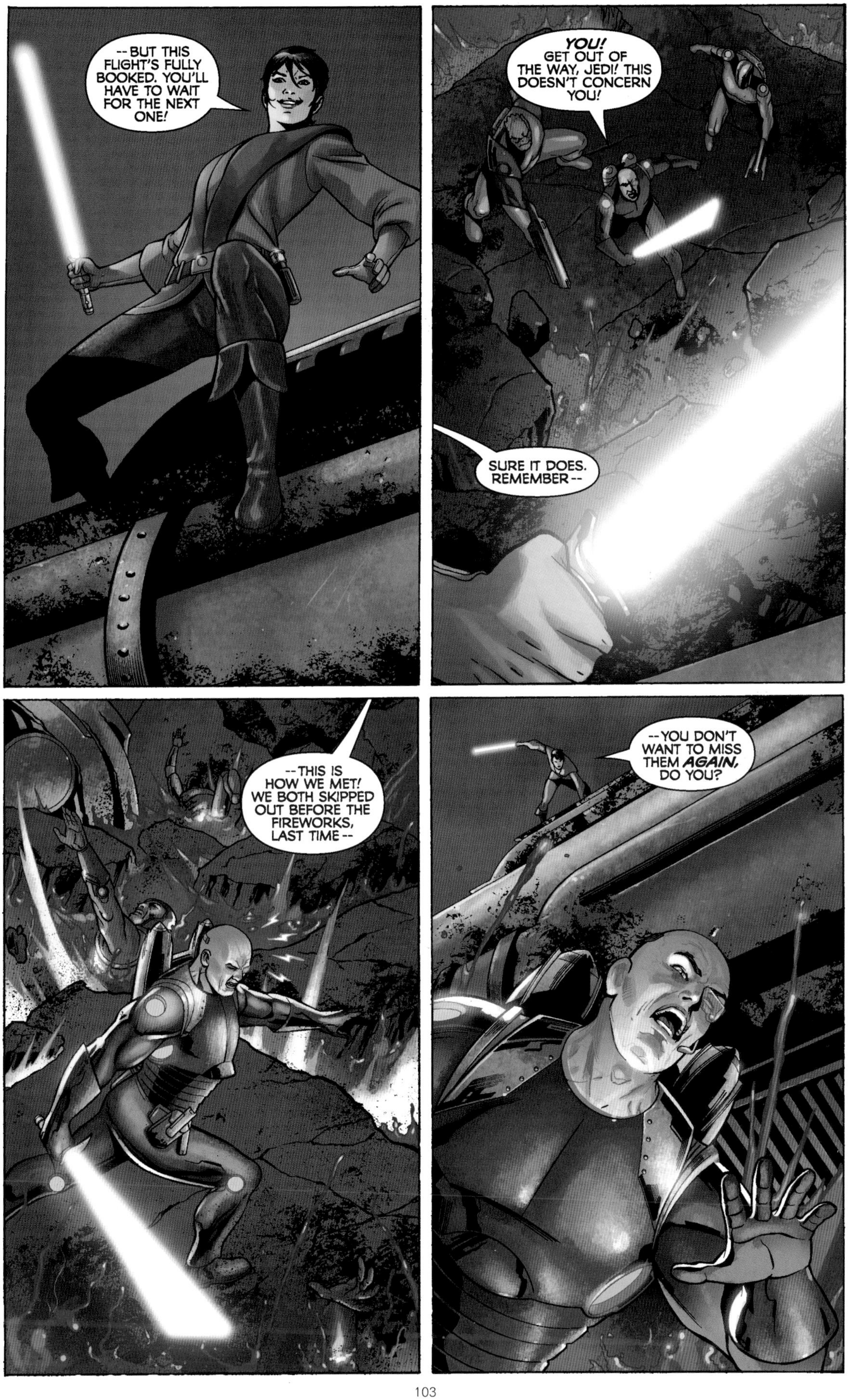
--BUT THIS FLIGHT'S FULLY BOOKED. YOU'LL HAVE TO WAIT FOR THE NEXT ONE!
YOU! GET OUT OF THE WAY, JEDI! THIS DOESN'T CONCERN YOU!
SURE IT DOES. REMEMBER--
--THIS IS HOW WE MET! WE BOTH SKIPPED OUT BEFORE THE FIREWORKS, LAST TIME--
--YOU DON'T WANT TO MISS THEM AGAIN, DO YOU?

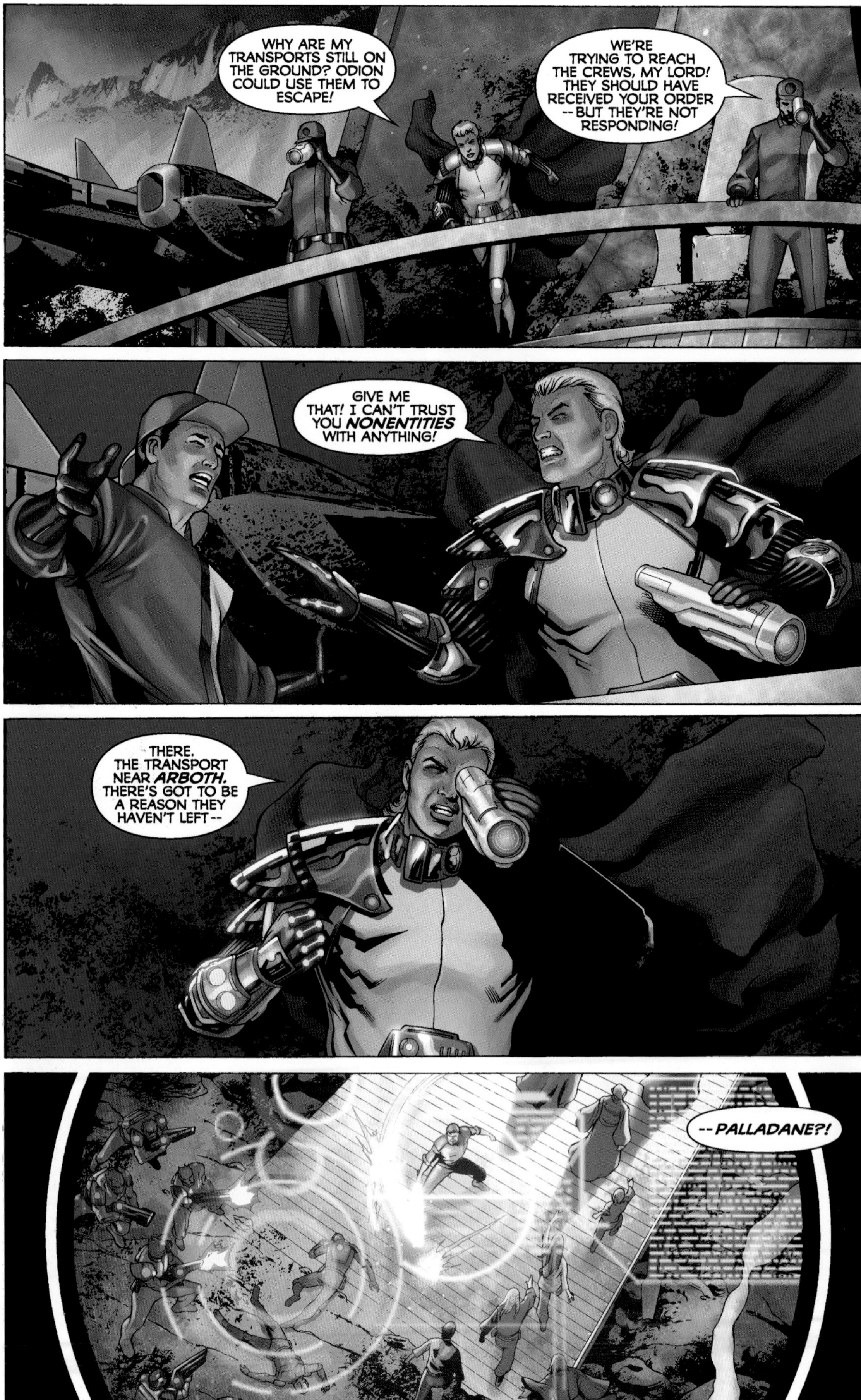
WHY ARE MY TRANSPORTS STILL ON THE GROUND? ODION COULD USE THEM TO ESCAPE!
WE'RE TRYING TO REACH THE CREWS, MY LORD! THEY SHOULD HAVE RECEIVED YOUR ORDER --BUT THEY'RE NOT RESPONDING!
GIVE ME THAT! I CAN'T TRUST YOU *NONENTITIES* WITH ANYTHING!
THERE. THE TRANSPORT NEAR *ARBOTH.* THERE'S GOT TO BE A REASON THEY HAVEN'T LEFT--
--*PALLADANE?!*

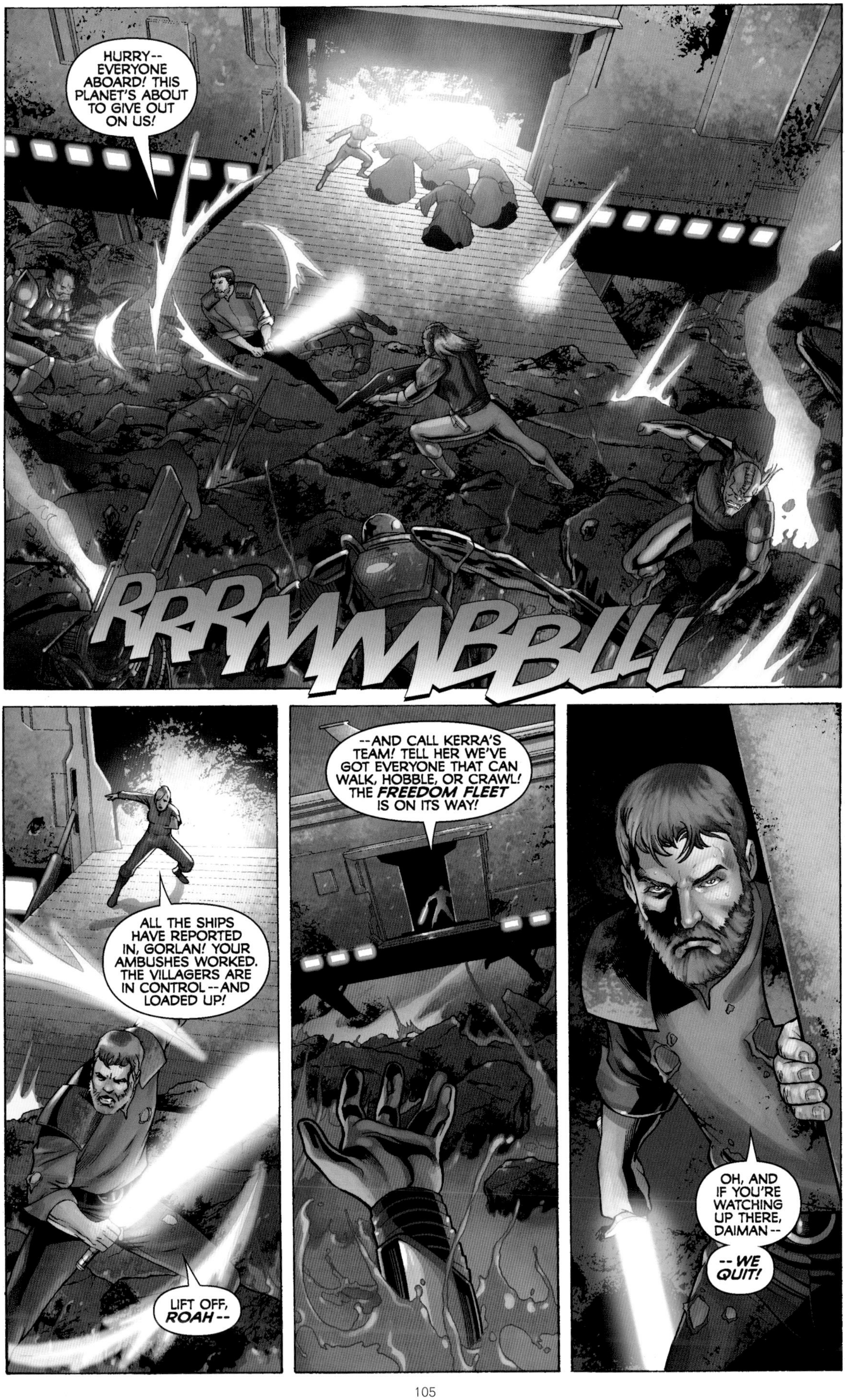
HURRY-- EVERYONE ABOARD! THIS PLANET'S ABOUT TO GIVE OUT ON US!
RRRMMMBBLLL
ALL THE SHIPS HAVE REPORTED IN, GORLAN! YOUR AMBUSHES WORKED. THE VILLAGERS ARE IN CONTROL --AND LOADED UP!
LIFT OFF, ROAH --
--AND CALL KERRA'S TEAM! TELL HER WE'VE GOT EVERYONE THAT CAN WALK, HOBBLE, OR CRAWL! THE FREEDOM FLEET IS ON ITS WAY!
OH, AND IF YOU'RE WATCHING UP THERE, DAIMAN --
-- WE QUIT!

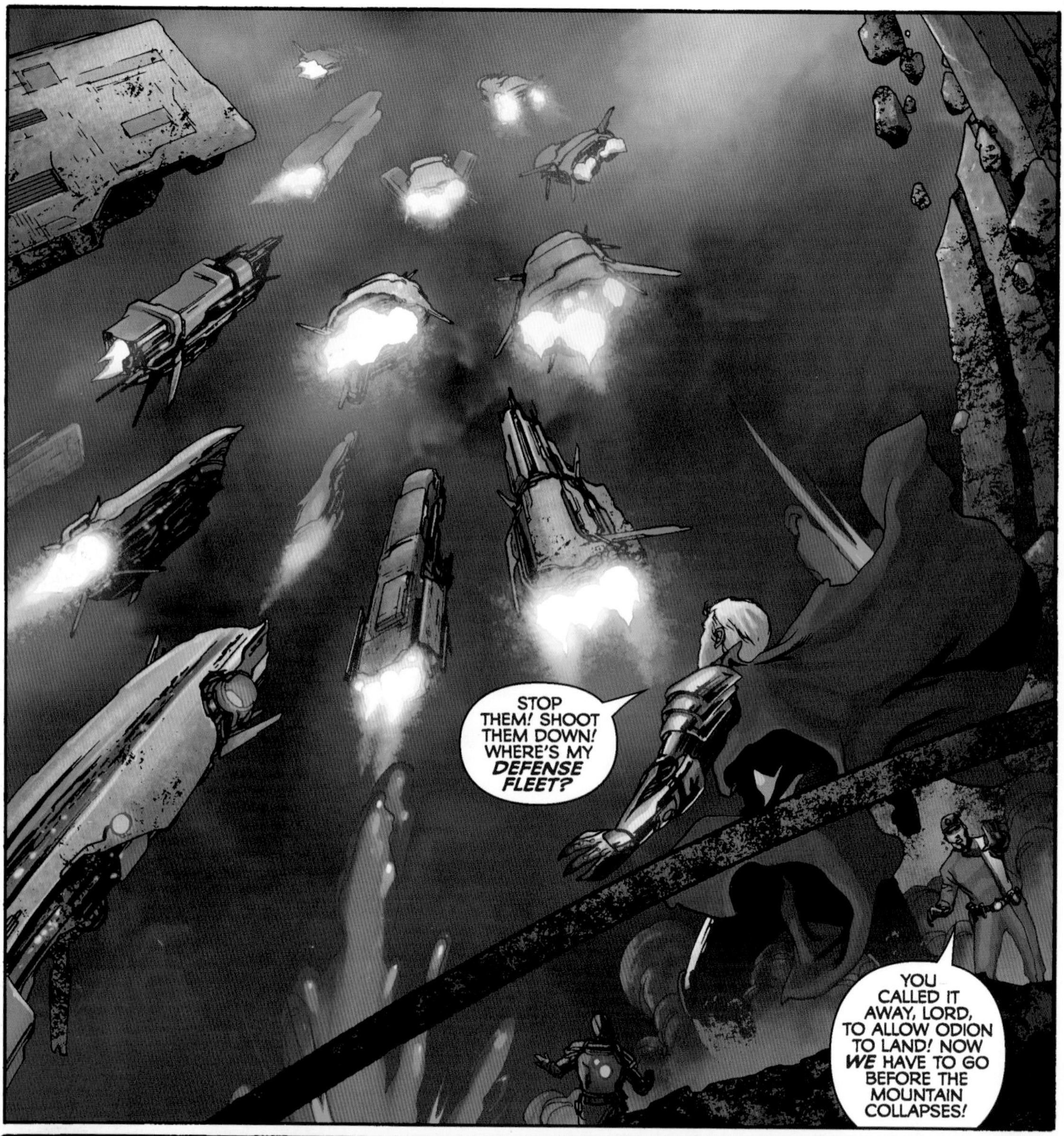
STOP THEM! SHOOT THEM DOWN! WHERE'S MY *DEFENSE FLEET?*
YOU CALLED IT AWAY, LORD, TO ALLOW ODION TO LAND! NOW *WE* HAVE TO GO BEFORE THE MOUNTAIN COLLAPSES!

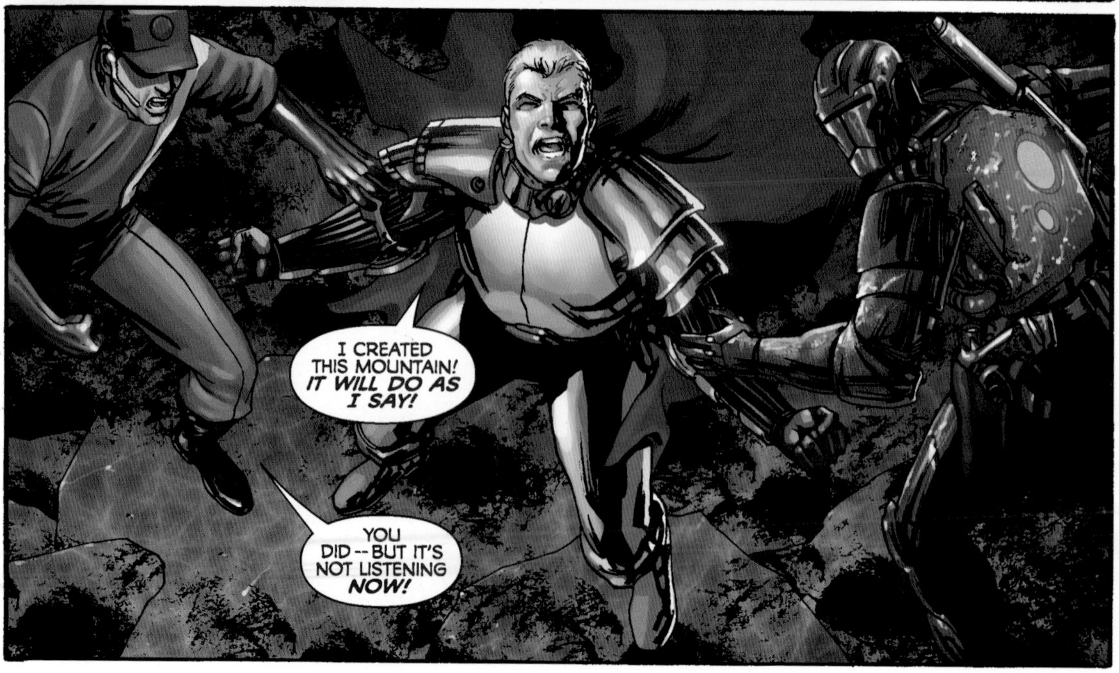
I CREATED THIS MOUNTAIN! *IT WILL DO AS I SAY!*
YOU DID -- BUT IT'S NOT LISTENING *NOW!*

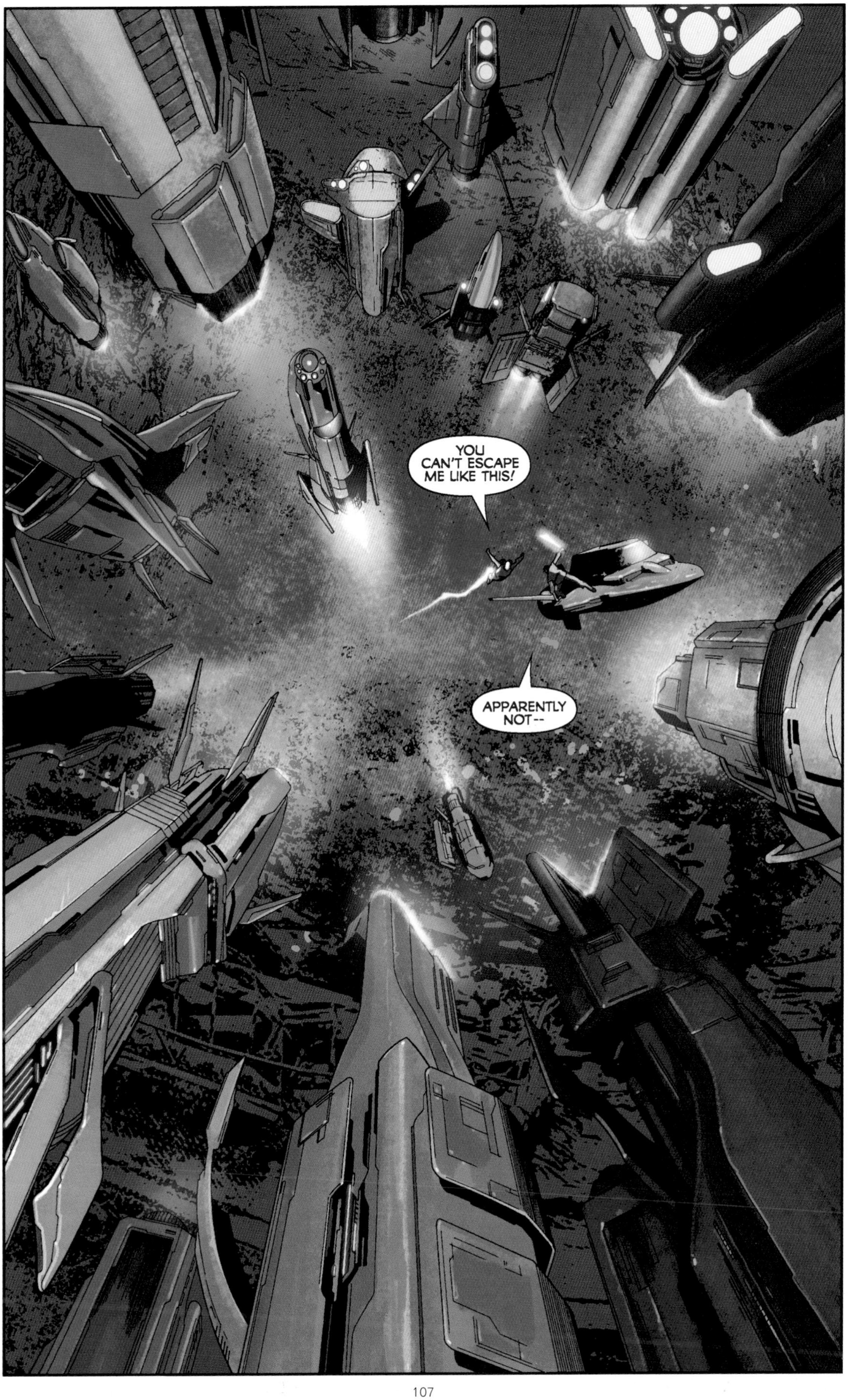
YOU CAN'T ESCAPE ME LIKE THIS!
APPARENTLY NOT--

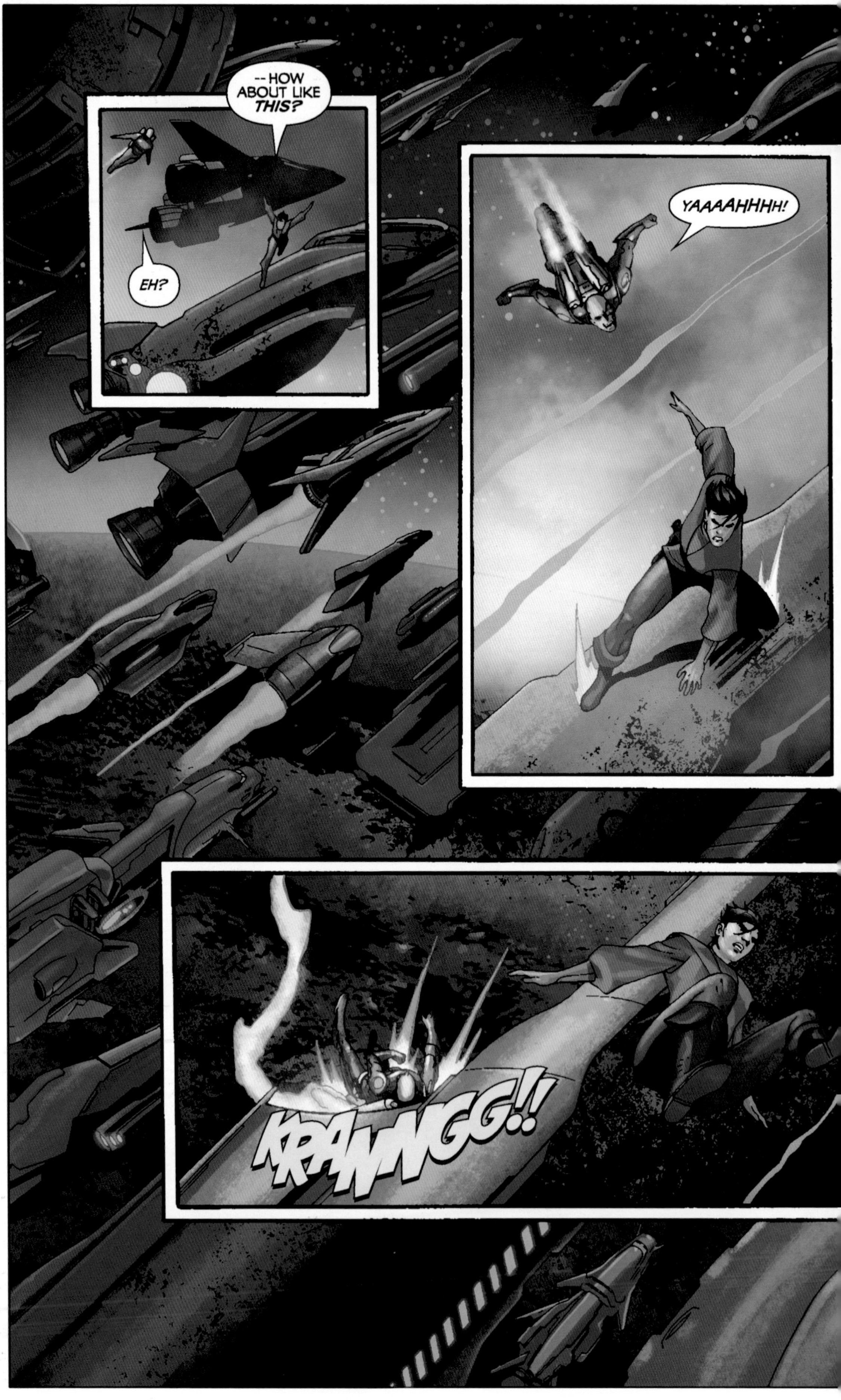

-- HOW ABOUT LIKE THIS?
EH?
YAAAAHHHH!
KRANNGG!!

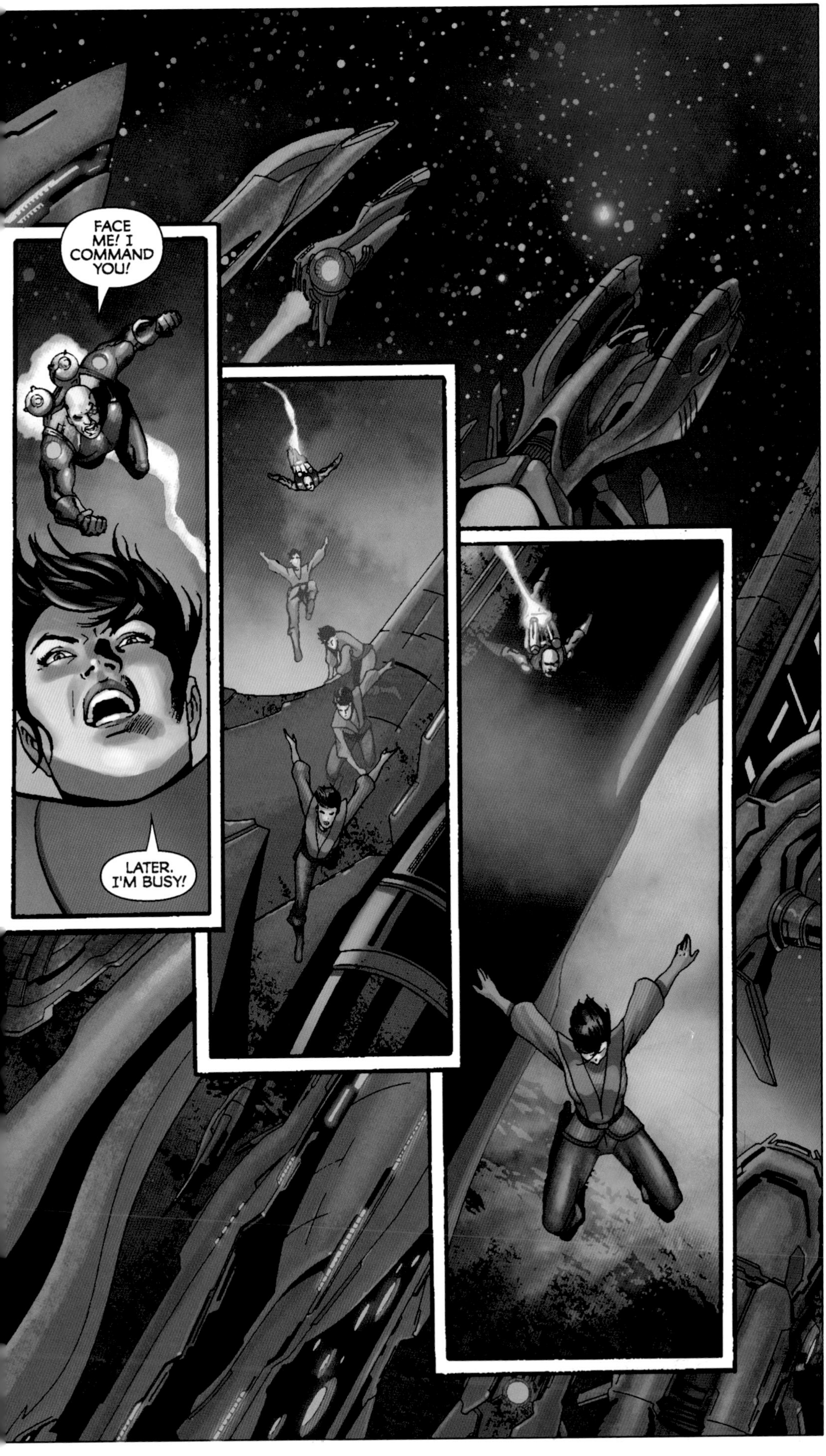
FACE ME! I COMMAND YOU!
LATER. I'M BUSY!

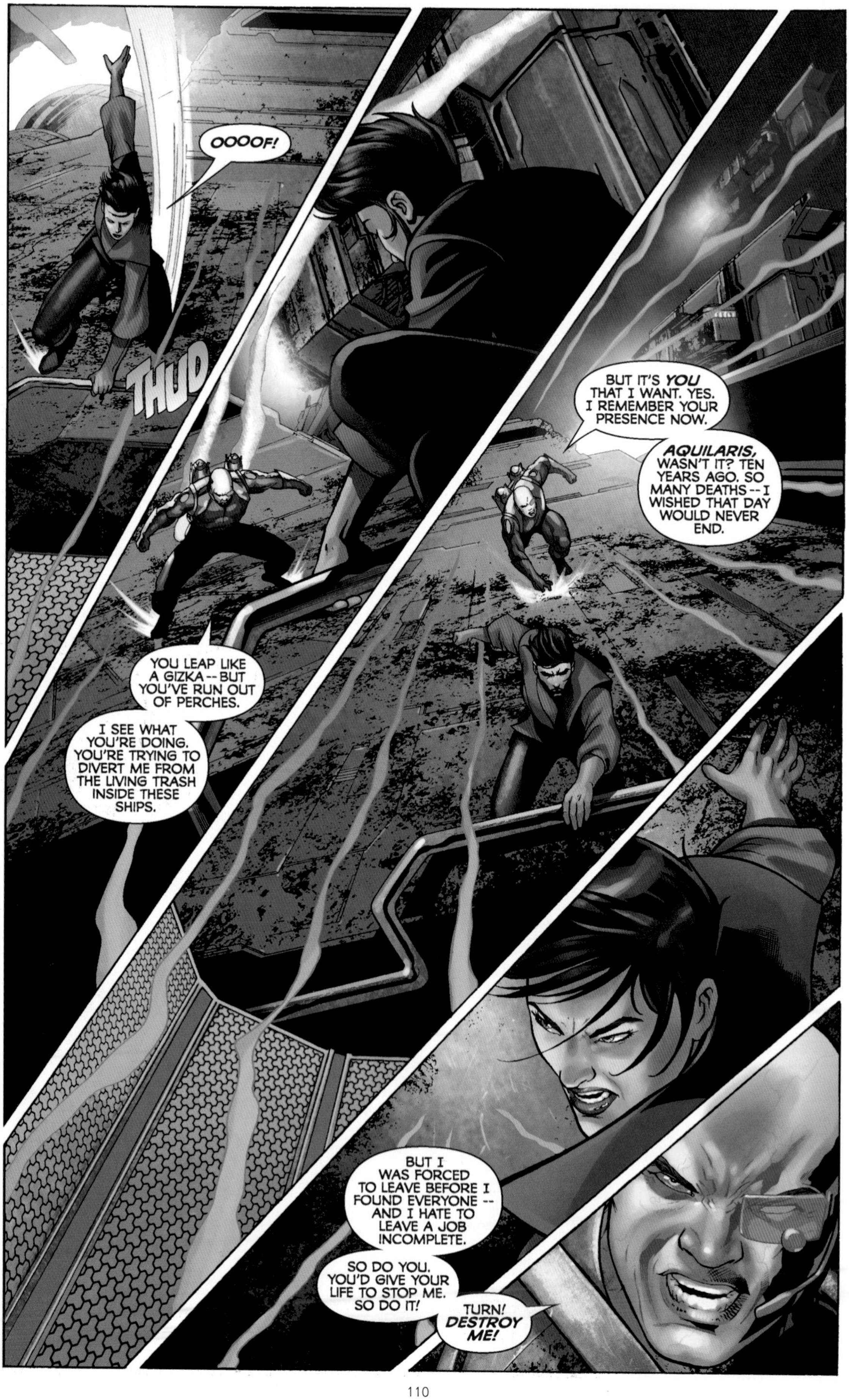

OOOOF!
THUD
YOU LEAP LIKE A GIZKA -- BUT YOU'VE RUN OUT OF PERCHES.
I SEE WHAT YOU'RE DOING. YOU'RE TRYING TO DIVERT ME FROM THE LIVING TRASH INSIDE THESE SHIPS.
BUT IT'S YOU THAT I WANT. YES. I REMEMBER YOUR PRESENCE NOW.
AQUILARIS, WASN'T IT? TEN YEARS AGO. SO MANY DEATHS -- I WISHED THAT DAY WOULD NEVER END.
BUT I WAS FORCED TO LEAVE BEFORE I FOUND EVERYONE -- AND I HATE TO LEAVE A JOB INCOMPLETE.
SO DO YOU. YOU'D GIVE YOUR LIFE TO STOP ME. SO DO IT!
TURN! DESTROY ME!

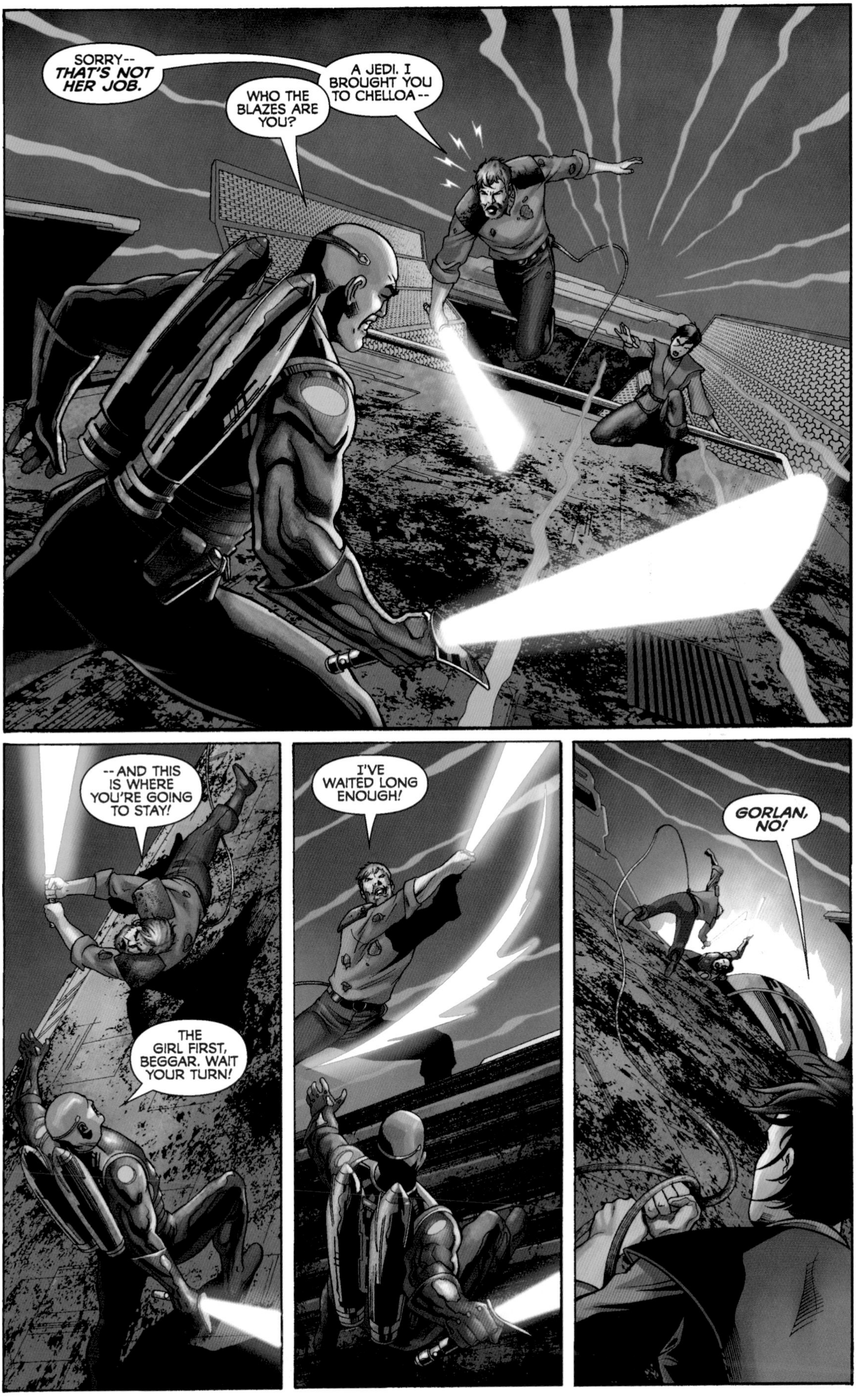
SORRY-- THAT'S NOT HER JOB.
WHO THE BLAZES ARE YOU?
A JEDI. I BROUGHT YOU TO CHELLOA--
--AND THIS IS WHERE YOU'RE GOING TO STAY!
THE GIRL FIRST, BEGGAR. WAIT YOUR TURN!
I'VE WAITED LONG ENOUGH!
GORLAN, NO!

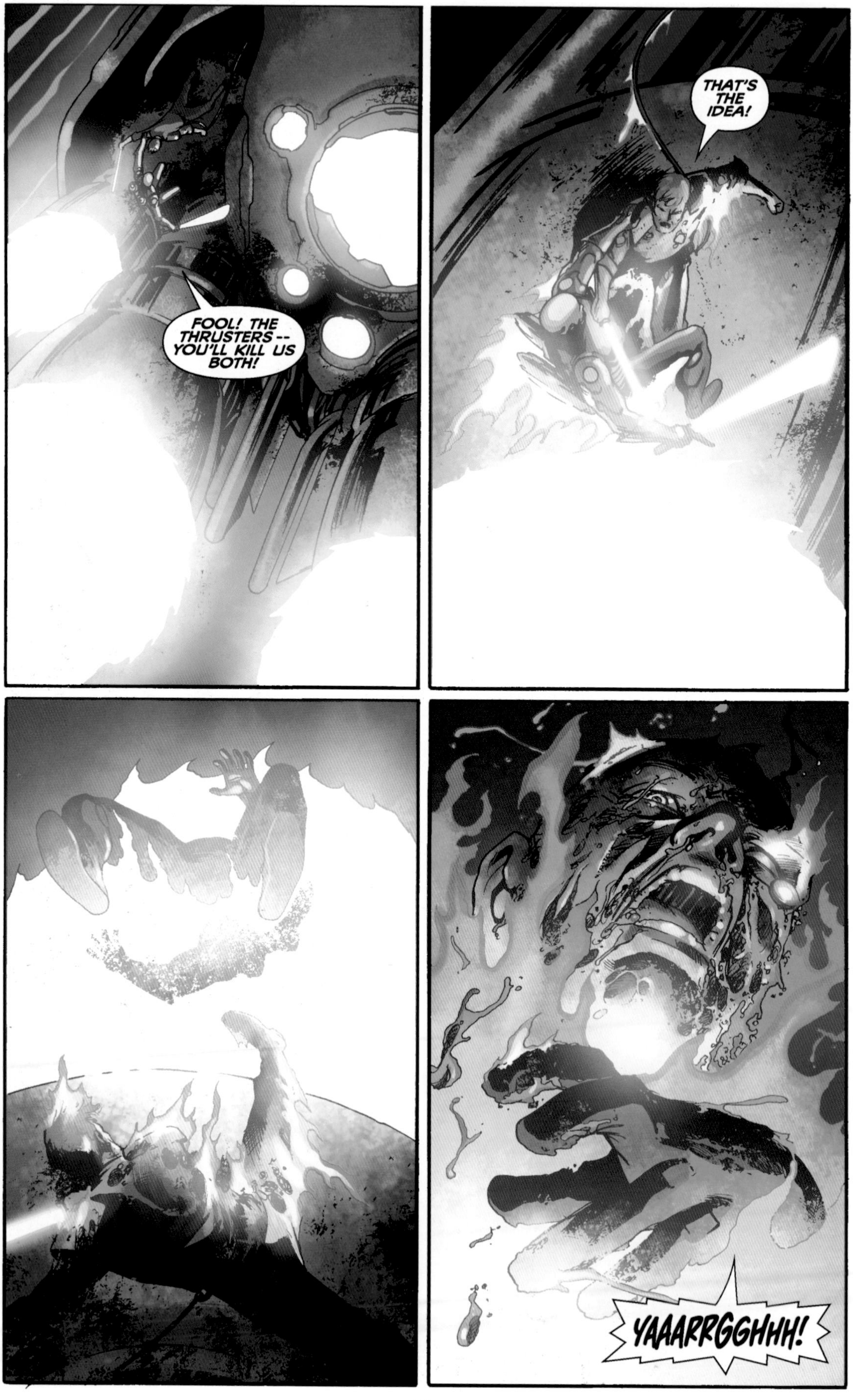
FOOL! THE THRUSTERS -- YOU'LL KILL US BOTH!
THAT'S THE IDEA!
YAAARRGGHHH!

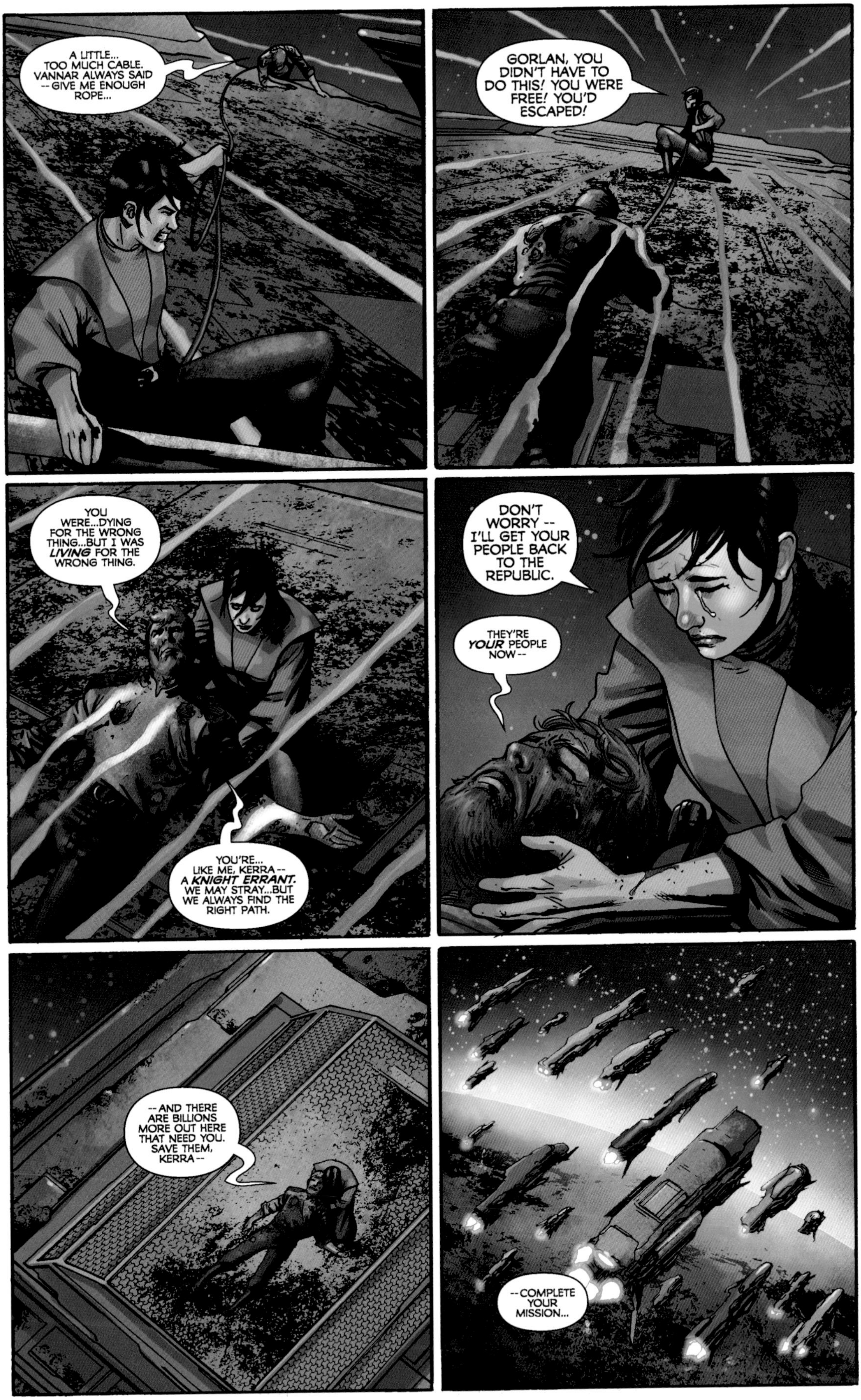
A LITTLE... TOO MUCH CABLE. VANNAR ALWAYS SAID -- GIVE ME ENOUGH ROPE...
GORLAN, YOU DIDN'T HAVE TO DO THIS! YOU WERE FREE! YOU'D ESCAPED!
YOU WERE...DYING FOR THE WRONG THING...BUT I WAS *LIVING* FOR THE WRONG THING.
YOU'RE... LIKE ME, KERRA -- A *KNIGHT ERRANT.* WE MAY STRAY...BUT WE ALWAYS FIND THE RIGHT PATH.
DON'T WORRY -- I'LL GET YOUR PEOPLE BACK TO THE REPUBLIC.
THEY'RE *YOUR* PEOPLE NOW --
-- AND THERE ARE BILLIONS MORE OUT HERE THAT NEED YOU. SAVE THEM, KERRA --
-- COMPLETE YOUR MISSION...

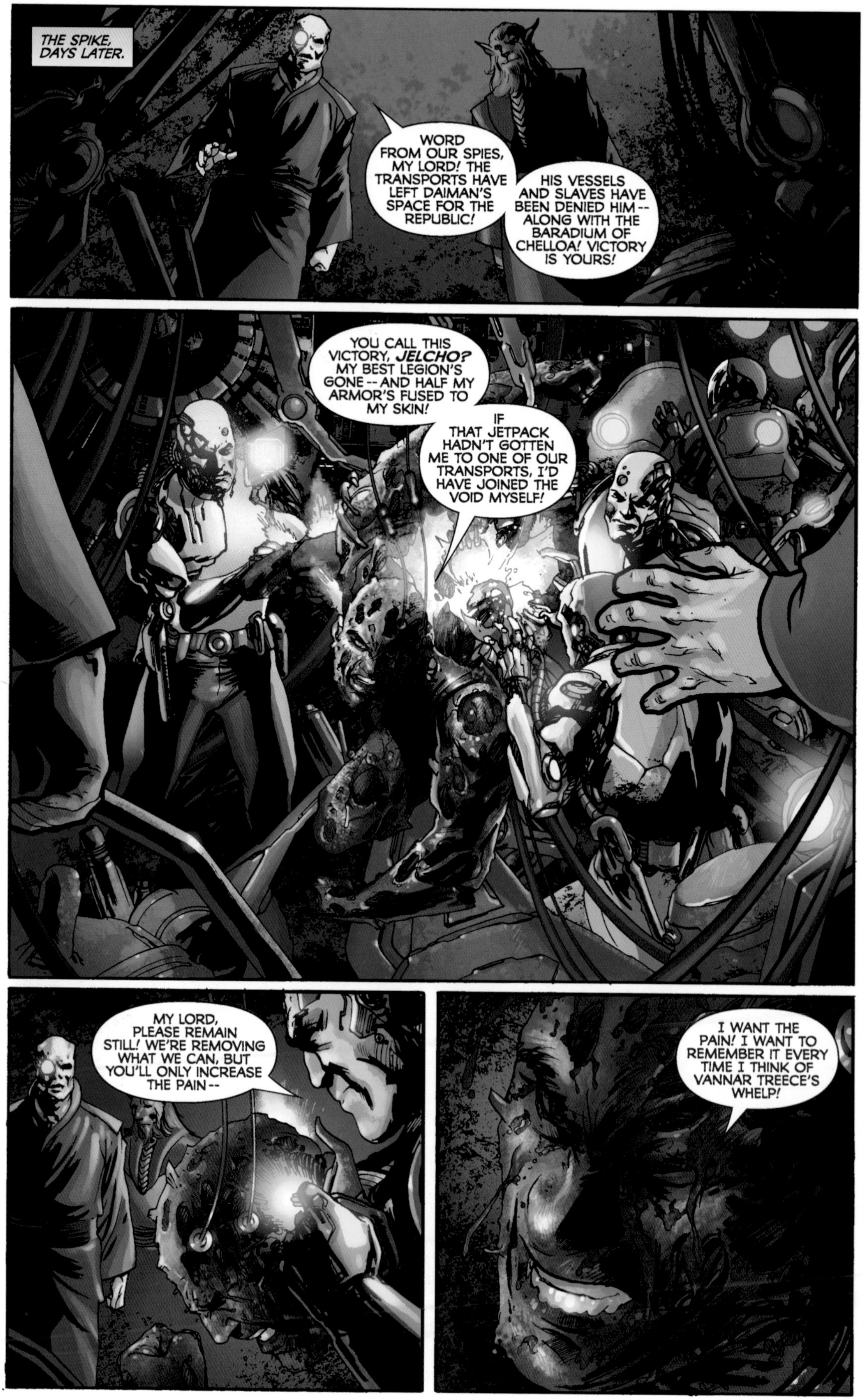
THE SPIKE, DAYS LATER.
WORD FROM OUR SPIES, MY LORD! THE TRANSPORTS HAVE LEFT DAIMAN'S SPACE FOR THE REPUBLIC!
HIS VESSELS AND SLAVES HAVE BEEN DENIED HIM -- ALONG WITH THE BARADIUM OF CHELLOA! VICTORY IS YOURS!
YOU CALL THIS VICTORY, JELCHO? MY BEST LEGION'S GONE -- AND HALF MY ARMOR'S FUSED TO MY SKIN!
IF THAT JETPACK HADN'T GOTTEN ME TO ONE OF OUR TRANSPORTS, I'D HAVE JOINED THE VOID MYSELF!
MY LORD, PLEASE REMAIN STILL! WE'RE REMOVING WHAT WE CAN, BUT YOU'LL ONLY INCREASE THE PAIN --
I WANT THE PAIN! I WANT TO REMEMBER IT EVERY TIME I THINK OF VANNAR TREECE'S WHELP!

NILASH, A WORLD IN THE DAIMANATE.

AS MY LORD KNOWS, PRODUCTION HAS SUFFERED HERE AND ACROSS THE REALM--

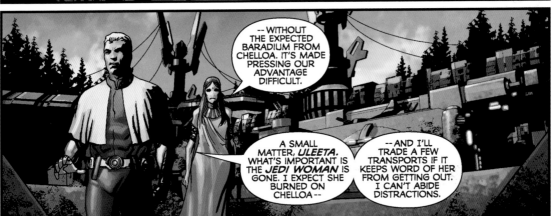

--WITHOUT THE EXPECTED BARADIUM FROM CHELLOA. IT'S MADE PRESSING OUR ADVANTAGE DIFFICULT.

A SMALL MATTER, *ULEETA.* WHAT'S IMPORTANT IS THE *JEDI WOMAN* IS GONE. I EXPECT SHE BURNED ON CHELLOA--

--AND I'LL TRADE A FEW TRANSPORTS IF IT KEEPS WORD OF HER FROM GETTING OUT. I CAN'T ABIDE DISTRACTIONS.

THAT'S WHY THE ADMINISTRATOR HERE CALLED, MY CREATOR. SOMEONE ENTERED THE MUNITIONS PLANT AND FREED THE NATIVE WORKERS LAST NIGHT.

WE BELIEVE THE SLAVES SIMPLY MELTED BACK INTO THE JUNGLE.

NO AGENT OF ODION'S WOULD FREE SLAVES. WAS ANYTHING MISSING?

ONLY A SINGLE HIGH-POWERED LASER, MY LORD, DESIGNED FOR CUTTING CORTOSIS. IT'S HARD TO SEE THE STRATEGIC IMPORTANCE.

IT'S A *MESSAGE.*

TO ME.

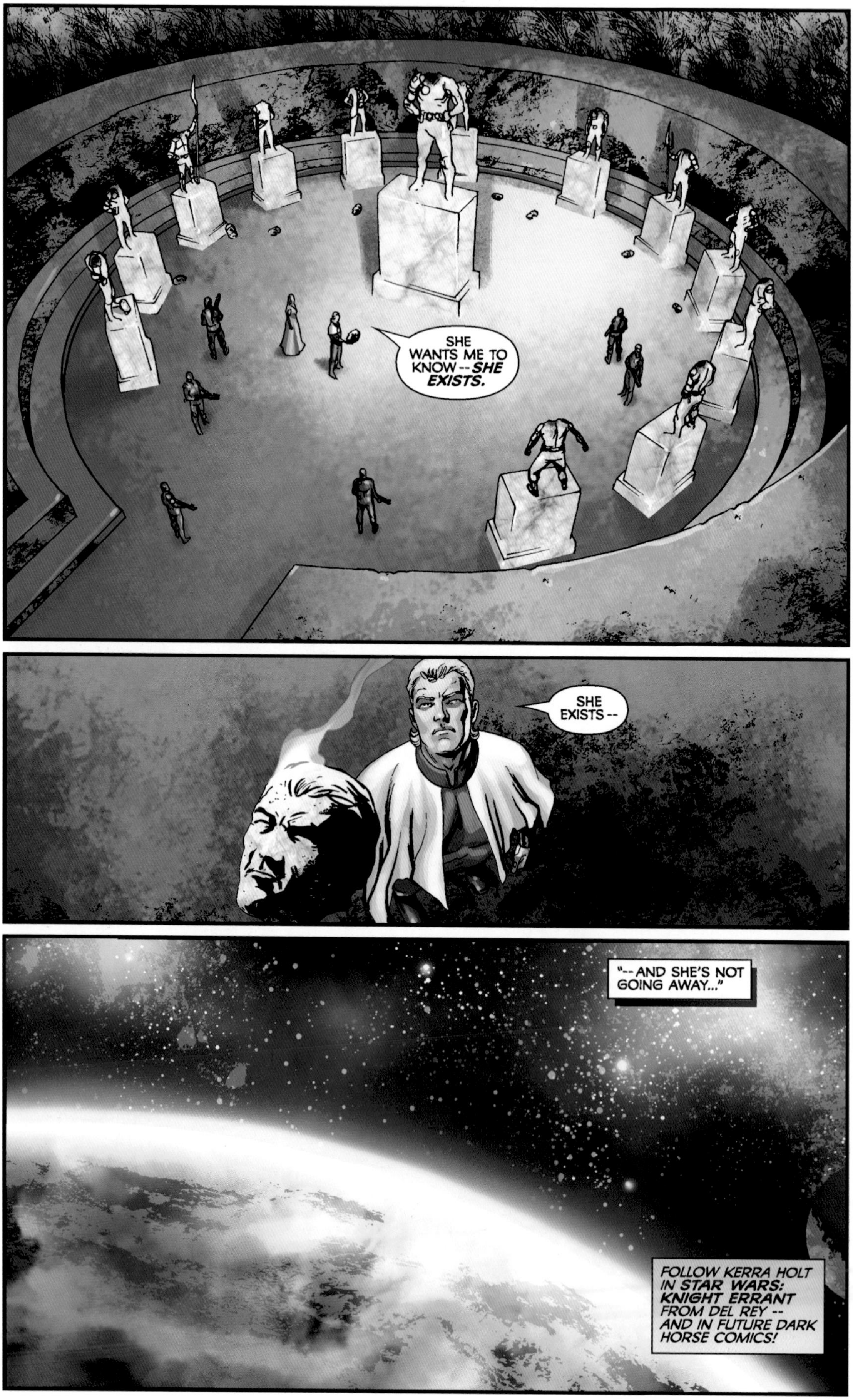
SHE WANTS ME TO KNOW -- SHE EXISTS.
SHE EXISTS --
"-- AND SHE'S NOT GOING AWAY..."
FOLLOW KERRA HOLT IN STAR WARS: KNIGHT ERRANT FROM DEL REY -- AND IN FUTURE DARK HORSE COMICS!

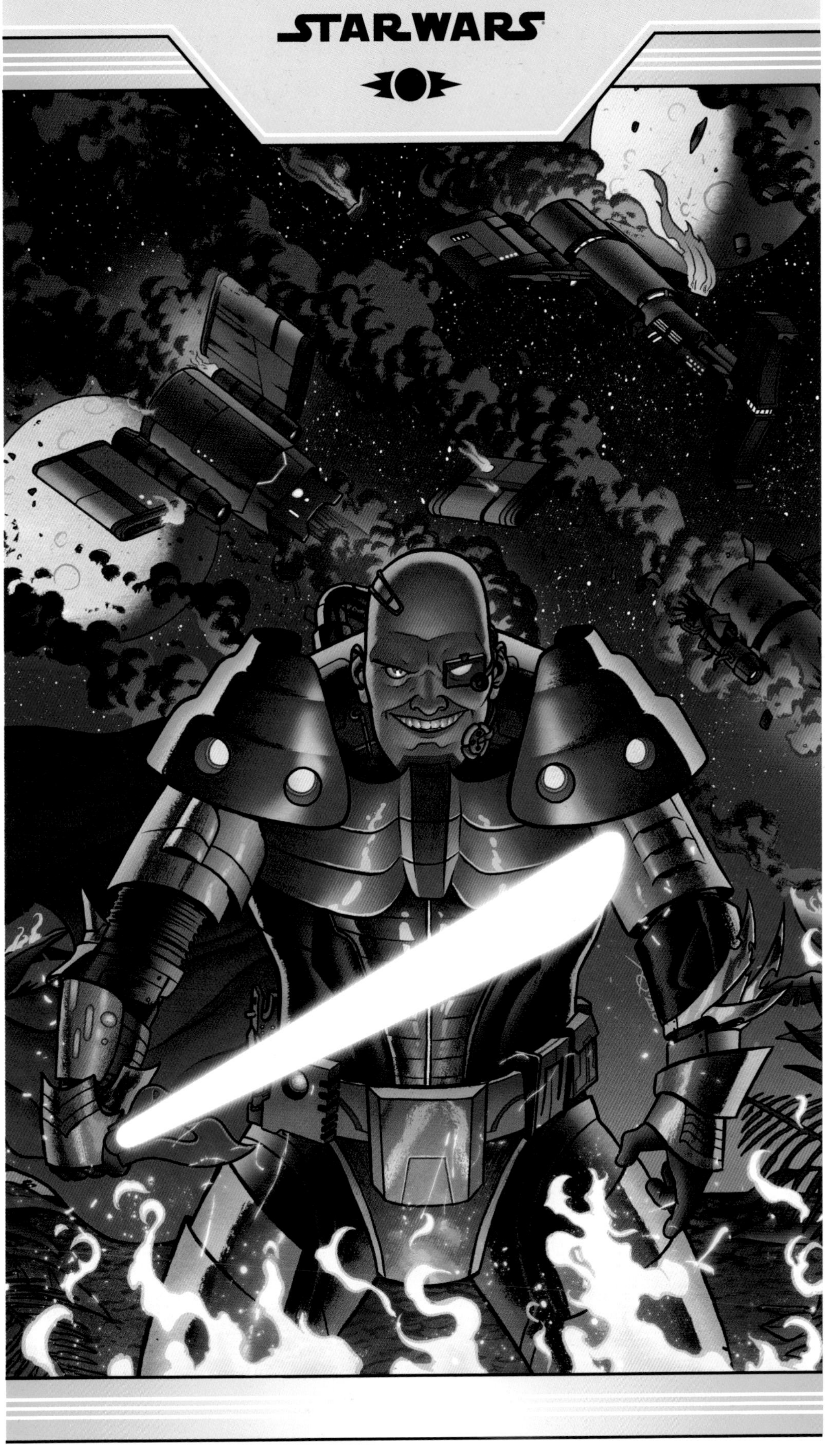
STAR WARS

ILLUSTRATION BY JOE QUINONES

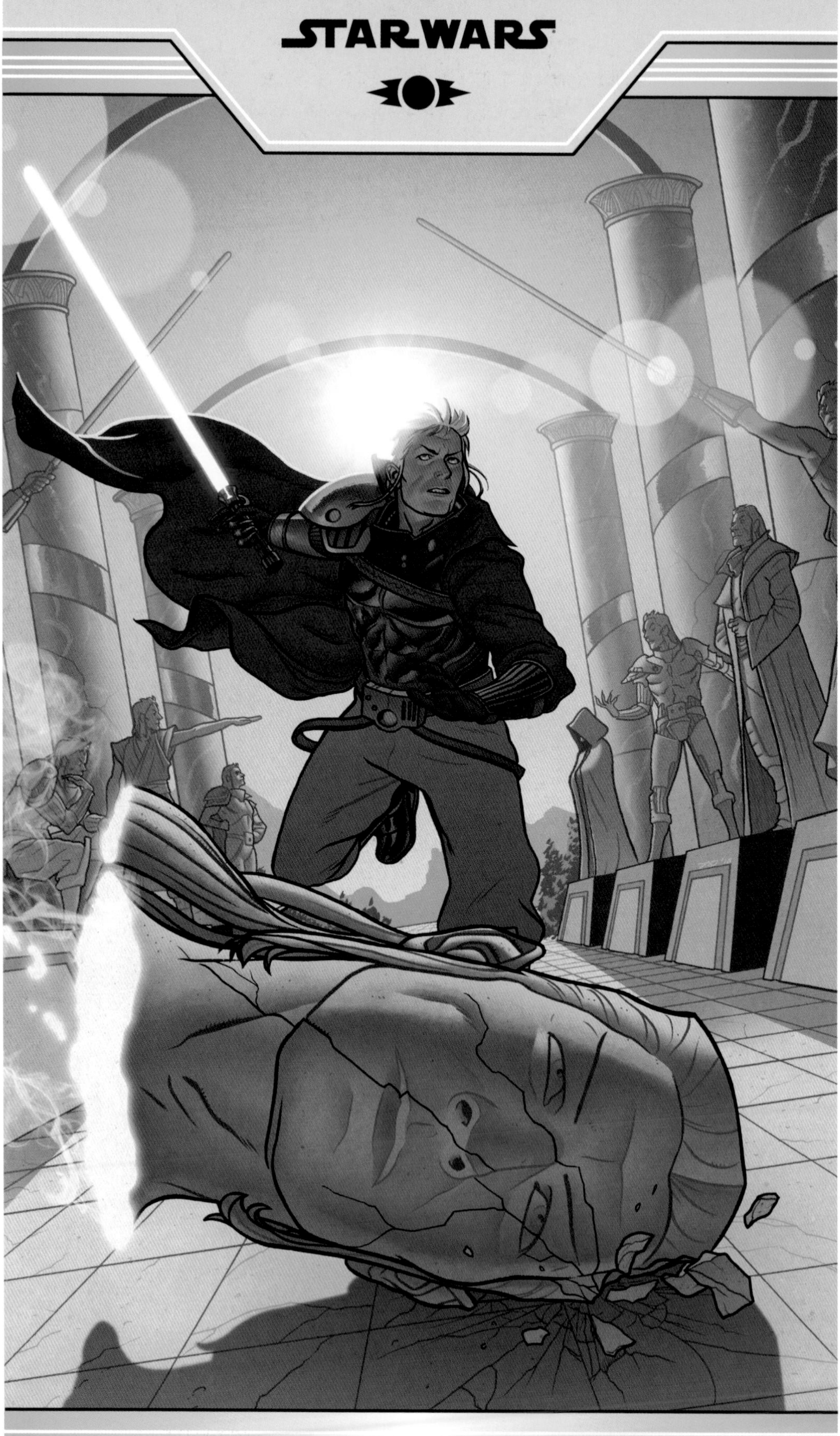
STAR WARS

ILLUSTRATION BY JOE QUINONES

STAR WARS GRAPHIC NOVEL

TIMELINE (IN YEARS)

Omnibus: Tales of the Jedi—5,000–3,986 BSW4

Knights of the Old Republic—3,964–3,963 BSW4

The Old Republic—3653, 3678 BSW4

Knight Errant—1,032 BSW4

Jedi vs. Sith—1,000 BSW4

Omnibus: Rise of the Sith—33 BSW4

Episode I: The Phantom Menace—32 BSW4

Omnibus: Emissaries and Assassins—32 BSW4

Twilight—31 BSW4

Omnibus: Menace Revealed—31–22 BSW4

Darkness—30 BSW4

The Stark Hyperspace War—30 BSW4

Rite of Passage—28 BSW4

Honor and Duty—22 BSW4

Blood Ties—22 BSW4

Episode II: Attack of the Clones—22 BSW4

Clone Wars—22–19 BSW4

Clone Wars Adventures—22–19 BSW4

General Grievous—22–19 BSW4

Episode III: Revenge of the Sith—19 BSW4

Dark Times—19 BSW4

Omnibus: Droids—5.5 BSW4

Boba Fett: Enemy of the Empire—3 BSW4

Underworld—1 BSW4

Episode IV: A New Hope—SW4

Classic Star Wars—0–3 ASW4

A Long Time Ago . . .—0–4 ASW4

Empire—0 ASW4

Rebellion—0 ASW4

Boba Fett: Man with a Mission—0 ASW4

Omnibus: Early Victories—0–3 ASW4

Jabba the Hutt: The Art of the Deal—1 ASW4

Episode V: The Empire Strikes Back—3 ASW4

Omnibus: Shadows of the Empire—3.5–4.5 ASW4

Episode VI: Return of the Jedi—4 ASW4

Omnibus: X-Wing Rogue Squadron—4–5 ASW4

Heir to the Empire—9 ASW4

Dark Force Rising—9 ASW4

The Last Command—9 ASW4

Dark Empire—10 ASW4

Boba Fett: Death, Lies, and Treachery—10 ASW4

Crimson Empire—11 ASW4

Jedi Academy: Leviathan—12 ASW4

Union—19 ASW4

Chewbacca—25 ASW4

Invasion—25 ASW4

Legacy—130–137 ASW4

Old Republic Era
25,000 – 1000 years before
Star Wars: A New Hope

Rise of the Empire Era
1000 – 0 years before
Star Wars: A New Hope

Rebellion Era
0 – 5 years after
Star Wars: A New Hope

New Republic Era
5 – 25 years after
Star Wars: A New Hope

New Jedi Order Era
25+ years after
Star Wars: A New Hope

Legacy Era
130+ years after
Star Wars: A New Hope

Infinities
Does not apply to timeline

Sergio Aragonés Stomps Star Wars
Star Wars Tales
Star Wars Infinities
Tag and Bink
Star Wars Visionaries

BSW4 = before *Episode IV: A New Hope*. ASW4 = after *Episode IV: A New Hope*.

STAR WARS®
KNIGHTS OF THE OLD REPUBLIC

Volume 1: Commencement
ISBN 978-1-59307-640-5 | $18.99

Volume 2: Flashpoint
ISBN 978-1-59307-761-7 | $18.99

Volume 3: Days of Fear, Nights of Anger
ISBN 978-1-59307-867-6 | $18.99

Volume 4: Daze of Hate, Knights of Suffering
ISBN 978-1-59582-208-6 | $18.99

Volume 5: Vector
ISBN 978-1-59582-227-7 | $17.99

Volume 6: Vindication
ISBN 978-1-59582-274-1 | $19.99

Volume 7: Dueling Ambitions
ISBN 978-1-59582-348-9 | $18.99

Volume 8: Destroyer
ISBN 978-1-59582-419-6 | $17.99

Volume 9: Demon
ISBN 978-1-59582-476-9 | $16.99

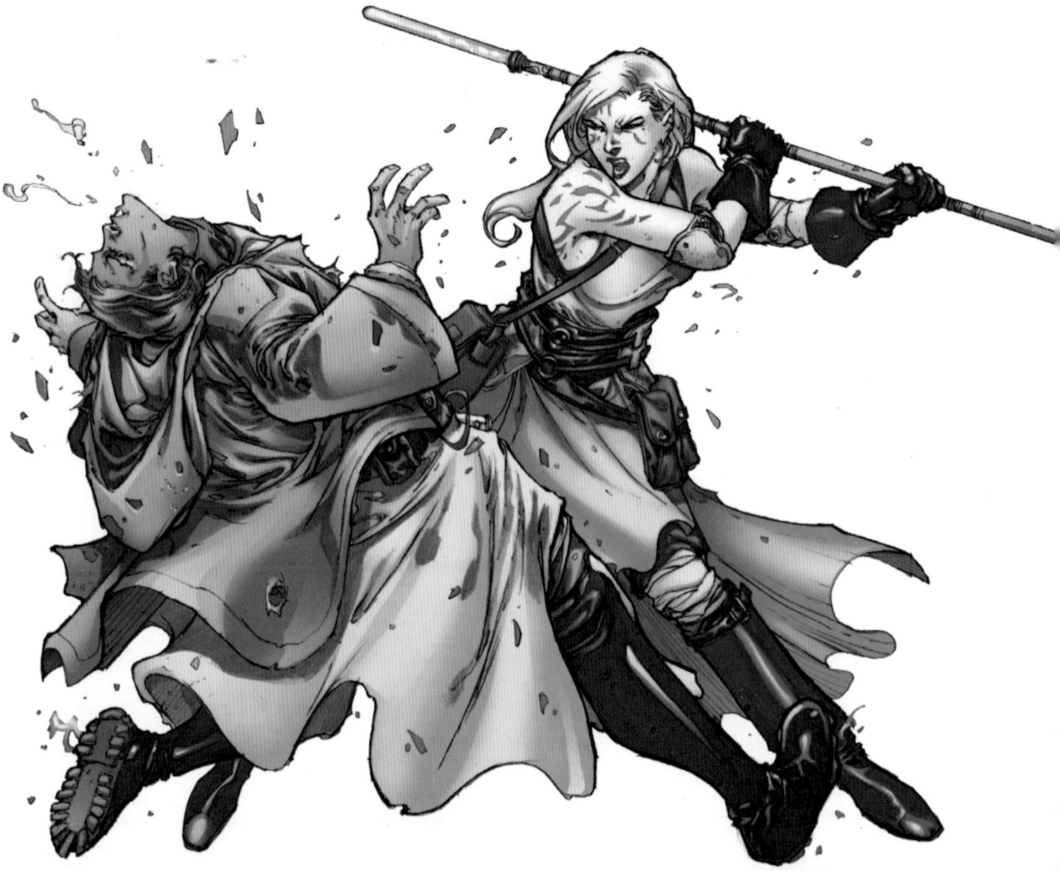

DARK HORSE BOOKS

TO FIND A COMICS SHOP IN YOUR AREA, CALL 1-888-266-4226.

For more information or to order direct: *On the web: darkhorse.com *E-mail: mailorder@darkhorse.com
*Phone: 1-800-862-0052 Mon.-Fri. 9 A.M. to 5 P.M. Pacific Time.